MEMOIRS OF A
TRAVELING ECONOMIST

MEMOIRS OF A TRAVELING ECONOMIST

Stories from the Remote Corners of the World

KJELL A. CHRISTOPHERSEN

Published by Canon Press
P.O. Box 8729, Moscow, Idaho 83843
800.488.2034 | www.canonpress.com

Kjell A. Christophersen, *Memoirs of a Traveling Economist: Stories from the Remote Corners of the World*
Copyright ©2020 by Kjell A. Christophersen

Cover design by James Engerbretson.
Interior design by Valerie Anne Bost.

Printed in the United States of America.

Library of Congress Cataloging-in-Publication Data

Christophersen, Kjell A. (Kjell Arne), author.
Memoirs of a traveling economist : stories from the remote corners
   of the world / Kjell A Christophersen.
Moscow, Idaho : Canon Press, [2020] | Summary: "This book
   chronicles the career of an economist traveling with USAID and talking
   about the pros and cons of how it is offered" — Provided by publisher.
LCCN 2020045944 | ISBN 9781952410734 (paperback)
LCSH: Christophersen, Kjell A. (Kjell Arne) | United States.

   Agency for International Development. | Economists — United
   States — Biography. | Economic assistance — Developing countries. |
   Economic development projects — Developing countries.
Classification: LCC HB119.C495 A3 2021 | DDC 338.91/730092 [B] — dc23
LC record available at https://lccn.loc.gov/2020045944

21 22 23 24 25 26 27 28   10 9 8 7 6 5 4 3 2 1

CONTENTS

PREFACE

This is not a thematic book in the genre of "managing your retirement," "the ultimate exercise manual for couch potatoes," "the do's
and don'ts of investing" or anything remotely similar to that. Rather, it
is a diverse collection of experiences or stories, vignettes ranging from
growing up in Norway to humorous anecdotes and some suspense-
ful stories of economic development experiences in the Third World.
These stories have remained in my mind for years, begging to be written down before they are too embellished or completely forgotten. I
have been encouraged to do this for many years by my wife, kids, and
others who seem to enjoy hearing them—so here it is. My own take on
this is that my career has been, at least ... well ... unusual.

I spent a lot of my working career in and out of Africa, Asia, the
Caribbean, and the Middle East in some of the most remote corners of
the world. For more than twenty-five years I was an international consultant traveling to and working in nearly seventy countries "solving"
all sorts of problems for various clients. My assignments were many—
from economic analysis and modeling of large-scale forestry and agriculture projects in Ivory Coast, Gambia, Senegal, Mali, Guinea, and
Niger, to training needs assessments, to wildlife economic assessments
in the national wildlife parks of Kenya, Botswana, and Tanzania, and

to biomass energy assessments in Rwanda and Vietnam and Thailand and many other countries.

Working as an economic development expert in the Third World is a job that can be very exciting if you are a high octane adrenalin producer. If you can meet the report deadlines, cope with constant jet lag, and you don't mind working in a totally unstructured environment characterized by Murphy's law — "if things can go wrong, they will" — you will be OK. Most can't, though, so I wouldn't wholeheartedly recommend this line of work to sane people whose focus should be on having a regular job, earning a regular salary, and living a life with at least some semblance of normalcy.

Typically, the sequence of events for me would be to travel to country A, spend two to three weeks there, write a report with hastily thought-up recommendations, come home for a week or so, and then head on out again to country B to repeat the process. On the way back from country B, I would often stop in countries C and D to set the stage for upcoming work there. And so it went for about twenty-five years. While on the road I somehow survived on heavy doses of adrenalin and lots of coffee, only partially recovering from jet lag, and often just barely escaping from countries where civil unrest had broken out.

On rare occasions when I had home time, we were invited to events (the kind where you juggle drinks and paper plates and spill the hors d'oeuvres) where I found myself talking with "regular" people. The conversation would usually go something like this:

Q: "So ... what do you do"?

Me: "Uh ... Umm ... I am an international consultant — I work overseas most of the time."

Q: "Really? So ... where do you work"?

Me: "Well, it varies; it depends on the assignment. Mostly in Africa, though ..."

Q: "Africa, wow, is it safe there? What kind of work? That sounds sort of secret. Is it government stuff? You a spook or something? Any connection with the CIA? — haha ..."

The inevitable CIA connection usually popped up, often accompanied by slightly nervous laughter depending upon the questioner's level of paranoia. He might think, "Here's a guy who routinely goes overseas to strange Third World countries (whose revolutions and coups d'état I occasionally read about in the newspapers) on assignments I cannot in any way relate to; he must be privy to some secret goings-on."

Me: "Nah ... I do a lot of work for USAID ... and the World Bank, and such ..."

Q: "What was that ...?"

Me: "The US Agency for International Development ..."

Q: "... Oh, I've heard about that — that's the foreign aid stuff, right?"

Me: "... Right, thanks for keeping me employed ... haha ..."

And so it goes. Usually it degenerated from there. By then his eyes had already begun to glaze over. Our interests had begun to diverge and he drifted off, particularly if the hostess had just brought in a fresh supply of snack food. There was little common ground, little to relate to, little opportunity to discuss any of this further, and he might say: "... Uh ... I went to Sweden a couple of years ago ... had a wonderful time. Ever been there?"

Sooner or later you realize you're a loner lacking somewhat in the kinds of social skills needed to be on the cutting edge of local issues, or even on the same wavelength as the regular folks whose life experiences are as far apart from yours as the east is from the west. You can't articulate the stuff you "do" in those countries in any meaningful way, or at least in ways that would keep them fascinated and eager to hear more. It was exactly the same way for the family when we came home on furlough every summer. We all just pretty much didn't talk about it. It was doubly challenging when it became clear that I was an economist grappling with a subject matter that defies a prolonged fascination by most people.

After moving to the US from Norway in 1963 to become a student at the University of Idaho, I actually embarked on what turned out to be a fairly ambitious academic career that spanned eleven years and resulted in BS and MS degrees from the University of Idaho and a Ph.D. from Washington State University. This time was interspersed with work that put food on the table, paid school loans, and kept me financially just about at the poverty line. I felt like a perpetual student, not unlike so many foreign students who get accustomed to the easy student life and opt to continue their academic careers forever rather than enter the workforce. In my own case, it wasn't as much a reluctance to enter the workforce that made me delay my working career; it was simply the uncertainty about what to do with my life. Should I become a businessman selling my soul to the corporate world as everyone in my family in Norway expected me to do, or should I become a teaching and research economist? After a long period of academic soul searching I chose the latter, not knowing what was in store for me later on. When it was all over, I actually found myself doing some interesting stuff, some of which is written about here.

So how did I get here to this point in 2020? Before embarking on the international work, my chosen career after my educational pursuits was in academia, which thankfully only lasted for three years. I was a professor of natural resource economics at the University of Idaho, plus I had a one-year appointment at the University of Santa Clara in California as an international agribusiness professor. Thank God I escaped this way of making a living. University campus politics is not for the faint of heart. They argue vehemently over so little—virtually nothing is at stake—but the rhetoric flows nevertheless. Tenure reigns and mediocrity breeds. But I digress.

My last career lasted nineteen years before I "retired." Along with a business partner of similar vintage (and a brilliant economist to boot) we founded a company by doing economic impact analyses of higher education institutions, because someone with money and a vision contracted with us to build the model that would do this in a cost-effective way. Our company grew from two to sixty people in eight short years. Then, we spun off another company with ten of our employees, and today the company employs more than 225 people, all young and incredibly smart. At my now advanced age (seventy-eight), I'm probably having more fun than is legal watching all of this. Who says life begins at forty? When you're over the hill (sixty, that is), you pick up speed.

So, this book is a memoir of sorts—a look in the rear-view mirror that aims to flesh out some highlights of a life lived a bit out of the ordinary, from childhood and through my career(s). It includes some amusing work-related stories, and some economic development lessons I've learned the hard way over the years which, at least in my mind, don't reflect too well on the economic development donor community.

My life has indeed been blessed with family, friends, church, and work. It has not always been smooth sailing and I have made plenty of mistakes along the way, but I do have many stories to tell that can probably entertain, edify, teach, or amuse. My life experiences can have value only when communicated to others with a good dose of humility. So that's my aim here: not to extol myself or claim that my life and work has made a lot of difference out there. I hope it has made a difference to me and my family, but with respect to my work as an international consultant, well … I'm not sure it went far beyond grasping for the wind in terms of the lasting differences it made. All is vanity, as is said in Ecclesiastes, and that certainly holds true in most pursuits of a livelihood. We are far less important than we think we are.

I am a Christian who came to the faith as an adult in 1974. This indeed was an unlikely event given my nationality and cultural background. Growing up in Norway was akin to living in an agnostic Mecca. Christianity, or any religion, was rarely discussed — or if discussed, usually scorned. Only old people attended the State church regularly and, as we so intellectually claimed, they didn't matter anyway.

In Norway our experiences with Christianity were confined to three events: confirmation as young adults (this essentially was a social, not a religious experience), reluctant attendance of a Christmas service once a year, and the lighting of candles on the graves of departed loved ones at Christmas time. And, of course, the final visit: a funeral. Christianity, as it was considered by us — the intellectually anointed ones — was for people who had drug abuse habits, ex-cons, drunks, or other social misfits who needed a crutch of sorts to lean on. We knew this because the people we met who tried to witness to us had tattered clothes and — the clincher — most of them did not come from Oslo (the center of all happenings in the universe). In other words, they were either ex-criminals or uneducated country bumpkins, or so we arrogantly thought.

Religion or Christianity was as far from my mind as it possibly could be when I made the trek to the US to go to college, the University of Idaho, in 1963 to begin my studies of international business and foreign trade. It wasn't until I had been married for a few years and was well under way with my Ph.D. studies that I became a Christian. Now, in retrospect and with some forty years behind me in my Christian walk, I can clearly see God's hand in every aspect of my life — He guided me through the many difficult times, blessed me with times of abundance, patiently worked on my highly sinful nature, and kept me safe through many potentially dangerous situations in Africa and Asia. God's existence is so obvious and real, and for people to believe otherwise is the real mystery to me. It requires an enormous leap of ... should I say ... faith? ... to be a non-believer.

In 1964 I met my wife-to-be, Judi, at the ski lodge in McCall, Idaho. She was a student at the University of Idaho, and an excellent skier, and we fell instantly in love. We were married in August 1966, but were promptly voted the couple least likely to make it for any meaningful duration. Not only did we come from completely different cultural backgrounds, Judi's dad also didn't like me very much in the beginning (in retrospect, I can understand why). Her mom thought I was okay but she needed to have many heart-to-heart talks with me to sort of knock off some of my pointy edges ("she must have done something wrong because I'm mad at her"). Judi herself really had no idea of how my life in Norway had over time built layers upon layers of baggage that I really needed to unload from my system.

Well, as of this writing it is 2020, we're still here, some fifty-three years later, three grown kids and nine grandkids and still going strong. So to all of the doubters: you were wrong. She stuck with me during all those years that I, let's face it, abandoned my family while traveling around the globe to do my work; she tolerated my attempts to steer the kids into competitive sports while quietly steering them into academic excellence and keeping the family intact with a steady hand. She had none of the childhood baggage of the kind I brought to the marriage and which life has been busy purging from my system. I will soon be able to claim victory, since I am really no longer competing against my family and relatives, at least as long as I am here in the USA.

So that's my story in a nutshell. Now let's unravel things a little.

CHAPTER 1: GROWING UP IN NORWAY

WAR YEARS

I was born on January 6, 1942, in Oslo, Norway. It was cold and snowy on that day, I am told, so I have to give my dad credit for getting my mom to the hospital after curfew while evading German soldiers at roadblocks all over town. It was in the middle of World War II, and the invading Germans were everywhere, menacing everything and everyone. Food and consumable items were rationed, and young families had to be innovative in how to make ends meet.

The earliest of my fragmented memories were from the last days of the war. Most vividly I remember family meetings when Dad taught us how to use the gas mask—a very scary looking thing that made Darth Vader-like sounds when you breathed in it.

Another early memory is the loud explosions of the bombs the Royal Air Force (RAF) planes dropped on German targets in the harbor area where their warships were anchored near our apartment complex. The harbor was within easy walking distance from our top floor apartment in a five-story apartment building close to downtown. The bombing usually occurred at night, so everyone in our building had to hunker down in the basement serving as a bomb shelter, listening to the planes roar just a few feet above our building as we sat on wooden benches in the dark. The very loud booms and the bright illumination as the bombs exploded were spectacular. I clearly remember the noise and the frightened faces of my parents and our neighbors as they endured the experience while quietly praying for deliverance.

I can also conjure up from my earliest memory that I too did my part in the Resistance movement. Although my parents had told me to stay far away from German soldiers, I was a rebellious three-year-old bent on breaking the rules. So, on one occasion when I saw a German soldier patrolling outside our apartment building I, in a moment of temporary insanity, picked up a small pebble and threw it at him while his back was turned. My throwing prowess had already begun to manifest itself at my very young age, and the pebble hit him smack on the helmet with a clang. My intent was to disobey the rule of not making any contact with any German soldiers whatsoever, and not for the pebble to actually hit its mark.

Upon impact, however, the damage was already done, and as I tried to make my getaway the soldier caught me in full stride. I probably expected to be thrown into prison or worse, and I awaited my judgment while bawling at maximum decibel levels. But instead of beating the daylights out of me he reached into his pocket, pulled out some candy, gave it to me, smiled, and walked off. Wow! Now that was confusing for a three-year-old. Candy, along with all other foodstuffs, was severely rationed, so it was an immense treasure when we had any. I naturally inhaled it and in my excitement told my parents everything. Big mistake, because it was then I received the beating from my mom which I had fully expected from the soldier. So, my own personal war effort had begun and ended in mere seconds. But at least I did my part.

LIFE AT HOME

My family was middle class, a bit on the upper middle side, sort of enough to be comfortable, but short of having enough to be part of the much-celebrated upper crust of Norwegian society. We used to have money before I was born, I'm told, but the family didn't manage to hold onto it and probably made some bad investments along the way.

And it didn't help that the government decided to nationalize the wine and spirits industry in which my grandparents were so successful.

But we survived. My dad owned and operated a hardware store in downtown Oslo, and my mom was stay-at-home. That was the norm of the day — one income families. My brother, Jon Erik, was two-and-a-half years older than me and circulated in an entirely different world. He and his friends were older and looked down on me as a little useless runt (they probably weren't far off). I duplicated this attitude toward my younger sister, Ann-Elina, and her friends. We, the three siblings, lived in three entirely separate universes, and my parents lived in their fourth universe. It wasn't until full adulthood that we actually developed close and lasting relationships with each other. I can't say that our family was particularly close or exhibited any warm and fuzzy family characteristics of the *Father Knows Best* kind.

My home was a small three-bedroom apartment near downtown. It had a spectacular view of the harbor area and innermost area of the Oslo Fjord. It was my neighborhood; all my friends lived there plus lots of kids who formed into cliques and gangs, terrorizing the neighborhood with boisterous playing, bloody noses, fights, and accidents. It was also characterized by moms who carried ointments and Band-Aids in their purses to render emergency aid and comfort to their kids as they earned their merit badges in the tough streets of Oslo. Well, at least we thought they were tough, and indeed we had our versions of street rumbles leading to bloody noses. Home was only a place where we ate, slept, and recharged our batteries; real life was lived on the streets, hanging out with friends where we generally raised a lot of hell.

My cousin Peder was my closest playmate during the early years, because he and his family lived in the same downtown apartment complex at the time. We did everything together. Our maternal grandparents lived a couple of miles away in a house we really liked to visit. They had a garden, fruit trees, berry bushes and plenty of space to play hide-and-seek. When there we gorged ourselves on unripe apples and berries, paying the price by getting sick.

Playing in our neighborhood was fun since we had a lot of friends, but it wasn't nearly as carefree as being at Grandma's house and benefitting from her generosity with edibles (particularly the sweet kind) or enjoying my grandparents' apparent disregard for the kind of corporal punishment so often meted out by our parents for seemingly small infractions. It was great to be there, to play endlessly, eat food and candy, and occasionally sleep over. So when our rich uncle from America gave each of us a super cool red trike for Christmas we began to plot. Now that we had transportation we had freedom and could go to Grandma's house just about any time we wanted.

One fine day in spring we found ourselves playing outside with our trikes and decided on an impulse to go see Grandma. We knew that it didn't take long to get there in a car, so how much longer could it take on a trike? We knew how to find our way, since we knew that the tram traveled on a track, and that the track passed reasonably close to our grandparent's house. All we had to do was follow the tracks. Telling our parents of our intentions didn't occur to us.

So we set off, following the track in the middle of heavy car traffic, trams, buses and fast-moving motorcycles. It was a slam dunk — about two hours later we showed up at Grandma's house on our bright red trikes, tired and ready for some sustenance. Grandma, of course, had received panicked calls from our moms, I think the authorities had been alerted, and a 1946 version of an Amber Alert had probably been issued to the police. Phone calls were exchanged, and while the panic subsided in all of the adults, it began to rise in us. We realized that we had caused havoc and we were due for a serious talking to and probably a spanking. Right on both counts — I think we learned a lesson that day.

During my entire childhood, adolescence and early adulthood, competitiveness was important, particularly in sports, much less so academically. My mother's younger sister and her husband urged their son, Peder (and best friend), along in sports, particularly sailing and alpine skiing. And it worked — he became an Olympic sailor with gold and silver medals to his credit in 1960 and 1968. He was also a great skier, winning races right and left. His parents, too, were accomplished sailors, both with an Olympic silver medal to their credit as skipper and crew member in the 1952 Olympics. My mother's younger brother also earned a silver medal in the 1952 Games in a different boat class.

Not to be outdone, my mother too participated in the 1952 Olympics in equestrian riding. Although she didn't earn a medal, she placed in the single digits (not bad). So the family had four participants in the '52 Olympics who harvested a lot of medals and accolades. It was a privilege to be a member of such an accomplished sports family.

Privileged, yes indeed, but this was also a double-edged sword. My sports prowess as a skier and sailor was probably above average, but not nearly up to the level of my cousin and his parents and their siblings. The memories are vivid — my struggles to become more like them, to excel, to become an Olympian, to compete at high levels were dreams never to be realized. I tried to compete, but always came up short.

One particular incident I remember well was when, on a rare occasion, I actually won a cross-country ski race. I remember being delirious with joy as I recounted the feat to my aunt. "Well that's great, I'm so happy for you," she said, "but, this was a school race, so none of the really good kids competed, did they?" Wow, what a joy crusher. Of course, my aunt had no intention to kill my joy; she only wanted me to build my confidence so I could tackle the really good kids later on. But, in the here and now, all I heard was the joy-crushing part — and it stuck with me for decades. My mom often implored me to be more like my Olympian cousin who had attained fame and fortune and made everyone proud.

Oddly enough, I don't think I resent any of this now, despite my obvious comparative deficiency in sports. This taught me valuable lessons that became very important later in life, even though they were probably badly misused as I applied them to my own family much later. At the time, though, my inability to measure up caused a lot of inadequate feelings that were difficult to overcome.

Growing up in Norway was not ostentatious, but certainly comfortable. As with most Norwegian kids, we had a great deal of freedom. Home was like a gas station where we filled up at mealtime and then left to hang out with friends. I fought a lot with my siblings; in fact my sister sometimes chased me with whatever weapon she could find, fully intent on inflicting lethal damage. Once I so frustrated her that she was ready to do me in. I scared her to death one day when I arrived at our apartment and heard her in the kitchen singing at the top of her lungs. Something evil stirred in my consciousness as I slowly inserted the key and pretended it didn't fit, pulled it out, inserted another key, juggled it around, and repeated this process two or three times. The singing stopped abruptly and was followed by a deep silence from inside. I knew I had her. I inserted the key again and again, slowly turned it, and then finally … click, the door opened and creaked just at the right decibel level, and I entered the apartment. Breathing heavily so she could hear it, I stepped inside and slowly advanced to the corner of the kitchen. I knew she was there and that she was probably close to panicking, so I took my time to savor the moment before I jumped into the doorway and yelled something like … "Boo!!!"

Well, upon seeing me, her face contorted into one of pure rage as her raw fear was instantly replaced with an uncontrollable urge to kill me. She grabbed a large bread knife and proceeded to chase me through the apartment. I discerned the urgency of the situation and headed for a different room while slamming the door behind me. She was right behind me. She kicked in the hollow door and made a large gaping hole in it, while screaming at me that my turn would come. Her intent to kill eventually subsided and I quietly left the apartment for a safer environment outside. I gained a healthy respect for her that time. Although we fought like cats and dogs when we were kids, now decades later, I love both of my siblings.

During my formative years I vividly remember the daily spankings administered by my mom—all well deserved. This, of course, was because I never really obeyed. I was always in trouble for exasperating my sister, forgetting stuff, lying, whatever reason (and there were many). And these weren't just spankings with bare hands; they were administered with wooden spoons which I had to select before the punishment was applied. It really hurt!! Where were political correctness and laws against corporal punishment when I really needed them?

At school I was less-than-mediocre because I had such a strong aversion to studying. Struggling along in my early school years, I tried to keep pace with my peers and to advance to the next class when they did. It was, more often than not, a lucky accident if I made it to the next level. That was all that counted, and it meant we hadn't wasted any effort. There was also a bit of sound strategy in all of this, since my parents had come to expect a poor performance from me over the years. So when I came home with the occasional (well actually, very few) As or Bs, I received praise and rewards.

I struggled valiantly with subjects like math and science in the early years but excelled in languages. Why I eventually pursued a Ph.D. in economics with a quantitative orientation is still a mystery to me. I truly understand the meaning and utility of remedial training — whatever I didn't learn during the earlier years came back to haunt me big-time in my graduate studies and had to be picked up painfully and with a lot of embarrassment.

In our pre-teen years ice hockey was big during the winter months. We filled the large playground sandbox next to our apartment building with water and fashioned an ice hockey rink of sorts, using large stones as goal posts and ill-defined out-of-bounds markers. If the puck got stuck in the adjacent shrubbery it was so obvious that we all agreed it was out of bounds. We formed teams and had more brutal ice hockey brawls than are seen in most NHL games today. Once I was hit in my forehead by a puck, which resulted in a severe case of bleeding. The injury itself was insignificant, but the bloody mess it caused convinced me that I was in mortal danger. I abandoned all dignity, bawled at the top of my lungs, and headed for home leaving a bloody trail in my wake.

Home was on the top floor. There was no elevator; all five flights of stairs had to be climbed, and a significant trail of blood was left on every step. Enter my mom, who had been out shopping. She quickly spotted the bloody trail, and, as she climbed the stairs, her anxiety increased as she gained the realization, with every flight, that it surely was one of her kids that had left that bloody trail. She had never climbed those stairs faster than she climbed them that day.

And then, there was the day that the temperature had descended into the lowest abyss of the scale when I solidly glued my tongue to the metal handle bar on the ground floor entry door to my apartment building. I did this precisely because my mom had told me not to touch my tongue to any metal when the temperature was sub-zero. So there I was, bent over and very stuck, feeling as stupid as is humanly possible. Luckily, we had an intercom, so I could call my mom and somehow confess my predicament in very garbled language. I can remember to this day her vague attempts to hold back hysterical laughter while attempting to commiserate with me as she freed me from the handle bar with a pot full of warm water. And yes ... I also did touch that electric burner on the stove after having received a similar admonition from my mom. I think I was probably a very stupid kid who would only learn the hard way.

We did a lot of skiing in Nordmarka, a beautiful wilderness area inside the Oslo city limit, where we could cross country ski and downhill ski for hours on end. It is a spectacular natural resource jewel which I sorely miss to this day. Skiing in Norway isn't just a way to pass the time; it is probably classified as a religion, or at the very least it is obligatory by law. During the long and dark winter season our evenings were spent night skiing on Nordmarka's floodlit slopes to which we all trekked after dinner. Television wasn't around then, at least not among my circle of friends, so the only potential distraction from our skiing passion was homework. Everybody would be done with dinner around 5 p.m. and still have plenty of time to grab skis and poles, hop on the tram, eventually arrive at the mountain area, and finally trek uphill for twenty minutes or so to the ski slope destination. We could be there within one hour and fifteen minutes after leaving the dinner table. There we would ski for fun or in races until after 8 p.m.

Skiing is a matter of national pride. We always do well in the Olympics in the skiing events. We don't mess around internationally with figure skating and curling and events, which require art and finesse (unless you count Sonia Henie — the Norwegian figure skater Olympian of the '30s and later movie star), and instead we focus more on the "brawn" disciplines like cross country skiing, ski jumping, and alpine racing. I was caught up in this passion and became a reasonably adept skier, although not of the caliber that floats to the top internationally.

I started in many races, crashed and burned a lot, got myself ready for the next event, crashed and burned again, and so it went.

I habitually competed against my older brother, my cousin, and all of my friends. If anything, this built and honed a competitive spirit that has remained with me to this day, much to the chagrin of my wife and family. I hated to lose, and everything became competitive; one-on-one outings of any kind, hikes, bike rides, tennis matches, skiing, whatever — which probably sapped the joy from whomever I was with (unless I was with someone of the same ilk, then it spoiled my joy if he or she beat me). Much later in life, my wife played one game of tennis and one round of golf with me and then decided never again. Now, in my advanced age I think I have mellowed some, so here it is honey: I am sorry — I apologize profusely — it will never happen again ... wanna play a round of golf?

In the Norwegian summer the sun sets for only a few short hours, and the ice hockey rink-sandbox playground was the main venue for at least twenty-five to thirty kids to carry out Armageddon-like warfare between cowboys and Indians late into the evening. It was always cooler to be a cowboy, because we had six-shooters that actually made noise when we pulled the trigger, so we died less and could fire our guns more. Come to think of it, the way we played with toy guns and rubber knives in those days would today be fodder for newspaper stories and expert psychological warnings about fostering real violence.

Indians, with their clumsy bows, stick arrows, and rubber knives, were a bit hapless and more prone to getting hit. So when they did get hit, we cowboys told them to fall over and stay put until we declared victory. They talked funny just like Indians did in the movies, which we amplified by embellishing Indian-speak with Norwegian. I think the cowboys always won — that's why it was always cooler to be on their team. We had guidelines classifying a gunshot hit as fatal or flesh wound, so arguments abounded on that subject. How we managed to survive all this without getting into real fights is still a mystery to me.

During the adolescent years, my best friend was Jan Børre Sundene, or Børsen for short. He was one year older than me. We did everything together — chased girls, partied, drank too much, smoked, and generally acted as most Norwegian juveniles did those days. We shared a love for modern jazz, particularly the Oscar Peterson trio variety. We could sit in his bedroom for hours and listen to Oscar Peterson records on his gramophone-outfitted state-of-the-art stereo system and know every possible musical expression and rhythm emanating from the solo performances of Ray Brown on bass, Herb Ellis on guitar, and Oscar Peterson on the piano. We had a strong passion for such things, which I sorely miss. If we had a collection of three or four records we felt rich and would listen to them repeatedly, eventually knowing every beat, note, and nuance.

Børsen and I attended every big name jazz concert we could, especially the Oscar Peterson trio with Herb Ellis and Ray Brown, Ella Fitzgerald, the Dave Brubeck Quartet, Sonny Rollins, Stan Getz, and many others who often toured Europe. Since I played the drums in the school marching band I also developed some (albeit small) skills as a jazz drummer. This led to filling in with established bands on dance gigs in and around Oslo on several occasions. I even got paid sometimes.

My foray into the world of jazz music with Børsen and several of my other friends who had similar tastes and who were also budding jazz musicians, hatched the idea of creating a jazz club. We had the perfect venue for this—a seldom- used theater hall in our neighborhood that could accommodate up to 200 devoted jazz fans, and a stage where the performers did their thing. The club was launched, and for about two years we hosted weekly events with different jazz musicians, charged an entrance fee, and sold soft drinks like crazy. Our membership reached 150, not bad for a bunch of sixteen-year-olds who put this together.

For the most part the musicians entertaining us were local and probably not very good. Every now and then, however, the US Navy docked for several days in Oslo, and we were the first ones showing up to recruit American jazz musicians from among the sailors. More often than not, the sailor musicians were black, which of course surpassed everything in coolness—we were the hottest ticket in town. We all felt on top of the world as the old theater hall was magically transformed into an international venue brimming with great soul and blues music late into the night. Those were fun days indeed.

Børsen and I did everything together, including long sailing excursions during the summer. Once we borrowed a Grimstadjolle for the summer — a 15-foot sailboat with no outboard motor and only a small paddle to power us forward in case of no wind. The boat had a small deck, so we had some cover while sleeping. It was truly great — total independence, eat and drink whatever, go to sleep whenever, or stay up all night if we wanted. We usually sailed during the night, since that's when a gentle north breeze powered us along as we proceeded on a southward course. Navigation was handled with a small compass and knowledge of the waters, as long as we hugged the coastline.

We had friends at vacation homes all along the coastline, and we made sure to stop to see them so we could pick up a free meal, a dry place to sleep, and just hang out. Come to think of it, all of our friends mooched off of other friends' families. We too had a vacation home in the mountains and we had friends coming to stay with us, eat our food — we all did it to each other. It never occurred to us that our parents might have had something to say about all of this. Perhaps this was their way of doing things in their younger days as well so they weren't too bothered. Money was very scarce and so we made excellent use of our extensive network of friends vacationing at their parents' summer homes along the coastline for all of our needs.

One particular trip took us away from home about two months. I think I called once from a payphone, which was about the extent of the communication I had with my parents. I am still trying figure out what my parents were thinking when they allowed me, at the mature age of fifteen, to go on an unsupervised sailing trip involving some open ocean crossing in a tiny 15-foot sailing boat with my sixteen-year-old best friend. The only explanation I can come up with is that we weren't the only ones. I had other friends the same age doing the same thing. We often met up while on the water and sometimes ended up in convoys of two or three boats. This was just the way it was. Parents supported us with food, shelter, and small allowances rather than nurture and supervision. Friends were everything; hanging out with them was the alpha and omega.

THE CULTURE

Norway's youth culture during those years probably wasn't unlike the culture in the US. We liked rock n' roll music and went wild when Bill Haley and the Comets came on the scene. We didn't "cruise main street" in cars; we instead roamed main street on foot or on bikes. Our transportation consisted of local buses and trams, bicycles, and for the few of us with some money, a Vespa scooter, or a moped. I was of the moped variety, always borrowing (stealing?) my mom's to run around.

I was very much caught up in the euphoria of the emerging rock and roll scene, but never really liked Elvis because his appeal reso-nated much more with the kids from the "other side of the tracks" on the east side of the town. We were incredibly snobbish—the kids from west side—because we came from white collar families, while the east side kids were largely blue collar. They were prone to settle arguments with their fists; we attempted to settle them with our vastly superior (or so we thought) intellects. The real truth is that we probably rarely engaged with the east side kids for fear of being pulverized.

Where my family lived, however, wasn't west enough. We lived near downtown but on the west side, so that was good. Further out west but still in Oslo, however, was where the really privileged kids lived. They attended the cool schools and were members of the much-coveted skiing and sailing clubs established in their neighbor-hoods. Soccer was considered proletarian (practiced extensively by the east side kids) and the really cool kids had little to do with it. I was secretly fond of the sport (because I was pretty good at it), but that wasn't an acceptable sport in my sought-after elite circle of friends.

In our early teen years we all smoked cigarettes and drank lots of very cheap liquor. Smoking was cool then, and nobody had yet fig-ured out that it was unhealthy. All of my friends' parents smoked, as did all of the adults in my extended family, and everyone drank a lot of wine and hard liquor because Norwegians love to imbibe while socializing—that was the prevailing culture. When my parents hosted a dinner party guests would be greeted with a cocktail or two for start-ers, followed by two or three different wines with dinner, followed by coffee and cognac in the living room. After that was when the real drinking would start—the gin and tonics, the scotch and sodas, the rum and cokes, and so on. It would typically last until two or three in the morning. For a dinner party of eight, I am sure at least eight packs of cigarettes would be consumed—all non-filtered. So, any heart-to-heart talks with us about the evils of smoking and drinking obviously had no effect at all.

The funny thing about this was that my parents didn't get obnox-iously drunk despite the fact that they consumed a lot of alcohol in various forms (wine, beer, hard liquor). Drinking and smoking were simply a part of the social fabric of the stretched out partying—over long hours of social interaction with lots of food accompanying the booze. As I remember, the adults seemed to know how to handle it—a result of much practice. We (the teens), however, had not yet devel-oped the skills needed to hold our liquor, as it were, nor did we have the money to buy quality booze, so we experienced very frequent bouts with over-indulgence and hangovers. Many of my friends have indeed developed alcohol problems since those days.

A major part of the culture we all dreaded was the draft. Many of us waited for as long as possible hoping the draft would end; others enlisted early just to get it over with. I was in the latter category. I en-listed and became a radar operator in the military—the Royal Norwe-gian Air Force—as a young man during the early '60s. I was on active duty during the Cuban missile crisis and remember sitting in the mess hall, eyes glued to the black-and-white TV, as we watched Kennedy's speech announcing the embargo on all ships sailing to Cuba. Perhaps it hadn't been the best of all ideas to have volunteered for military ser-vice at that particular time, we were all thinking.

We were routed out of our bunks in the middle of the night during this crisis to run around in the woods playing war games, throwing live grenades, digging trenches, and preparing the perimeter around our base against attacks. At the time, we all thought this was the real thing. The Russians were about to descend on us in the early stages of

World War III. After all, our small military base—a radar operator station—located inside the Oslo city limits was part of NATO (the North Atlantic Treaty Organization), sure to be attacked first by our neighbor to the northeast.

Needless to say, the tension during those days was palpable. We woke up every morning thinking that this could be the day when we would be called on to defend our land. But it didn't happen, so the worries began to abate. The whole experience made me sympathetic to what our troops in Iraq and Afghanistan must have gone through every day.

After spending my obligatory eighteen months in the military I focused again on exploring my academic career options. It was not because I wanted to learn; it probably had to do with wanting to catch up with my buddies who had postponed their military service. Many of them had remained in school while I valiantly defended them as a radar operator, and I so desperately wanted to catch up in order to experience the month-long partying following graduation with them, rather than with the younger kids whom I didn't know. So I chose to attend a private school specializing in collapsing three years of orderly study into one year of highly intense and chaotic study. The school had a reasonably good reputation, but it was hard. The flunk rate was about 70%, so we all expected to repeat the experience. But that was OK. What was important was the partying with my contemporaries. True enough, I was among the 70%, so I had to repeat the year. The second time around I passed with flying colors and was now eligible to attend a university.

At this point, though, I had reached the inevitable fork in the road. Culturally, all of us looked outside the country for study opportunities, because they were very limited at home. My accumulated experiences in the military and working off and on in my dad's hardware store were not enough. I could have been groomed for an eventual takeover of the family business, which was tempting because of the income. But alas, it was also a double-edged sword, since it entailed actually having to earn my pay. How dreadful. So, after much soul-searching and listening to my friends, I decided in favor of higher education. I knew that with my rather mediocre grades I wouldn't be admitted into the line of study I wanted to pursue — business — at the university in Oslo. The only real possibility was to apply overseas. Many of my friends had chosen to enter a business curriculum in St. Gallen in Switzerland, which I also considered. But another large contingent of friends had successfully applied to universities in the US, not only to study, but also to race on the university ski teams. Now that sounded great. Besides, I considered my English to be far better than my German, and the US was sort of cool, as my returning-from-vacation friends told me with their newly-acquired American swagger and mannerisms.

So that was it — I wanted to study in the US and at the same university where many of my friends were. I began applying, dreaming, counting my money, and talking my parents into the prospect of my leaving home and heading for the great unknown.

CHAPTER 2: EARLY STUDY AND WORK YEARS

STUDYING IN THE US

"I have been accepted at the University of Idaho, and ... I will get a partial scholarship to be on the UI ski team!" I shouted as I opened the letter.

This was a big deal. I had friends already there, and they had told me tales of their exciting experiences which made me want to go there like nothing else I had ever wanted before. My English, I thought, was fairly fluent (which it wasn't), my skiing skills were right up there (which they weren't), and I had always been good as a student just getting by and making it to the next level. Little did I know. Surely I would do well, get my degree, do some serious partying as a university student, and then come home to a spectacular job paying an astronomical salary—or better yet, work overseas while being based in the US. That letter conjured up an infinite number of possibilities—all very good.

Being on the university ski team is how many Norwegians made it to the US as students in those days. Our high school diplomas were roughly equivalent to slightly less than two years at a university in the US, so technically we should all have started as juniors. But, language difficulties and a lack of similarity in subject matters studied in Norway and the US resulted in fewer approved advanced credits, so I started as a sophomore with three years to go before earning my BS degree.

The summer was spent counting the money I had set aside or needed to raise for this eventuality, procuring the best skiing equipment and clothes that would make me blend in well in America, and looking into the cheapest possible mode of transportation. Late July 1963 finally arrived, and I took the suitcase I had packed months before, my skis and boots, and headed for the airport. There I said goodbye to my worried parents and boarded an old Icelandic Airlines DC 6 to begin a 24-hour flight to New York, with refueling stopovers in Reykjavik and Newfoundland. I'm sure we barely arrived at each stop coughing in on the remaining fumes in the tank. And hey, guess what, we didn't have any airport security, no TSA gropers, and no electronic tickets. We just showed up and boarded the plane after producing a valid paper ticket.

Hello, New York! Getting off the plane and retrieving my luggage is just a blur in my memory. The sight of me standing in the taxi line carrying alpine skis and cool Munari ski boots in stifling New York late July heat must have been a something to behold. Needless to say, the New Yorkers stared at me. I was lucky to eventually find a taxi driver willing to accommodate long skis and a big suitcase for the trip to downtown Manhattan. I had the address of a friend who worked in the shipping industry there, so that's where I was headed. I remember the taxi driver letting me off about a block from where the office was, and I had to walk the rest of the way in the heat of midday, skis on my shoulder, boots hung around my neck, and carrying a heavy suitcase without wheels. This was my entry into the US.

Two days in New York City was followed by a week or so with my family in Darien, mother's younger brother and his wife and kids. Basse (his nickname) was already well on the US east coast, having graduated from Dartmouth and Harvard, and was on a fast climb in the corporate world. He was the one we all wanted emulate. All of his friends and neighbors in Darien were presidents and/or CEOs and so he managed to hitch a ride for me on a corporate airplane that was traveling to Los Angeles. That's the only time I took a ride on a private plane with bigwig corporate executives. It was a memorable trip.

I spent most of my time in the cockpit with the crew while all of the executives in the back got tanked on way too much booze.

Upon arrival in LA I found my way to the Greyhound bus depot to catch my ride to Idaho. By now I was used to the stares and occasional laughter from people who clearly didn't appreciate the beauty of Munari boots and the latest in ski equipment, even though it was late summer and very hot. Finally, I arrived in Moscow, Idaho, on August 3, 1963. I had the address and a phone number of some friends from Norway and managed to locate a bed in their apartment where I began to settle in. My life as a student at the University of Idaho had begun.

The choice of international business as a major was easy for me. It fell in line with what I really wanted: to get my green card, live in the US, and work in international business. What could be better than earning a good US salary while working in many different countries on assignments that always varied so you wouldn't simply ossify and perish from pure boredom, and you would be able to learn foreign languages to boot? I already had a head start on the languages, so that made it even easier to decide on this line of study. In Norway I had already completed nine years of English, five years of German, and five years of French before I moved to the US to attend college, in addition to my native fluency in Norwegian and the other Nordic languages. In my chosen field of study linguistic competence was strongly recommended. So I figured I had an edge since languages were the least of my worries (well, this is what I thought—it is amazing how quickly one forgets everything if practice is abandoned).

However, one semester in and it quickly dawned on me that business and foreign trade weren't my cup of tea. Business, management, marketing and all of the associated stuff that accompanies a business curriculum just didn't resonate, so I began to gravitate toward what I saw as a related field—economics. After all, it's all about the money, right? My first foray into the world of economics, however, was to take a required Principles of Microeconomics class from an instructor whose mission in life must have been to make a fascinating subject matter excruciatingly boring and complex so that I completely abandoned any attempt at studying, which resulted in a big fat F on my transcript. I had to repeat the class, but this time from an instructor who had a different approach, and I was hooked forever. Not only did I decide to pursue economics, I decided to go to graduate school and in the end I managed, against all odds, to get my Ph.D. in Agriculture and Natural Resource Economics in 1974 from Washington State University.

I was a less-than-mediocre student as an undergraduate, finishing my first semester with a 1.83 GPA. The second semester wasn't much better. Throughout my career as an undergraduate student, though, I somehow managed to do just enough studying to keep myself out of serious academic trouble while, at the same time, not sacrificing any of my priority to party. I ended up graduating with a stellar GPA of 2.13 in 1966, not exactly a proud moment. So I admit it—I didn't shine academically. I was more into hanging out with friends, preparing for the ski season, playing on the university soccer team, and doing a lot of partying. I guess this wasn't atypical for college students during those days, because I sure had a lot of friends and fellow students doing the exact same thing.

I met Judi in 1964 in McCall, Idaho on a skiing weekend, only one year into my studies. Urges to get a bit of seriousness and responsibility soon began to creep ever so slowly into my sub-consciousness since she actually agreed to go out with me. She was a truly smart lady with matching good looks, and one who actually studied and was used to getting excellent grades. She was also totally different from anyone else we—the Norwegians—were chasing every day and I think it didn't take very long before I was head-over-heels in love. I had to shape up and increase the quality quotient in my personhood to win this one. So I began to change my ways. Miraculously, I graduated. And so, armed with a spanking new and shiny BS degree in business, I was ready for the job market.

I first landed a job with Shell Oil Company, and Judi and I decided to get married and our journey together was launched. The job with Shell Oil didn't last long as I sorely missed the student life. We soon found ourselves returning to the UI for a master's degree after I literally begged my way back in. After two more years of study, that goal was reached in 1970, and now I was truly hooked. Being an almost perpetual student and gaining in intellect by leaps and bounds from book learning, I had grown very comfortable in my lifestyle. Judi was working and made enough for us to live and eat, and I held temporary jobs as an economics instructor, or did research for pay—probably minimum wage. We cobbled together enough work to be able to live in reasonable comfort, yet maintaining our image as poor students with lots of friends in the same boat.

Life was good in academia, so why not go all the way and get a Ph.D.? I had had an awakening as an academic and had discovered the joys of actually studying and learning something. Economics at the master's level was fascinating, economic theory assumed a life of its own in my consciousness, and intellectual discussions with friends about anything connected with economics were abundant. We (my friends and I, not Judi) were oh … so … nauseating.

With my stellar performance at the MS level (3.9 GPA), it was easy to be admitted into the Ph.D. program at Washington State University (WSU), just across the border, nine miles away. My chosen field was agricultural economics, majoring in natural resources and agriculture—as far removed from my European background as conceivably possible. What did I know about agriculture, or natural resources? I was an urban kind of guy from Norway and my knowledge about earthy things extended to my visits to the grocery store to buy fresh vegetables. Somehow, though, I was drawn into applied economics and I was determined to make a career out of land, trees, and water and all associated economics. My Ph.D. was completed in 1974, which marked the end of my academic career that had begun eleven years earlier.

SHELL OIL COMPANY

I think I fit well into the category of people who can't hold down a regular job. Growing up in Norway I held part-time jobs just to get cash I could spend during vacations when not mooching off my friends' families at their vacation homes. In the US I had to get special work permits so I could remain in-country for up to eighteen months while gaining work experience. With my first job with Shell Oil Company in Seattle, the 18-month clock started ticking. During the interview with Shell I had stated my intention to gain work experience in the US and then be transferred to Shell's offices in Europe. Other Norwegians had done exactly that before me, so it really wasn't a wild idea. Even back then, my mind was fixed on an international career.

My salary was set at $500 per month, which was big money for me at the time. Just to have money on a regular basis was a true novelty and I was looking forward to embarking on a career in business, following in my family's footsteps. After the honeymoon, Judi and I packed up our meager belongings and headed for Seattle in our rickety 1955 Studebaker I had bought for $200. There we found a small one-bedroom apartment on Queen Anne Hill, not far from the Space Needle, and set up house. I think our rent was a whopping $90 a month, gas cost $0.32 per gallon, and groceries cost us another $100 per month. Judi had a job, and we taught skiing on weekends. We actually had plenty left over for skiing and fun.

It quickly dawned on me, however, that a career with Shell Oil wasn't going to become my cup of tea. Frankly, it was a miserable job and I wasn't very good at it, because I made all the mistakes imaginable. My vision of a job for a college graduate back then was one where I could wear a suit, get a company car and have an office and a briefcase full of important papers. Of course, that's not what happened. I and all of the other young sales folks hired at the same time were told we needed on-the-ground training in the business before we were allowed to wear our suits and carry briefcases and … get that all-important company car.

The training was humiliating; we complained. We were fitted with service station uniforms (we called them brown monkey suits), assigned to a Shell service station (when gas stations actually offered tires, batteries, and accessories — or TBA in our company lingo — in addition to mechanical services), taught to serve the customers (checking oil, fan belts, tires, and cleaning the windshields, etc.), and actually performing the services needed.

"Your oil is low, ma'am, and it is dirty, how about pulling it into the bay and we'll fix it right up for you?" Or, "… I checked one of your spark plugs and you really need a tune-up, ma'am. We have an opening in one of our bays right now, so how about it? It won't take long and there's coffee in the waiting room …" Although I have a very low aptitude for car mechanics, I learned to do oil changes, tune-ups, brake jobs, pack wheel bearings by hand, change tires in record time, and other car fixes. And, I also learned how to clean gas station toilets (I don't recommend the latter as a long-term occupation).

I said earlier this was a miserable job. In retrospect, however, it was probably one of the best jobs I've ever had. At that time, I was as snobbish and entitlement-prone as young men today are, thinking they own the world and should have everything handed to them on a platter. They don't know — and I certainly didn't — that when they are lucky enough to actually get a job, they will be completely useless in most occupations until they learn what makes that business tick. I needed to learn the car business, the oil business, sales, marketing, and customer service from the ground up. And that meant getting your hands dirty until the management deemed you were ready to get your own sales territory.

I finally graduated from this basic training to become a sales-man-in-training. This meant I was working under the supervision of a real salesman in his territory. More importantly, I could shed my "monkey suit" and dress in my own duds. And now I could drive around in a company car and have an expense account. Things were looking up a bit.

After six months in Seattle, we were transferred to the Shell regional office in Sacramento, California. This was my return to the monkey suit to become the manager of local (problem) service stations that had lost their dealers. Some stations were flourishing because they were in great locations; others were problem stations because of mismanagement, or their locations had become less desirable as traffic patterns changed. Every city and every oil company would have stations like this and they had to be kept open. So managing these stations became my job.

In the '60s, service stations were known for their generous special events: free cokes, free steak knives, free drinking glasses, and most importantly Blue Chip stamps or S & H Green stamps with any purchase over eight gallons. We had lines of cars waiting to be served, and I was there from dawn to dusk pumping gas, doing brake jobs, tune-ups, and oil changes, and, at the end of the day, the books. While I remember hating every minute of it, this was a great job in retrospect. It taught me so many good things that would come in very handy later in life. Nevertheless, back to school we went.

FMC

After completing my MS degree, we briefly traveled to Norway to (sort of) look for a job. It really was a tepid job search because my heart was still in academia and the good student life, so the trip actually became a fairly long vacation with a lot of traveling rather than an intensive job search in my native country. So we returned as soon as we found out I had been accepted by the Ph.D. program at WSU, where I spent the next four years studying and working.

My first real job just out of the chute with a brand new Ph.D. in agricultural economics in 1974 was with FMC (known before as the Food Machinery Corporation), based in San Jose, California. FMC at the time had a division that manufactured and sold agricultural processing plants and farm equipment all over the world, and this was the division that hired several of us from the WSU Agricultural Economics Department. My new job was to work for a just-created consulting arm of this division.

This literally was a dream job. It had all of the attractions that I had always wanted: international travel, good pay, fascinating work, interesting people to work with, and a chance to wear a suit and look important. No workday would be the same as the previous one, no boring routines, and ample opportunities (I naively thought) to apply everything I had learned in academia to the real world. The excitement quotient was high and Judi was eager to get started with this life as well. I think the clincher for accepting the job was the possibility for Judi to travel with me as a non-paid employee of the company but

with all of the costs covered. What a deal. Besides, the market in academia for agricultural economists had dried up.

The dreams were plentiful and vivid, the anticipation high. We
knew before we moved to the Bay Area in California that our first assignment would be to travel to the Middle East and Eastern Europe
to work on three potential projects. One was an irrigated vegetable
farming project on 300,000 feddans (1 feddan = 1.038 acres) of desert
land between Cairo and Alexandria in Egypt. Another was a range
re-vegetation project in northern Iran. The third was an ongoing vegetable farming project in Bulgaria. My job, as one of the project economists, was to establish the economic and financial feasibility of these
projects, activity by activity, sector by sector, and then sell these results
to the decision-makers holding the money so that we could build food-
processing plants all over the world. It certainly made sense—what
could be more logical than to first consult on what to do for clients and
then to recommend that FMC plants and equipment would be just the
ticket to get the jobs done?

So we packed up and moved to San Jose, California, where we
promptly moved into the hip Oakwood Garden Apartment complex,
complete with pools and exercise rooms and all sorts of social infrastructure. We were ready to join the international jet set and the apartment complex was full of like-minded young people.

As soon as we had settled in, I was tapped to embark on my first
trip to Cairo and Tehran. The moment of truth had arrived; it was time
to start negotiating the contracts for the Egypt vegetable production
and the Iranian range re-vegetation projects. Many important people
were involved in the Egyptian project including the then Vice President of Egypt, Hosni Mubarak, plus several ministers of various de-
partments and many others from both the private and public sectors
who were politically or economically there for a piece of the action. In
Iran we were to meet with the upper echelons of the Ministry of Agriculture as well as other ministries. These were the days in the mid-'70s
when Anwar Sadat and the Shah of Iran were firmly in power in Egypt
and Iran, respectively. The excitement was high octane and everyone
involved anticipated great things out of these projects.

And then there I was, with my brand new shiny Ph.D., now a member of this high-powered team. I was told to get a dark suit and a haircut, and to act as if I were truly urbane and sophisticated with lots of experience and possessed tremendous negotiating skills despite my youthful appearance. After all, I was the economist who needed to convince the powers-that-be that these projects were the real deal and that they would indeed solve a lot of economic woes in both countries. I was already trembling from the anxiety of having been so rapidly removed from my safe cocoon of academia into such a politically charged and high-flying environment as this.

To add fuel to the anxiety fire, I was given another assignment on this trip, namely to hand-carry a very expensive wedding gift from FMC to a young Egyptian man who was soon to be married to Anwar Sadat's daughter. This man also happened to work for FMC in Egypt as a local economist who, as it turned out, was to report to me. I was hand carrying this very expensive gift for him and his young bride-to-be, along with official letters from the Egyptian authorities to avoid any problems I might encounter with the custom authorities along the way. This all went well, and I arrived in Cairo with a sigh of relief as the gift was handed over to the right people.

Before leaving California I had run the numbers for all of the projects and so was at least reasonably well prepared in that department. All of the activities to be implemented, of course, involved our eventual supply of state-of-the-art processing facilities and equipment so that large volumes of vegetables could be efficiently turned into exportable final products in record time. Everything had been carefully considered and the analysis was ready, as were my talking points. On paper, therefore, it was a slam dunk. The projects were feasible and I was ready. I packed up the expensive gift, my dark blue suit, combed my now short hair, kissed my wife goodbye and was off to my first two-week trip beginning in Cairo and then on to Tehran.

Upon arrival at the Cairo airport, chaos ensued immediately. As I entered the building I saw a disheveled man with a four-day-old beard holding a sign bearing my name. He seemed to be in a hurry, and as I identified myself, he promptly demanded that I surrender my passport and some money to him. I figured I had no choice but to trust him and produced the passport and a $100 bill from my wallet (which was about all the cash I had in my wallet). He promptly told me to stay put, and he then disappeared into the chaotic crowd of people waiting to retrieve their luggage. Meanwhile, my luggage arrived, and I was immediately surrounded by porters who fought over the right to help me, never mind that I didn't want or need any help with my luggage.

One of them finally won, and we proceeded to the disorganized queue waiting to be processed through immigration. Everyone except me, I quickly observed, had their passports in hand ready to be processed. I was the only one without money and passport, and I began to experience the early onset of panic. I instinctively knew I had been had and was already beginning to think about how to contact the embassy from my jail cell somewhere at the airport.

But then miraculously and suddenly, my airport greeter appeared from nowhere with my passport and a huge wad of paper money in hand to usher me and my porter to the front of the queue. He was handing out money left and right from the thick wad. I just stayed as close as I could, now extremely thankful that my life had been fully restored and that my anxiety had all been for naught.

We got through the immigration barrier in record time, more money exchanged hands, and all of a sudden we were securely on the other side looking at the next barrier — the customs officers. Before we got to that point, however, I was once more told to stay put, and my anxiety increased as my greeter disappeared. Ten minutes later he reappeared with the porter, toting a case of scotch and some other bottles of booze he had procured at the duty free shop with my passport. This, of course, was odd in and of itself because we were in a Muslim country, so up went my anxiety level yet again because we still had to go through customs. But money solves so many things; the wad of cash became thinner and thinner as we proceeded through the maze, and soon we found ourselves outside the customs barrier, the wedding gift, passport, and luggage still in my possession, plus lots of liquor procured in my name to boot. A car appeared, more money was handed to the porter, and we loaded up and were on our way.

Despite the extracurricular activities at the duty free shop, we were actually the first ones to leave the airport. On the way to the hotel I asked the airport greeter who he was and what had happened to the cash. He laughed, told me he was the personal assistant to one of the ministers we were supposed to meet with, handed me the remaining cash and said he had spent about $20 out of the $100 I had given him. Over the next week he functioned in the role of a remarkably effective expediter and also became a close friend.

As we began our work in Cairo, it had the earmarks of intense political and international intrigue from the very beginning, and I was right in the middle of it, not just as an observer, but as an integral member of the team. To put it mildly, I was frightened to death and found myself often longing for the safe environment of being a university professor somewhere. What if I flubbed up and was guilty if the project were not funded? What if all I knew and applied in the analyses as an economist for these projects was regarded as nothing but equations and academic jargon? Would I be able to function out there in the real world without my academic security blanket? What if I committed a political faux pas in the presence of these high-powered movers and shakers? These and many other questions ravaged my brains during the sleepless nights in Cairo.

The first lesson I learned very clearly during the meetings was that political realities always trump economic realities. Although we think we walk on water many times, our economic analyses are often rendered moot as soon as the political realities emerge. I remember vividly one social occasion where several ministers attended and business was transacted in a polite and jovial manner over food and drink. It soon came to pass that all of my economic feasibility measures I had so carefully prepared evaporated rather quickly, as did my eloquent talking points.

Obviously, the ministers involved in the project had a stake in the action. Whereas they extolled the soundness of the main project component—the irrigated production of vegetables in the desert area between Cairo and Alexandria—they didn't see the need to establish new processing facilities because they already had their own fully functioning ones up and running already, thank you very much. Well, of course both they and we knew quite well that their processing facilities were in a dismal condition and could not in any way, shape or form even be retrofitted to handle the increases in volume, let alone meet the strict food-processing standards required in the export market.

What to do? Their feigned reluctance to new processing plants had to be overcome. The president of our division explained to me that this was all a standard and expected part of the process of doing business in the Middle East. The ministers wanted a part of the action, and in order for us to proceed with the project we would have to secure their cooperation in different ways. So, after the dinner and before the social event was over, arrangements had already begun to shore up this potential deal-breaker, and the amount tentatively settled upon, with a clear implicit understanding of what was going on but hidden under a thin veil of legitimacy, was roughly $1.5 million. With that bit of news handed to me during one social dinner on the day before I was to make my presentation, I realized that my analysis of the much-anticipated project was at risk of being obliterated. I didn't know if the additional $1.5 million of cost would break the economic feasibility bank. Not fully cognizant of the fact that this was all probably illegal, but suspecting so nevertheless, I stammered that I would have to rerun the numbers to see if the project could withstand a $1.5 million cut off the top while still remaining feasible.

That night I stayed up and recalculated everything by hand (we didn't have any handy laptop computers or hand calculators that could do cash flow analysis then), accounting for an additional $1.5 million worth of costs to see if indeed the project could withstand the higher costs. Whew!!! Yes, it could — the project would still be strongly feasible.

Another meeting was also quite memorable — the one when we were picked up at the hotel by a large official car with flags on the hood and a motorcycle escort. I was in my brand-new dark blue suit, a matching tie with the appropriate dimple, hair combed, a briefcase full of important papers loaded with talking points. We hit the streets with horns blaring; the motorcycle escort cleared the way and we arrived at our destination in record time. This was the office of the then Vice President of Egypt: His Excellency, Hosni Mubarak. He had agreed to meet with us because this project was deemed both politically and economically important and he wanted to give it some visibility.

After waiting the appropriate amount of time in the office ante-room, our entourage was ushered into the inner sanctum – the VP's office – where he met and greeted us. Hands were shaken and pleasantries were exchanged, and just as I thought we would be getting down to business, the TV crews were ushered in. More handshakes, more photo ops, more pleasantries, but no business was transacted at all. Soon we were back in the limo with the motorcycle escort blaring through the streets of Cairo back to the hotel.

So that was my meeting with His Excellency, Vice President Hosni Mubarak. I must say I wasn't really that impressed with getting so close to the center of power in Egypt. I had fully expected to be called upon to wax eloquent about the economic benefits of this project, but alas … no glory for me.

And so it went during this hectic week in Cairo, from meeting to meeting, more political realities to deal with, all contributing to sleepless nights, far removed from the safe academic cocoon of which I had been a part in my previous life. Besides the business aspects and all of the associated adrenalin-producing moments these meetings engendered, being in Egypt was fascinating. Cairo is a bustling city filled with people, commerce, cars, buses and taxis, all honking their horns at the same time. The horn definitely is the most important piece of equipment on any vehicle in Cairo. Drivers with faulty horns would not venture out on the clogged streets and roads at all, I was told. The rest of the week in Cairo was filled with meetings and more meetings, and our team left Egypt reasonably assured that the project was in hand. And so we were off to Tehran to repeat the process there.

******

In Iran, the experience was totally different. This was during the days when the Shah of Iran was in power and Tehran was teeming with western business visitors, all wanting their piece of the plentiful oil revenues. We were in that mix and had traveled to Iran to promote the merits of our proposed range re-vegetation project to the Ministry of Agriculture. This was a project the Iranians had wanted to see implemented, but it became increasingly apparent after several meetings with the Ministry officials that our approach would not be the winning one. Perhaps it was the fact that we didn't offer a sufficient amount of "baksheesh" or unofficial encouragement, which cemented our failure to win this project.

The Iranian experience also ended on a tragic note — all of the Ministry of Agriculture officials we met with at the time, including the minister and his deputies, were executed a few years later by the Ayatollah Khomeini regime that took over when the Shah was ousted.

******

On our next trip overseas, two of the three projects were still in play: Bulgaria and Egypt. Judi was traveling with me this time as our official team secretary, and she was a Godsend. We were as modern and efficient as we could possibly be, armed with a small, but cute, portable manual typewriter, typing paper, and Dictaphone. I was a seasoned businessman by this time, accustomed to staying in 4-star hotels, dictating on the balcony while Judi transcribed on the portable typewriter. Our mission in Europe was to conduct market surveys for the canned foods we were about to export from Egypt and Bulgaria. So we contacted all sorts of importers, sent them questionnaires, recorded their responses, and Judi typed the reports I dictated.

The trip began in Brussels, then on to Paris, over to Sofia and Plovdiv, Bulgaria behind the Iron Curtain, and then down to Cairo, Beirut, and finally back to Europe again — to Rome. It was a great trip and especially so because Judi traveled with me at no cost.

Funny things happened everywhere on this trip, though. First, in Paris we stayed at one of the downtown Hilton hotels in a room on the fourteenth floor. I was an avid jogger at the time, and this hotel was in the perfect spot, because right across the street was a soccer stadium with a jogging track. So dressed in my jogging shorts and shoes, I told Judi I was going on a run just across the street. Looking pretty scruffy, however, I decided to forego the ride down the elevator with all of those impeccably dressed European dignitaries, and instead ran down the 14 flights stairs until I reached the street level.

The exit door was locked, however, and displayed one of those signs that said in French : *This is an emergency door only – don't open, it is wired to the hotel alarm system.* But at the time even my latent French expertise didn't kick in so I promptly grabbed the door handle and pushed the door open. It *was* wired to the alarm system. The hotel exploded in a cacophony of loud alarms while I, now safely outside with no one having seen the idiocy I had just perpetrated, found out that I could really run fast when I had a purpose for it. My purpose was to get as far away as possible to avoid being associated with this deed. Safely on the jogging track across the street I kept listening to the alarms howling away at the hotel for seemingly an eternity, at least for two to three laps around the track. When things had finally quieted down, I put on my innocent face and returned to the hotel lobby all sweaty and breathing hard only to ride up the elevator to the fourteenth floor with impeccably dressed European dignitaries who all seemed to be quietly saying to themselves, "He really should be riding up in the service elevator." I found out later that the hotel staff had apparently begun the process of evacuating the guests before they found out where the alarm had been triggered.

******

After Paris we traveled to Sofia, Bulgaria on an old and noisy Air Bulgaria aircraft manufactured by Aeroflot, probably twenty to thirty years earlier. To put it mildly, the plane was decrepit. The paint was peeling, the fuselage had huge cracks, and the inside had not been refurbished since the day it rolled off the assembly line. We decided to risk it and stepped on board along with the other risk-taking passengers who all seemed to have accepted their fate, whatever it might be. I firmly believe that some people, particularly in the Eastern bloc countries, accept much higher probabilities of airplane crashes or mishaps than do Westerners. They really don't have a choice.

Immediately upon takeoff we could tell that Bulgarian pilots (or perhaps they were Russian pilots) never took the course on gentleness in flying, or how to ensure the well-being and comfort of their passengers. The noise was deafening and far exceeded any standards that would have been set by FAA, and the climb to cruising altitude was near vertical. We all held on to our seats until our knuckles were white. The cruising altitude carefully chosen, I firmly believe, was the one with maximum amount of turbulence and discomfort. The service consisted of a glass of tepid water and some dry crackers as we bounced along, spilling the water and holding the barf bags in readiness just in case.

Then, without any warning, we began the descent into Sofia, again nearly vertical and nearly weightless, knuckles again as white as they could be. Finally, we touched down on the tarmac and the brakes were applied with full force. In the cabin, this aggressive braking set in motion a massive dominolike collapsing of empty metal chairs inside the cabin since no forward stopping mechanism on the chairs had been engineered. After the extremely harrowing flight, this last bit of noisy excitement nearly did us in. It wasn't until much later when safely inside the terminal that we regained just a little bit of composure to enable us to get through customs.

Sofia was just a welcome overnight respite; our destination was Plovdiv, a day's ride by car the next day. Reasonably well rested, we embarked on this journey with a chauffeur who spoke very limited English, so we just enjoyed the scenery and marveled at the differences between west and east Europe. Arriving in Plovdiv in the afternoon we checked into the hotel and met up with the rest of the team already there. On the agenda for that day were some short team meetings and a dinner at the hotel restaurant. We really looked forward to the latter since we were both starving, not having had the opportunity to eat anything the whole day.

The hotel restaurant was the "in" place in Plovdiv. All the Plovdiv elites dine there, the restaurant had many waiters, and it had a huge and very attractive menu. The restaurant itself was a partially inside/outside massive terraced expanse in the back of the hotel with a large dance floor located in the middle. Life was good. The whole team was in place, the live band was playing dance music. It was pleasantly warm, and we studied the menu page after page until we finally settled on our choices.

The waiter appeared with pencil and paper in hand to take our orders, and that's when the fun started. First, none of the French wines listed on the menu were available; we could only have the Bulgarian wine. Well, OK. We ordered enough wine for the entire team and proceeded with the orders of the three to four course culinary extravaganzas listed on the menu. Well, again ... nothing on the menu was available. We went through everything listed and the waiter politely informed us that it was not available. Exasperated and now very hungry, we asked if anything was available, and to our delight, the waiter said meatballs. I looked around at the other tables and saw that everybody was eating meatballs, and so we quickly ordered ours hoping they wouldn't run out, as the restaurant was quickly filling up.

The Bulgarian wine and meatballs appeared, and both were, in fact, quite good. The wine flowed and gladdened the heart, we finally had something to eat, and the mood was ebullient. Trying the Balkan Swing on the dance floor was next, and then off to bed after a great dinner with probably a bit too much Bulgarian wine.

Then came the discovery that all of the hotel rooms occupied by our team members were bugged. The team leader had learned this and told us to be careful in what we were talking about in our rooms, because every word would be recorded. So, I guess whatever was said there is duly recorded and safely tucked away in the KGB archives somewhere in Bulgaria.

We stayed in Plovdiv about four days and suffered through endless meetings with very little accomplished other than attempting to overcome the suspicion clearly implied by the Bulgarian authorities that we were probably spies. They were reluctant to provide us with any vegetable yield and production data, and so with little success in this endeavor we left Plovdiv and traveled on to Cairo next.

******

What a change this was. Cairo was miserably hot, and despite indoor air conditioning, the time spent outside moving from one meeting to the next wore us down rather quickly. We stayed at the famous Shepheard Hotel in downtown Cairo, which was later destroyed by fire. While there we enjoyed belly dancing and great meals at the rooftop restaurant of another hotel. The suffocating heat, however, negated any daytime tourism excursions we had planned and so we began to inquire about tourism visits at night. On top of our list was to see the pyramids at Giza. While daytime temperatures hovered around 110°F, at night it cooled all the way down to about 100°F, obviously a much more bearable temperature. So we inquired of the concierge at the hotel:

"Do they show the pyramids at night?"

"Oh yes, indeed they do ... and it is only a short taxi ride away."

"Are the pyramids lit up at night?"

"Certainly ... and here is your taxi."

While we were talking he had summoned a taxi and soon ushered all five of us into a small vehicle, where we piled in on top of each other. Off we went on a nighttime tourism excursion to the Pyramids at Giza. Well, it became obvious very quickly that the taxi driver was in cahoots with the concierge in working with unsuspecting tourists. The drive itself was a little nerve-racking because none of the drivers used headlights at night unless they suspected an approaching vehicle. As soon as we arrived in the vicinity of the pyramids (we had seen some vague outlines in the distance) the taxi peeled to the right and drove into a compound where we were surrounded by white clad Arabs, begging children, and vendors of all sorts. We were literally pulled out of the taxi and ushered toward four huge kneeling camels. There, in total darkness, Judi and I were plopped onto one camel and our colleagues onto one each. We didn't have any choice in the matter because the camels all stood up on cue, and the tour started before any of us could launch a protest.

So there we went, en route to the pyramids in pitch dark, on four camels, far too many guides all expecting to be paid handsomely, and followed by a trail of vendors who spoke fluently any language you preferred. Were there floodlights at night? Not on your life; we saw absolutely nothing. Well, not exactly; our taxi driver was off in the distance positioning his cab so his one functional headlight shone on one eye of the sphinx and later on a stone of one of the pyramids. So we got the full-fledged tour on camel in pitch dark, seeing absolutely nothing, accompanied by a large entourage of guides, vendors and children trying to sell us scarabs. Out of the distant darkness we heard a comment made by one of our colleagues, "I think we lost control on this one!" Afterwards we paid far too much money and drank soft drinks with the lead tour guide in his home. We asked him if he had ever done the same for other tourists and he said no, this was the first time. In retrospect, though, I wouldn't have wanted to have it any other way. Who can top that experience?

While our project negotiations in Egypt took place, there was also a lot of shuttle diplomacy going on at the same time. Henry Kissinger was flying in and out of Tel Aviv, Cairo, Damascus, and Beirut to avert various crises, so the situation was actually quite tense. We probably naively thought that our project would be a great tension reliever and so were optimistic that we would soon have a contract in hand. That is, until Bill Simon, the Secretary of the Treasury under President Nixon, flew in and out of the Middle East and made some insulting declaration about Arabs and the Arab world. All of a sudden, politics ruled and the project we had been working on for such a long time was declared dead because all promised funding had been withdrawn overnight.

******

After this bit of stellar news we traveled to Beirut, where we had an FMC field office, to lick our wounds and come up with some sort of strategy to salvage the situation. The timing for this visit was about two weeks before the civil war in Lebanon broke out in 1974. The

situation in Beirut was tense; the Israelis were flying over the PLO refugee camps constantly, travel to and from the airport was stressful
and dangerous. As Judi and I were walking a little distance from the
hotel one evening, the police stopped us and cautioned us to go no
further in that direction.

The president of our division, who had been brilliant in the negotiations during our stay in Cairo, was an alcoholic. He had been on
the wagon for two years prior to this, but the failure to land the Egypt
project got to him and he fell off the wagon big time. About 2 a.m. one
morning, Judi and I received a phone call from him, where he simply
stated in a very slurred voice that he had just committed suicide by
ingesting all of the pills in his bottle of prescribed medication. We immediately mobilized the hotel staff and forced our way into his room,
retrieved the now empty bottle of medication and ushered him to the
hospital where his stomach was pumped. He survived the ordeal but
sadly did not get back on the wagon again.

While in Beirut, we visited the archeological site of ancient Byblos.
Later, we were "yachted" to Tripoli by the mayor of Beirut. After a
pleasant trip on the water, our group dined at a restaurant on the shore.
Judi was served chicken liver brochettes and was seated between two
men who smoked cigars after the meal. Amazingly, for her, she took
the boat trip well, but the chicken livers and cigars did her in. After
returning to Beirut, our host let her lie down in a quiet room while the
rest of us continued the party.

After Beirut, Judi and I limped off to Rome on the final leg of our
journey. There was work to do, because we still hoped that there might
be a possibility to salvage what had gone wrong, perhaps in different
forms or with different funding sources. In Rome, Judi and I checked
into a luxurious hotel near Via Veneto. She still felt a little queasy, either wanted food "right away" or didn't want it at all. Our first suspicion was that it was Montezuma's revenge, and we decided to call for
the hotel doctor. After knocking on the door, in strode Dr. Frank Silvestri to handle the case. He was American, probably from the Bronx,
but had lived in Rome for the past thirty years. He spoke English with
a distinct Italian accent.

"Wassa matter?"

"Well, we just flew in to Rome after spending a couple of weeks in Bulgaria and the Middle East … must have been something she ate. She can't hold anything down — see there she goes again …"

"Hmmm, lettee me have a look …"

And he poked and prodded, asked some more questions and then fished in his bag for the prescription pad. He wrote out a prescription to calm the stomach and headed for the door. Before exiting, however, he turned around and said with a thick Italian accent:

" … Are you sure she's'a not'a preganant?"

I think I laughed and said something condescending about how our very fine and modern doctors in the US had already determined that Judi could not get pregnant. I patiently described the procedures she had gone through, the results, and so … no, there was no chance.

"… Hmmm … I'ma not so sure. Lettee me have another look," he said, and I think I rolled my eyes a bit but patiently let him back in.

"I think'a she may be preganant. Bringa me a sample today and comma to my office tomorrow for the results."

That night we couldn't sleep. We talked all the time:

"What if?????? Do you remember what the doctors at home said, that it could be possible?"

"Yes, but not if we're up and down in airplanes, or in hot climates, eating strange foods and hauling luggage and all, remember that?"

"Why do you think Silvestri suspected you might be pregnant, especially after I told him about the verdict we received in the US?"

"No idea at all!"

"I wish it were tomorrow afternoon right now." We kept on talking about this during the whole night.

"This is just to cover all of the bases," we said aloud to ourselves, while in our hearts of hearts, we both fervently hoped that some miracle really had occurred.

The next day, the morning hours passed excruciatingly slowly. I was attending some short meeting. Finally, the afternoon arrived and I was off to see the doctor. His office was right around the corner from the hotel and I was ushered right into Dr. Silvestri's office. He took one long look at me, scowled, and said with his heavy Italian accent:

"Well, if they don't'a believe she's'a preganant in the US, you can comma to Rome and you can havva the baby here."

I think my jaw dropped and I made him repeat everything he had told me. It is all a blur now, but I think I stood up and hugged him, his receptionist, his nurse, and probably his other patients in the waiting room, while I was mentally doing the math; it was Plovdiv, Bulgaria, after the Balkan wine and the Balkan Swing, in the room that had been bugged.

To make a long story short, we stayed in touch with Dr. Silvestri for many years after that—corresponding with him and sending him pictures of our first daughter and of our other two children who arrived on the scene two and four years later.

******

To close the chapter on this very exciting year with FMC, it all started with anticipation and enthusiasm, but it was short-lived. None of the contracts materialized and soon the entire consulting division of which I was a part was dissolved. Many of the employees were let go, including me. It had been one year of blinding excitement and international intrigue, but all was for naught.

By now, however, I had been severely bitten by the international bug—the FMC gig had been intoxicating. This is what I wanted to do—travel to different countries and work on different projects where I could apply my now well-honed economics skills. I had one year of solid international experience under my belt so I very much gravitated toward job opportunities that would take me to different places. The prospect of ending up doing the same kind of work day in and day out for a paycheck which increased only by the cost of living was frightening. That's exactly what would have happened if I had remained an academic.

Teaching was OK, but my conservative bent didn't sit well with many of the students who held strong negative opinions about capitalism or even fundamental economic principles. Teaching in academia became a mixed blessing, and basic research was far less rewarding than I had anticipated. What counted in the academic world of publish or perish was peer-reviewed articles published in reputable journals, most of which contain articles written by academics for academics addressing nuances of interest to very few readers. I know, I know ... this advances knowledge at the margin and the peer-reviewed process is important.

But it wasn't for me; applied research was a great deal more rewarding to me since it had a much wider readership, and it often led to actual changes happening in the field. Academic research requires near perfect information, while in the real world information is imperfect so we have to make do with what we have. How do you estimate the probable extent of the European market penetration for processed vegetables grown in the desert region between Cairo and Alexandria and at which pricing point, without a lot of credible data to support your analysis? Well, you make assumptions based on the most applicable theory available and then derive the results upon which you base very costly production decisions. That was the reality in which we lived and worked. Academics assume the availability of perfect information to prove or disprove a theoretical point or nuance, and perfect information is often unavailable in the realities of fieldwork where you have to get your hands dirty. Maybe that's why research universities are sometimes referred to as ivory towers.

And so, one thing I learned very quickly at FMC was that the real world didn't easily lend itself to intricate analysis, so I quickly tempered my attempts to filter every assignment through my academically-derived econometrics expertise and highly technical equation-driven write-ups. This kind of approach obviously didn't always resonate with my colleagues and clients, and much to my chagrin, it also left me a lot more vulnerable since I would be outside my comfort zone. There is some perceived measure of security in having knowledge/ skills that few have (i.e., the ability to wow people with stuff they don't understand, or as I found out, don't care one twit about), so I let go and actually tried to hone my people skills by speaking in lay terms instead of in equations. Problems can be articulated so people understand, and solutions don't need to be complicated. Not every problem needed an econometric solution, and not every report needed long chapters full of equations and economic jargon.

I was unemployed for only two hours when the FMC division dissolved because I was invited to take a one-year position as a visiting Assistant Professor of Agribusiness at the University of Santa Clara. The University was just then looking for credentialed teaching expertise in international agriculture and business for their agribusiness MBA program, so the timing was perfect. But it was indeed a huge letdown after the hectic days with FMC. Besides, I wasn't a Catholic, so my advancement possibilities there probably weren't the greatest.

NORCONSULT

After the one-year appointment in academia at the University of Santa Clara, it was time to move on. The time was ripe to do what I had always wanted to do since coming to the US: go back to Norway and really give it a try. Judi was willing, my family was eager to have us back and sweetened the prospects by helping us find a place to live in Oslo. Moreover, a large international consulting firm in Oslo — Norconsult — was courting me to work for them on Middle East and other projects. I guess I was an attractive candidate since I had a Ph.D. and the one-year-long Middle East experience in Egypt, Lebanon, and Iran. One thing led to another and the deal was cemented — we had decided to move to Norway.

The excitement was definitely there. Norconsult was very much on the international cutting edge, and most of their projects were overseas. I was eager to get involved. I was back home with my family again, a Ph.D. under my belt, a brand new daughter, Judi really enjoying Norway, and the work was challenging. All of the pieces of the puzzle fell into place.

The small apartment we moved into in downtown Oslo was centrally located with everything necessary within walking distance. But it was dark and depressing compared to what we had grown accustomed to in the US. We needed light and sunshine. So we quickly abandoned this apartment and moved to another smaller apartment by the water and away from the downtown area. It had floor to ceiling wall to wall windows that were actually sliding doors to a large veranda with a spectacular view of the Oslo fjord and all of the boat life that came along with it. Now this was more like it. Our social life soon picked up and it wasn't long before I was asked to crew on a sailboat in regattas in the Oslo fjord, some taking place just beyond our apartment balcony. Oh yeah, this was the life.

What begins well, however, doesn't always end well. My previous experience from Norway was simply the freedom of a kid growing up. I could do anything I wished, my parents fed and housed me, and I was hanging out with my friends. Now I had to pay ... shudder ... the Norwegian taxes, and ... shudder again ... get used to the Norwegian prices for everything. My salary from Norconsult wasn't that great, it turned out. I had thought it would be sufficient, but I soon found out that there was always way too much month left at the end of the money. Counting pennies (kroner) became the norm, as did foregoing vacations and replacing our decrepit Volkswagen bug. Peanut butter sandwiches, eggs, and fish pudding were the affordable food staples, and keeping an eye on the red electrical power-use needle an important money-saving factor. Work was fun though. The project to which I was assigned had nothing to do with agriculture or natural resources, so it extended my skills as an economist to include large scale urban development in Manama, the capital of Bahrain. Not only did this project wake up my imagination, it also put us in contact with high-powered financiers in London.

As the project economist, I had to develop estimates of square footage of different kinds of floor space based on the demands for offices, luxury apartments, shopping centers, and service facilities such as clinics, garages, and open air markets. Then, working with architects, engineers, and construction experts, we put together a full and detailed plan of what the project would consist of, where, when, and how, including all of the costs and the revenue projections. The architects even built a model to scale, which we toted around everywhere — to London to show to the financiers, and to Bahrain to show it to the clients. The model was really impressive, as was the brochure we made with the perspective drawings and pithy analysis. It was truly a work of art.

But as happens so often, the project didn't get any legs and the momentum sort of bled away over time. Maybe we didn't have enough bribing money to hand out, so the project just quietly expired.

By mid-year in Norway it had become abundantly clear to me that there is something to the saying that you can never really go home. I had been away too long, I was married to a non-Norwegian and my cliques of old friends had moved on. Besides, even if my old cliques still existed, a "mixed" marriage re-entry would leave me on the periphery, not in the thick of things. Getting back into the Norwegian social life outside the immediate family was not easy. Friendships are cliquish and newbies, particularly of the mixed marriage kind, will find full acceptance very difficult. Only mixed marriage cliques were open to us, and that's where we found some very good friends. But it didn't return me to my Norwegian roots one bit—we remained international in the friendships we cultivated, our outlook on life and our politics.

To add to the difficulties, we were also both new Christians when we lived in Norway and the prospect of living in an agnostic, borderline atheistic culture was overwhelming to me. To be frank, I had one foot in the Christian camp on Sundays, and on other days I was every bit the pagan I had been while growing up in Norway. In retrospect, I can't say that I had very many good moments in my Christian walk during those days. I was a wimp and far too cowed by my family to stand up for what I believed. Now, years later, however, they all know differently and life goes on—"If it works for you dear ... then I am happy for you ..." And so it goes.

All of this made me think often and hard about moving back to the US once again—settling back into the Norwegian lifestyle I had known as a kid and young adult wasn't at all in the cards. Worse, by now it began to seem like I was a drifter, someone who couldn't hold down a job anywhere—one year here, one year there, and then move on. It was always greener on the other side of the fence and my preoccupation was rarely on the here and now. Wherever I was, I always wanted to be somewhere else. "Enjoy what you have and don't cast sidelong glances at everything around you," was Judi's advice. Yes, good advice, indeed, but advice I couldn't heed until much later in life.

For me, there was always something out there worthy of pursuit. Although Norconsult provided me with a great job, it didn't pay nearly as much as I perceived I needed for a semi-comfortable lifestyle, given the extremely high cost of living in my home country and my unrealistic estimation of my own worth.

Judi, on the other hand, was perfectly happy in Norway. She had friends, we had a brand new daughter and she didn't have to work (she did work for a few months until it became evident that the Norwegian government took her entire salary in taxes), she wasn't involved in the feuds of my family, and we lived in this fantastic apartment with a view to die for. Things were good, Judi was happy, but I was casting sidelong glances everywhere, looking for better opportunities back in the US.

When Dr. John Ehrenreich, the Dean of the College of Forestry and Wildlife at the University of Idaho and his wife, Dixie, showed up in Oslo to attend a World Forestry Congress, we spent as much time with them as they had available. Yes, they were looking to hire economics faculty members who could teach natural resources and forest economics and yes, "why don't you apply?" In fact, he really encouraged me to apply, particularly after he had fallen totally in love with Kari, who took her first steps and said her first word in his presence. One thing led to another and I was picked for the new faculty position at the college and we were on our way back to the US.

PROFESSING AT THE UNIVERSITY OF IDAHO

I wasn't done as an academic yet, since the holiest of holies had been offered to me on a silver platter—a tenure track academic position. Yes indeed, I was looking at a full-time tenure track position as an Assistant Professor of Natural Resource Economics at the University of Idaho teaching one course per semester plus doing research. Oh goody, now I could really play the part and wear corduroy jackets with leather patches on the elbows, wear cool bell bottom pants, smoke corncob pipes, let my hair grow (particularly the sideburns) and become just like the young professors on all university campuses during those days. The carefree university days were back, but with two major differences—I wasn't a student myself, I now had power over them in my classes, and I had money to spend. The pay wasn't great, but it sure beat the less than minimum pay I earned while working for professors as a graduate student, grading papers, substitute teaching, and doing research.

The College of Forestry and Wildlife Resources (FWR) also had an active international program, both in terms of foreign students and consulting opportunities overseas. The natural resource management (NRM) field was also very much in vogue in developing countries, which opened up numerous opportunities to work on USAID and/or World Bank projects all over the world. So yes, professing on a tenure track trajectory and still being able to indulge in my preferred propensity for international work didn't sound bad at all.

I taught my classes, undoubtedly alienating many of my students, did my research for two full years at the University of Idaho, and published what I needed to publish. I think I was a pretty good teacher, although I hadn't discovered political correctness yet. The simple fact was that nearly all of the students in my classes were what I affectionately called "tree huggers," had a radical environmental orientation, and were political leftists. It was a grievous sin in their mushy brains to ever: a) cut down a tree, b) convert any wooded areas to farmland, c) reclaim any wetlands for commercial crop production, d) stop wildfires from devastating the forests (because they are natural occurrences), all regardless of the circumstances. Capitalism is evil, profits are more evil, and anyone espousing the merits of either one is the most evil of all. Come to think of it, it doesn't seem that much has changed since then.

I, on the other hand, am an economist whose job it is to identify and quantify the economic consequences of resource allocation decisions. As such, I think my bent was diametrically opposed to that of the large majority of my students. I actually enjoyed provoking them with hardcore economic principles in the classroom, often leading to heated debates. I guess in retrospect that is what college should be like, although you have to live through those moments, and a 90 (students) to 1 (me) battle isn't always fun.

The best part of all this, however, took place many years later when some of my old students actually took the trouble to write to me to express appreciation for what had transpired in the classroom at the time. They were now gainfully employed, had seen the light, and had abandoned any affinity for socialism and extreme environmentalism. Now they were capitalists pursuing profit with gusto, for themselves and their employers.

Just to clarify, I'm not anti-environment. The exact opposite is true. In fact, I was very much hired at the university because of my economics expertise as applied to the environmental discipline. My environmentalism is best described by one word: stewardship. It isn't all about preserving and/or increasing biodiversity, it is also about generating the means to pay for that which you want to preserve or protect. Economics here can be the great equalizer — it forces the decision-makers to take a hard look at all aspects of the decisions they are about to make, including affordability.

I do indeed recognize that the environmentalist community is filled with highly reputable scientists, ecologists, biologists, and environmental economists (Herman Daly comes to mind, for example) who are not anti-everything, but knowledgeable professionals who have much of great value to teach conventional economists.

Extreme environmentalism of the kind I often encountered in my teaching at the university, however, would only look at one side of the equation while ignoring the costs, including the opportunity costs. What, for example, does it realistically cost society if you lock up forests and natural resources indefinitely for the sake of preserving the pristine habitat for some endangered flora or fauna species? Proper stewardship of our natural resources allows us to have both in most cases. The management of privately owned forests is a great example. They tend to be in excellent health while rich in both flora and fauna. Their owners often make healthy profits from timber sales. Publicly managed forests, on the other hand, are often managed according to the tenets of the latest environmental fads.

One of my like-minded colleagues related to me some comments made by a high-level Washington D.C. bureaucrat from the US Forest Service while they were flying over the checkerboard pattern of private/public forest land holdings in North Idaho: "So that section is a private forest, and that one over there is public, right?" and "Look, over there, that rich and diverse forest must be a public forest." You could literally discern the patterns of ownership from the air. The only problem was that his batting average was zero. All of the healthy, thriving, and diverse forests were private; all of the public ones were far less healthy.

The research to which I gravitated was a bit risky, because it often went against the grain of conventional environmental wisdom, including the strong opinions of most of my faculty colleagues. The state of Idaho is endowed with a tremendously diverse natural resource base, particularly our forests. The problem is that most of the acreage is held in public ownership, largely US Forest Service, the Bureau of Land Management, and Idaho Department of Lands. Back in the early '70s, the federal government wanted to lock up most of the forest land into wilderness areas — that was the environmental trend *du jour* — and we were asked by Boise Cascade (one of those evil profit-oriented corporations) to measure the economic consequences of doing this.

One project was all about the present and future productivity of Idaho's forests where we clearly documented huge economic losses if the forests could not be managed for commercial purposes, even when managing for multiple uses (timber, wildlife, biodiversity, recreation, etc.). And, if one managed to clear the political and environmental hurdles after several years of haggling in the courts to miraculously have a timber sale, the requirement would be to only harvest biologically mature trees, or in technical terms, to harvest at the biological maturity at the culmination of the mean annual incremental growth. Biological maturity is the foresters' mantra — any harvesting occurring prior to that is probably sacrilegious. From our (the conventional economic) perspective, however, profits could be maximized if trees were harvested at financial maturity, which often occurred ten to twelve years before the trees would be biologically mature. So the question is: what do we want, maximum biological growth or maximum profits? You can see the conflicts that can easily arise between the different disciplines.

But I digress again ... Back to the faculty job and the reality of being a university professor. There are the faculty meetings, next the committee assignments, then the bickering between fellow professors, and worse—the left political leanings of most of the faculty members. All of this was more than enough to drive me nuts. At a very early stage in a professor's life he begins to think like the others—if I only had a) that breakthrough publication that will really launch my academic career; b) that huge raise I truly deserve because of my excellent teaching evaluations; c) that coveted administrative position and huge raise that comes along with it in my department; d) that large slice of the collective conference attendance budget I need so I can travel more; and most importantly, e) the eventual achievement of that coveted trophy, tenure.

Yes, I have seen them, know them, and been their colleague—the professors aspiring to make tenure, and when they do, they really cannot be fired. Some continue along in brilliant ways doing excellent research and teaching. Many simply ossify, become nauseatingly opinionated, and never update their teaching materials. They are overpaid and underworked and always complain about this or that. Today I count my blessings every day for having escaped this way of making a living.

While at the University of Idaho, I always kept a keen eye on the international operations at the college. I was tapped once to go to Morocco with a forester colleague on a USAID short-term assignment, because I had said that my French was operational. I'm not sure it was a conscious lie because I did have a lot of French expertise; the only problem was that it was latent—tucked away safely in my inner consciousness from my long-since-forgotten high school days. I had earned good grades in French in school, so I always claimed to know the language. In any case, even if my expertise didn't surface while in Rabat or Casablanca, compared to my linguistically challenged forester colleague, my French was impressive.

The assignment actually didn't turn out that badly—we managed to put together the outlines of a forestry project in Morocco for USAID that it did indeed implement later. This only served to whet my appetite. I was now beginning to get to know people in USAID. We met contractors in the field, and we met with host country counterparts who were players in the economic development activities in their respective countries. All of this was good networking that would come in very handy later, and it was exciting.

USAID

The next stop was a natural — Washington, D.C. Academia sometimes operates in mysterious ways by providing aspiring young professors with lots of opportunities to advance their careers. One such opportunity was a mechanism called an Inter Personnel Assignment, or IPA, which allowed faculty members to accept temporary assignments away from the home campus. One of these was put in my lap — a one-year IPA to Washington, D.C. seconded from the University of Idaho to a US Forest Service team dealing with forestry issues in developing countries under a USAID contract.

For me, this was very exciting. For the taxpayers, however, it was probably a boondoggle. I didn't know, thinking all the while that I was doing good and important work. After all, who wouldn't want to know about the tasks I was given as part of a team, what the donors were doing in forestry in developing countries and how well they were doing it? This task consisted of sending two-man teams out to all developing country regions to document who does what in forestry. I went to Asia and Africa. Another team covered Latin America. We produced a thick report that few people read. And then, as true blue academics, we produced a refereed journal article summarizing what we had said in the thick report and then moved on to the next assignment.

Telling the story about what other donors did in the forestry sector gave me lots more experience to put on my resume. It involved lots of travel to many different countries, endless meetings with donor representatives, and weeks on end writing a huge report. More importantly, however, the IPA experience greatly augmented my international network in agriculture, forestry, and natural resources management. I now had names, phone numbers, fax numbers, and addresses for lots of people who would later turn out to be valuable connections.

I stayed in D.C. for two years working on this IPA assignment, after which I was supposed to return home. At the end of the second year, however, things had gone downhill at the University of Idaho to the point where it had declared financial exigency. When that happens, all rules are suspended. Tenure means little, people could get fired for no cause, and raises were unheard of. I received a letter from my dean urging me to stay out if I could find a way. I was strongly advised to seek yet another year on my IPA, or find something else and take a leave of absence, or be on loan from the University until the financial problems had been resolved.

In 1980, therefore, it was decision time. The opportunities were good: a) return to the UI but with no raise, and with no job security at all (even though I had been promoted to "Associate" from "Assistant" professor while in D.C.); or b) join a "beltway bandit" consulting firm who had a contract with USAID for a project in Senegal. After some serious family discussions, we decided to make the leap and move to Senegal for the Gambia River Development Organization project, or the OMVG as it was called — the Organisation pour la Mise en Valeur du Fleuve Gambie.

Africa, here we come.

CHAPTER 3: POINT OF NO RETURN

SETTING THE STAGE

By the time we moved to D.C. we had been blessed with two beautiful children and one on the way. We lived in a small condo in Falls Church near D.C. and were happy and comfortable. We had lots of friends, and had settled down to what we thought would be a one- to two-year stint in the nation's capital with my occasional work trips to Africa and Asia. All was well, but we had no idea of what was awaiting us — the grueling work schedules, the dangers in the places where I worked, and the incremental creep of my absences from the family as the traveling frequency expanded exponentially.

One year in D.C. turned into two, and the messages from the University of Idaho were clear: if you can, don't come back if you have other options. And so we did. We decided to move to Senegal — a developing country — and become a member of an expatriate technical expert team on a project there. It was a decision that marked a point of no return.

While reading the stories that follow in the several chapters below, it is easy to ask the question: where was your concern for your wife and kids while you were traveling about, often at the edge of life? And while your family was in Africa, how do you justify remaining in countries full of dangers and uncertainties while you travelled, leaving your wife and small children alone in places they most likely never imagined living, surrounded by unrest, robbers, poverty, etc., and in an alien culture? Why didn't you realize this and just quit your job and get something that kept you home in a "safe" environment?

Indeed, these concerns were front and center with all of us at the time while living overseas. It was often a conversation topic, but together we agreed that missing the experience would be a source of regret. We soon reached the same level of awareness that all expatriates reach: that you will always be a potential target for robbery, kidnapping, carjacking, and other crimes; you will be significantly exposed to serious health risks, and doctors aren't always at hand. Consequently, we made adjustments in our lifestyle that reflected awareness of our surroundings and the dangers facing us every day.

We were always on the alert (which I count as a good thing no matter where you live). Parents delivered kids to school, picked them up again for lunch at home, drove them back to school for the afternoon, and picked them up again at the end of the school day. Kids' socializing with friends took place inside homes or inside the home's walled gardens. The schools themselves were walled and well-guarded. Securing the house before going to bed became a formal routine, never forgotten. Wallets were always worn in front pockets. Bleaching vegetables and scorching the crust of the bread before consuming it became routine. Boiling drinking water was a necessity. Malaria pills were taken religiously. Immunizations and inoculations were kept strictly up to date. We knew there were dangers but took precautions to the extent we could, so life as expatriates wasn't fraught with the heightened kind of anxiety many would think normal. In fact, we felt more vulnerable in the suburbs of Northern Virginia after our return to D.C. than we had felt while living in Africa.

After we repatriated I continued to do the kind of work that required frequent travel and long absences from home. Why didn't I quit then and try to find a "normal" job? Since we both knew the dangers and risks, why did I continue with my seemingly hazardous journeys, leaving everything important in life back home for long periods of time?

My answer: alternative jobs were not available at the time. Living in Africa had taught us that God is our security and that we can trust in Him, incuding the dangers of traveling solo on short-term missions to unstable regions. Changing jobs because of the fear of future dangers never entered our minds as an option. When 9/11 happened and all overseas work dried up for months, God had already prepared the way for us. We had already moved back to the Pacific Northwest to work remotely for my D.C. firm, and for WSU at the same time, which provided some income during the lean months. Just before 9/11, I had also been contacted by the people who essentially triggered the creation of the company I founded with my business partner in 2000. The transition was seamless.

After the years I worked overseas with so much travel, so many absences, so much uprooting and moving of the family I don't hesitate for a moment to say that it takes a very strong woman in a marriage not only to tolerate, but also embrace the kind of lifestyle we lived. It wasn't "traditional," nor did it reflect what most churches would prefer for families. Judi, however, rose to the task and became supportive of my work, never urged me to find "home" work, and became strong enough to manage the void left behind during my absences. This is probably *not* ideal in the minds of most, I hasten to add, but it worked for us because God ordered our lives. And the rest is history, as they say.

AFRICA AND MY "CLIENTS"

I don't know of any African state where a power change hasn't taken place without some sort of civil unrest. Coups d'état were frequent and it wasn't a good idea to be caught in one (as I was in 1983). In Africa back then, the rebels weren't after Americans, so a valuable skill to acquire is knowing when to duck when bullets were flying.

Coups d'état notwithstanding, Africa has other problems, one being that it is plagued by suffocating heat. And, along the coastal regions you have high humidity to boot, which makes you feel you could slice through the air with a machete. Sweat is literally pouring from every pore in your body — there really is very little relief unless you spend your entire life indoors in air conditioning. And there is the dust that invariably finds its way into your computer to thoroughly clog it up, just as you are in the middle of saving your report for the last time before you head for the airport. In the beginning, though, dust wasn't a problem, because computers were virtually non-existent. In the US they were still confined to air-conditioned buildings staffed by nerdy-looking youngish and bespectacled men with crew cuts. Most of my "word processing" at that time took place on the airplane where I was well equipped with scissors (of the kind no longer allowed on the plane), scotch tape, lots of yellow pads and everything was written by hand and literally cut and pasted.

In Africa the electricity is dirty with frequent power surges. More often than not, it just quits for hours, and hours, and hours ... and then still some hours. In the rural areas plumbing is non-existent or not functioning. A "restroom" consists of a hole in the floor. The few hotels in the rural areas are suffocating heat traps with only occasional electricity to keep a rickety fan running during the night (if you're lucky) and even less reliable running water for that very essential end-of-the day shower.

Yet, despite the difficulties and the fact that I would seldom have any sort of creature comfort while on mission, I learned to love the work, the people, the camaraderie with colleagues and our African counterparts, the laughs we had, and most of all the stories we all have collected over the years. For me, the twenty-five years or so I put into this work was both fun and professionally rewarding.

Moving to Africa was a momentous decision in retrospect, even though it really didn't feel that way at the time. It didn't trigger any great emotional upheaval, since we were already steeped in a developing-country mentality—I knew the issues, by now I had an extensive network of involved people with whom I communicated regularly, traveling overseas had become routine, and the work was fascinating. Things at the University of Idaho hadn't changed, and the prospect of returning to a dismal academic situation without any hope at all of improvement was not exactly appealing.

While in D.C. and on the road, I was heavily focused on all things forestry, agroforestry, and natural resource management (NRM) in Africa. While there will always be crises in Africa, such as starvation, drought, civil unrest, locusts, and incredible poverty, the *crise du jour* as perceived by the donors in the '80s was energy, or the lack of bio-mass energy, to be specific. Fuelwood and charcoal are by far the most important sources of energy for cooking, lighting, and heating in the developing world. The palpable fear in the '80s was that they were quickly being depleted. The natural forests all over Africa were per-ceived to be degrading fast, and plantations couldn't keep up with the demand. As the population was increasing faster than the natu-ral resources' capacity to renew itself, the logical conclusion was that disaster was looming, that supply would simply run out, and then what would we do? Presumably, hunger and misery in Africa would quickly exacerbate, and we would have problems like nothing ever witnessed before.

The doomsday prognosticators were out in force applying their models predicting that the last tree in Sahelian West Africa would be cut down by August 3, 2012, by 3 p.m. (or maybe it was August 4 at noon — the models varied). They had myriad followers, including the donor community, which obligated enormous sums of money to grow fuelwood in plantations, to improve charcoal production efficiency, to improve the efficiency of cooking vessels (stoves, etc.), to use biomass fuels, and to introduce the concept of agroforestry to African farmers. It was a good time to develop expertise in any of these areas — it meant temporary job security.

It was around this time, just before we moved to Senegal, that I met Fred Weber, an Idaho-based (of all places) crusty African consultant, fluent in French, German, and Spanish with probably forty years of field experience in the remotest corners of the African continent. Fred became my mentor. I remember a full day spent in his old converted garage office in Boise, Idaho, sitting on an uncomfortable three legged chair, learning about the intricacies of African natural resources man-agement — what works, what doesn't work, why or why not. His shelves were jammed with books and reports on Africa, stacks upon stacks in total disorder, yet he knew where everything was. His collection of written stuff from Africa was probably richer and more varied than any library. He told me stories from a field perspective (no politics) about the importance of different tree species and the commercial uses one could extract from each, and he made sense out of claims that bush medicines were often far more effective than the medicines from pharmacies here in the US. His mind was extremely fertile, and he made my economic juices flow with project ideas, many of which were put to the test on later field assignments.

Fred was my hero—he energized me, was fun to be with, was universally respected, and really made me appreciate the line of work I had chosen. I also think I became his favored field economist over time, because I actually listened to his ideas and built them into the analyses we conducted together over the years. They made a huge difference and actually made the decision-makers stop and think a bit before they funded some projects that would have been harebrained.

Fred died in 1991 at the young age of sixty-seven, probably from having smoked at least three packs of cigarettes every day for more than forty years. Everybody who knew him will clearly remember his violent coughing fits, which seemed to threaten to lead to his demise right there and then. When over, however, he would calmly fish out another cigarette from his crumpled pack and inhale every puff down to his toes. This was soon followed by another violent coughing fit.

My kids were truly fascinated by Fred when he stayed with us at our home in Bobo Dioulasso in Burkina Faso, where we moved after Senegal. He told great stories of his travels while he sat on the floor between the couch and the coffee table. He was more comfortable there than on the furniture. One evening at dinner, the kids urged him to take his malaria pill without any water. Surely he wouldn't do that, they thought, and they kept egging him on. They always took their malaria pills in a spoonful of mashed banana so they wouldn't have to taste it. It was chloroquine—tasted awful. So Fred calmly picked up his pill, popped it into his mouth, and proceeded to chew and swallow it, without water. Now that was over and beyond—the kids' eyes almost popped out and their jaws dropped in unbelief. He did the same thing with one of the hottest red peppers on earth – the kind that spices up the African food with just a mere touch. This was even more impressive, if possible.

What follows in subsequent chapters are anecdotal stories and lessons that I learned while working with Fred and others in the field on many different assignments. But first, let me introduce Africa. There are fifty-three countries on the African continent (including the island nations), all of them different in culture, people, resource endowments, colors, smells, and degrees of poverty. It is a continent of contradictions, the poorest-of-the-poor live there as do the most generous people on the planet, eager to share whatever little they have — their food, time, and the meager crops harvested.

I have worked in at least a third of the countries in Africa, but it is in West Africa where most of my stories originate — in Senegal, The Gambia, Mali, Niger, Guinea, Burkina Faso, and Benin. Although 42% of all adults in West Africa are illiterate (the percentage is much higher in the rural areas), they are also extremely resourceful. If your car breaks down, for example, they will pop out of nowhere with a little satchel full of tools ready to *"depanner"* you — to fix your car right there on the spot. (The only exception to this is if you have the misfortune of driving an American car in Africa where parts can't be fixed, only replaced.)

In the rural villages the people live in mud huts and eke out a living on whatever they can produce on one hectare or less of depleted farmland. Typically, they will harvest two or three 50 kg sacks of millet or sorghum if the rainfall cooperates. For cash they sell one or two sacks and they consume whatever is left (after the rodents have had their share). The cash is used to buy soap, sugar and salt, cheap batteries, cigarettes, etc. There is rarely enough left to send any of the children to school. School is a luxury that few enjoy.

Families tend to be large for good reason. It is a reasonably functional social security system — chances are that the elderly will be taken care of by their offspring, even when considering the real fact that many of the children will die before they reach adolescence. A second reason is that children work the farm and don't get paid.

To put things in perspective, imagine what your life would be like if:

a.) You only owned the clothes and shoes (flip flops) you wore that day plus maybe one spare set of worn-out clothes to change into once a week.

b.) You have no money, only a few meager possessions — perhaps two or three sheep or goats that you can barter with or eat if you have no other food.

c.) You have no transportation — except perhaps a rickety old bicycle if you're lucky. You hoof it everywhere.

d.) You have no electricity, only a small battery operated transistor radio that goes with you everywhere.

e.) You have little energy with which to cook, other than fuelwood or charcoal on special occasions. Collecting the small bundles of wood for a day or two takes three to four hours every day.

f.) You have no private bedroom, nor do you have a bathroom of any sort — that business is taken care of in the bush.

g.) Your only source of clean water is that 50 meter deep (hand dug) well down in the center of the village, often a long walk away, so forget about that end-of-the-day shower.

h.) You live in a malaria-infested area — there is no way to escape the mosquitos unless you have a mosquito net (which few can afford), so the periodic onset of malaria is very certain and frequent.

i.) You have no access to medicines, so you can only rely on the traditional bush medicine.

j.) You have a very high probability of contracting AIDS.

k.) Your life expectancy is around forty-six years.

l.) You live on less than one dollar per day.

I only included twelve points here, but so many more could be added to characterize the typical rural African way of life. One feature that is difficult to comprehend is the huge chasm between males and females. Whereas the African man works hard during the farming season, he doesn't even come close to the work done by the African woman all year around. The rural African woman is a marvel — I don't think any middle-class American or western woman or man could walk in her shoes (or flip flops) even for one day. She rises painfully early in the morning to cook breakfast, clean the hut and court yard, take care of a crowd of small children, and then head out on foot for the next three to four hours to collect fuelwood, which she carries in a bundle on her head while having a baby or two strapped to her back.

After she deposits the wood, it's time to draw water for the day's needs. She heads down to the communal well and hauls up several satchels full of water; she waters the communal garden near the well, hauls up several additional satchels of water and pours it into a large water basin, which she carries on her head back to the house. All of this is done in 100°F heat or higher. Then there's the midday meal followed by the evening meal to prepare. Pots have to be washed, kids handled, the small garden in the back of the house tended, and assistance given in the farm field. Then finally a few short hours of blissful sleep on a thin mat on the ground before it all begins all over again.

So now I have introduced you to the people who were my "clients" for many years. Most of my work was done in remote rural villages with the poorest of the poor. The universal focus of the donor community during my days—USAID, the Swiss, the Germans, the UK, the World Bank, among others—was on improving the lot of the poorest among us by implementing projects or programs that offered assistance to them in the forms of direct gifts of various farm inputs, improved farm-to-market roads, technical assistance on improving crop yields, lowered costs, and improved seed varieties. The permutations of what to do for whom and where to do it were endless.

During project implementation—usually calibrated to a three- to four-year period—the landscape was soon inundated with self-important expatriate consultants (including me) running to and fro with their briefcases, vehicles, equipment, and frantic activity. Added to that were incoming TDYers (temporary duty consultants), the attachment of Peace Corps volunteers to the project, and the hiring of locals for a variety of tasks (chauffeurs, mechanics, accountants, counterpart foresters and agronomists, and on and on). Project offices were established, bank accounts were opened, and monies were disbursed in layers based on the successful achievement of benchmark project goals.

Looking back at this now conjures up all sorts of armchair theorizing about how one could easily think of far better and more efficient ways to spend the money and actually achieve some positive results. But, we live in the moment, and back then we all believed that what we were involved with was the best thing to do, given our supposed intimate knowledge of the problems we were tasked with solving.

The primary recipient of the development aid, of course, was the host country government. Once a project had been approved, there would be a signing ceremony, platitudes would be exchanged, and then the corruption would start. The personnel assigned to the project from the host country would be keenly aware of the—to them—huge amounts of money now placed under their control. It is a powerful elixir. Some would seize the opportunity to get as much for themselves as possible with many innovative cooking-the-books ways; others would be more modest in their approach.

In typical fashion, the host country project staff would provide employment to the maximum extent possible for their aunts, uncles, brothers, sisters, nieces, nephews, fathers, and mothers. I actually don't begrudge them this proclivity given the culture in which they operate. If one individual in the extended family is gainfully employed, it becomes incumbent on him/her to feed, clothe, and educate the nearest relatives. It is not uncommon to learn that one employed person may be expected to care for the immediate needs of forty people or more in the home village. If they have the possibility of getting employment for a relative, the burden on them will be lessened substantially.

Cooking the books is a favorite way of getting ahead. Every field project has a fleet of vehicles used by the expat staff and the host country staff. According to the USAID rules, all vehicles are supposed to be used strictly for business purposes, never for personal reasons. The way to control this is to keep a detailed logbook in each vehicle where every kilometer is recorded by date, the purpose of the trip, and who used the vehicle. Well, needless to say, that system didn't work as intended. The vehicles were used for personal reasons all the time, some probably even as off-duty taxis. The log books were then filled in with fictitious information to meet all of the USAID requirements.

As a chief-of-party (COP) for such projects, I was vigilant at first in attempting to restrict the use of the vehicles to business purposes only, but over the long haul it became evident that this was impossible. As we got to personally know our counterpart staff, however, and we told them we were aware of what was going on, we would eventually be able to settle down to a working equilibrium of allowing some personal use of the project vehicles as long as it didn't become blatant.

Another brief example where corruption is rampant: the procurement of project furniture and supplies. Once again, family matters. Figure this: the project needs twenty desks and fifty chairs of different varieties, twenty file cabinets, tables, and other sundry furniture items. In Africa, these things aren't necessarily bought off the shelf, they are built to specifications, and bids are solicited. There is a process involved and USAID's rules have to be observed. In the end, one bidder wins and, when everyone is satisfied, monies are disbursed.

Armed with African field experience, however, we knew that it doesn't cost $1,000 in the local currency to build a simple desk; they can do it for $250. Those who are selected to bid on the project are known by the host country staff and are invariably family or simply colluding with the project staff, both knowing they have great potential for great personal gain. So, the project gets billed for the entire $1,000 for a desk, $250 is actually paid, and $750 is shared between the project staff and the contractor according to some clandestine formula. The accounting only reflects the transaction: one desk procured for $1,000.

CHAPTER 4: WEST AFRICA

SENEGAL AND GUINEA
Robbed

My long-term field experience began in Senegal with the Gambia River Development Organization, or the OMVG as it was called — the Organisation pour la Mise en Valeur du Fleuve Gambie. Upon arrival in Dakar before Judi and kids arrived, I found a house close to the international airport and the beach. While I first thought it was a lovely spot with a great view of the ocean, it turned out that the view was the only thing lovely about it. The house was located very close to a fishing beach just up the road where fish were dried on hundreds of large racks. This produced swarms of large flies that hovered around and in our house and made life miserable. Not all the time, mind you, but at least when the wind came from the west, we had a huge and very annoying fly problem. The winds blew from the east on the day I looked at the house and fell in love, as well as on the day when I signed the papers. It blew from the west when we moved in. Months later, our front porch was fully enclosed with screens to keep the flies and mosquitos at bay.

The house was very close to the airport, in fact close enough to the active runway that we could almost see the faces of the pilots as they approached for landing, and the planes' headlights lit up the bed-rooms where two of the kids slept. It was pretty exciting for them, and we did get accustomed to it—even liked it.

There were undeveloped lots on three sides of our house, which I thought was a plus—it might allow us space, perhaps some area where we could put in a garden and such, and where the kids could play. Well, chalk it up to inexperience—it turned out that undevel-oped land surrounding us on three sides left us highly vulnerable to break-ins and all sorts of unwanted attention. On the fourth side was another house occupied by an American missionary and his family. Our children became great friends, and quickly learned to scale the walls between our homes by climbing on a huge box of small seashells.

Crime in Dakar was rampant. Break-ins were commonplace and expatriate houses were targeted, including houses that seemed like virtual fortresses. They had 24-hour uniformed guards, high concrete walls topped with pieces of broken glass, and *Bougainvillea* bushes (a particularly thorny and nasty plant) all along the inside periphery. All windows were heavily fortified with iron bars, and before going to bed all expatriate families would carefully lock every door and implore the guards to stay awake during the night.

To top it all off, I added to my protection by getting a gun that didn't shoot bullets, only tear gas. It really was a ridiculous thing, but the salesman convinced me it was the most effective way to stop would-be thieves while avoiding trouble with the local authorities. Armed with my tiny tear gas shooter, I decided to try it out by shooting off a couple of rounds, aiming at the incoming surf on the beach. On that day it happened that a bunch of young locals were playing soccer right out-side our compound. I swaggered out with my peashooter onto the up-stairs balcony, just like John Wayne, made sure they all watched while I aimed for the ocean and pulled the trigger. It fired, sure enough, but the little pop it made was overpowered by the surf. Nevertheless, the soccer-playing crowd got the point—they now knew I had a gun—don't mess with this house.

Needless to say, the gun proved to be no deterrent at all. After a few weeks our guard happened to be awake one night and was surprised by three menacing strangers inside the compound in the middle of the night. He proceeded to blow his whistle, fought with the three, yelled at the top of his lungs, woke us up, and total mayhem ensued. The three fled without having taken anything, our guard became our family and neighborhood hero, and we thought we had averted a disaster. The experienced Africans and expatriates around us, however, warned that our house was now marked. In about three months they would be back again, they said. We paid attention and doubled our security precautions.

I got into the habit of waking up at midnight every night to make a tour of the entire house, checking all of the doors and making sure the guard was awake. For three months exactly I did this every night without fail. The first night after the three months, however, I didn't wake up. That was the night they hit us again. The guard had either fallen asleep or had decided to hide to protect himself. This was not the same guard who had prevented the robbery three months earlier. The thieves came in the middle of the night and simply bent the bars, weakened by long exposure to salt air, to allow the skinniest one or a child to slip through to open the doors from the inside. They cut down the curtains in the living room and used them to wrap up the stereo and other valuables in the living room and kitchen areas. They were in our bedrooms while we slept, took things off the nightstands, and then calmly left with the loot.

Why we didn't wake up is still a mystery to me, but thank God we didn't. African and expat friends suggested with absolute certainty that the thieves had released a sleeping potion into the air conditioning system that kept us very cooperative during the entire time it took to clean us out. If we had awakened it might have meant immediate and certain death. We had heard of thieves in Dakar mercilessly killing people if disturbed during their "work."

We were beginning to get an understanding of the realities of living in Africa. We had thought we were secure as long as the guards were awake, but we weren't aware of poisons or potions the Africans could and would use against us. Because of this experience we began to develop a sense of self-preservation; we trusted no one, prayed for God's protection, and became very circumspect in our conduct and interaction with others outside the compound. In short, we were transformed into the likeness of other expatriates who had developed their version of a sixth sense based on similar experiences. Our missionary neighbors' solution to home security was a very large dog and a night guard inside their home at night. Ours was two outside guards to whom we gave very strong cups of coffee before we went to bed. By the time we left Africa our security measures had expanded considerably.

Politics

The OMVG offices were located in Dakar, the capital of Senegal, a fairly sizable city on the western most tip of the African continent. The Gambia (where the economic development was supposed to occur) is entirely surrounded by Senegal on the southern, northern, and eastern borders, and is bisected by the Gambia River running east and west for almost the entire width of the country, and bordered on the west by the Atlantic Ocean. Only this small western coastal region is not bordered by Senegal. To drive to southern Senegal would take almost a full day, heading east from Dakar and then south to the Gambia River, which had to be crossed by means of an entirely unreliable ferry. The average wait on each side of the river was about three hours, always in blistering heat with no relief in sight. Certainly no air conditioning was available. But I didn't starve; the street food was abundant, as were fruits of all kinds and cold Coca-Colas. Considering the number of times I crossed this river, I must have spent the equivalent of one full week at this crossing site.

The other route to southern Senegal was a road to the east, traversing Senegal the entire length of The Gambia, turning south into southern Senegal and bypassing The Gambia altogether. This was a very long and bumpy drive, much longer than the alternative, even with the minimum three-hour ferry wait.

The OMVG project was a political nightmare. Three countries were involved: Senegal, Guinea, and The Gambia — a fourth one, Guinea Bissau, wanted to be involved as well, because a small snippet of the Gambia River was located in that country. They were not included, however. The OMVG political structure—the High Commission—was staffed by high-ranking ministerial level self-important people. They were chauffeured around in Mercedes cars by personal drivers, and they had secretaries and all the trappings that come with perceived power. We were the expatriates, the technical people, the experts, all male and all white, and we had our assigned African counterparts who were experts in their own right. Our offices were fully staffed, and we had the latest in computers, printers and even air conditioning that worked occasionally.

The High Commission naturally pursued their individual country agendas as to how the Gambia River should be developed, and their individual agendas were in conflict with all the others more often than not. Our job was to determine where the hydroelectric dams should go, where anti-salinity dams should be built, where the irrigated perimeters should be located once the salt water problems had been solved by the anti-salinity dams, and how we could do all of this with minimum damage to the fragile ecosystems in the three countries.

These were formidable tasks indeed, and they were complicated further by the fact that our expatriate technical employer was USAID in Dakar. We were supposed to take our marching orders from US-AID, not from the OMVG High Commission. But we were also working for the latter, which did not bode well for this project. There wasn't a day without friction, political misunderstanding, and infighting with the technical experts caught squarely in the middle of the battles. US-AID required us to individually submit detailed work plans on how we would spend our time as technical advisors, whereas OMVG told us not to, at least not until they had worked out their overall plan.

So there we were, furiously writing detailed work plans in secret, knowing full well that these would eventually be rejected by OMVG, while also knowing that USAID would hold us accountable for the implementation of the work plans once they had been approved. It was a mess. In the end, most of the technical experts in this project either quit or were fired inside one year by the overzealous USAID administration because the work situation was utterly impossible.

My one year in Senegal, however, was a very rich learning experience, both in terms of what an economist can do under extremely difficult working conditions and how incredibly inept USAID can actually be. The culture is finely honed to include a delicate mix of arrogance and incompetence. For the mathematicians among us, this is akin to multiplying with fractions; eventually you end up with nothing.

Many USAID officials are ex-Peace Corps who gravitated towards international development work without having acquired any of the requisite skills in hard disciplines such as forestry, agronomy, engineering, or certainly not in economics. Their field experience obtained while in the Peace Corps, all of it relevant and excellent in many ways, includes precious little to qualify them for the serious work of managing funded projects and programs. They may hold BS degrees in political science or in sociology and can speak a smattering of the local languages, but many of them are unqualified to manage project portfolios funded by the taxpayers or to ensure that the technical benchmarks are accomplished on time and in a satisfactory manner.

The OMVG had such a USAID management structure firmly in place — people endowed with plenty of arrogance and disdain for anything emanating from the OMVG High Commission as to how resources should be allocated. We, the technical experts, were caught in the middle. In the end, I too had fallouts with the USAID folks and in the end was asked to resign from the project. Technically, that meant I wasn't fired, although it sure felt like it.

Fouta Djallon

One thing everyone agreed upon in the beginning, however, was the need to arrange for a field trip along both banks of the Gambia River, all the way to the source of the river, in order to assess potential dam locations, location of irrigated perimeters, and such. There were twenty of us, including the team from the main project contractor (the University of Michigan), and the technical experts.

The field trip was made quite hazardous by the fact that we were obliged to drive four-wheel-drive US Chevrolet vehicles. It was just a matter of time until they broke down. The African landscape is littered with dead and rusting GM, Ford, and Chrysler vehicles which roamed the countryside for a brief period of time. These vehicles just couldn't handle the brutality of the African bush that the Land Cruisers could. All US-funded projects had to procure US vehicles unless a waiver could be obtained, which the OMVG project did not get. Not exactly a ringing endorsement of the US auto industry prowess (but that has changed since then—US-made vehicles are far better now).

All food, medical supplies, gasoline, and other supplies had to be purchased in Dakar before departure. We loaded up the vehicles and set out for what was to become a most memorable introduction to absolutely unimaginable working conditions. Our trip east from Dakar took us all the way through Senegal to Kedougou and then south towards the Fouta Djallon region of Guinea.

Senegal's roads east of Dakar were, at the time, full of alternating pavement, dirt, and potholes. Compared to the Guinean roads, however, Senegal was a perfect picture of modernity. Our average speed between stops along the way was probably around twenty miles per hour. Crossing over into the Fouta Djallon region near Kedougou, the average speed slowed to around two miles per hour. There were dirt roads, but they were impassable. They hadn't been repaired for decades, ruts were sometimes four to five feet deep, none of the "roads" had ever been paved, and very few of the bridges at multiple tributaries to the Gambia River crossings looked like they could support any of our heavily loaded vehicles. We found alternate off-road solutions beside the "roads," driving on the laterite and in between the termite mounds. At river crossings we didn't risk driving across the dilapidated bridges but chose instead to cross the river itself when we found areas where we could drive down the banks and cross in shallow water.

The Fouta Djallon region was not only plagued with malaria-infested mosquitos, it also had a severe tsetse fly problem—the kind that causes sleeping sickness. Driving with the air conditioning on in the rural Guinean bush over-taxed the engines, so we didn't use the AC; instead we opened the windows to get air and somewhat escape the stifling heat. But at two miles an hour average speed, all sorts of flies and mosquitos would leisurely enter the vehicle. So, there we were, swatting every exposed surface and sometimes each other all the time and hoping we wouldn't get stung or bitten.

At night, the routine settled into an interesting dynamic. The expatriate technical experts preferred sleeping out in the bush on camp cots fitted with mosquito nets instead of trying to find a "hotel." Hotels were virtually non-existent anyway, and if one were located, the Africans would stay there, whereas the expats would set up the camping cots in the village square.

It was always interesting waking up in the morning with the eyes of the village kids intently trained on all the white and slightly rotund young to middle-aged consultants sleeping in their village square. It was difficult to find any private spot in the nearby bush to take care of urgent morning business without having a gaggle of kids following every move. Brushing teeth generated laughter, as did packing up our camp cots, grinding coffee, and drinking water out of plastic bottles. Everything was new and puzzling to these kids.

We soon learned that our African counterparts were terrified of any sort of wildlife. They all had horror stories of previous near-death experiences with monkeys and snakes, which were undoubtedly either untrue or heavily embellished. They tried to convince us all that it would be far better for all of us to seek some fortified shelter in town rather than camping out. Most of the time, however, we prevailed and set up camp in the bush. It was reminiscent of the old John Wayne movies when they circled the wagons to provide protection against attacks from the Indians. We too circled the Chevy Blazers and trucks laden with all our food and gasoline supplies—and built a bonfire in the center for evening light and, yes, to keep the wildlife away. Our African counterparts were quick to carve out their sleeping spaces— around the bonfire—and quickly set up their cots there in the center, mathematically clustered as close to the fire as possible. Many of the expats set up their cots outside the circle to be away from the bonfire heat and the noise.

This three week long field trip took us to the source of the Gambia River in the remotest corner of the Fouta Djallon Region of Guinea. According to Wikipedia, the Gambia River runs 1,130 kilometers (700 miles) from the Fouta Djallon plateau westward through Senegal and The Gambia all the way to the Atlantic Ocean at the city of Banjul. It is navigable for about half that length, but certainly not beyond about two-thirds up river in the country of The Gambia or on into Senegal and Guinea. The river becomes narrower and the adjacent land wilder and less populated. The source of the Gambia River is in a very remote and landlocked area of the Fouta where few vehicles dare venture, and where the villages are rarely visited by any foreign dignitaries or consultants.

My team was the one selected to go to the source of the Gambia River. I was the only expat consultant on this particular excursion, white as can be and totally mystifying to the local villagers. As we were driving on the off-road laterite and dodging the termite mounds on the approach to the village nearest the source, we were greeted by dozens of completely naked kids running alongside the vehicle. In the village we met with the village chief and other dignitaries and then gathered together in the shade of a baobab tree for a hastily arranged meeting.

Greetings were exchanged, and we explained the purpose of our visit—to see the source of the Gambia River and report back to our leaders and decision-makers where irrigated perimeters along the entire stretch of river from the source to the mouth by the Atlantic Ocean could be developed. After much commentary on this bit of news, the conversation turned to the possibilities of irrigated farming in their area and, in that event, wouldn't this also have to be accompanied by some road-building into the vicinity of the villages? This was, and had been for a long time, the most important issue for the villagers. The region was a major orange producer, but very few drivers would brave the terrain and elements to reach the villages in their decrepit trucks. The villagers estimated that about 70% of their crop was lost each year, simply to rot on the trees for lack of access-to-market roads.

The villagers were the most hospitable people we had met on the entire trip. They loaded us with several sacks of delicious oranges and some live chickens. Then they took us on a guided tour to the source of the Gambia River—a small indentation in the landscape some two kilometers from the village, where the ground water burbled up to the surface and began flowing downstream.

A Close Encounter

I had a very energetic colleague on the OMVG expatriate technical assistant team named Andre DeGeorges. Great guy, competent in his field, not married, and pretty much a daredevil. He was someone who thought he had an unlimited number of lives, so he hunted big game in Africa on foot, always getting himself into near-death situations. He was also an accomplished diver who actually enjoyed playing around with sharks.

As we waited for the political rifts between USAID and OMVG to get sorted out, Andre and I decided to propose for ourselves a three- or four-day field trip to the Niokola Koba National Park four hours' drive east of Dakar. The aim of the trip was to better understand the issues at hand in local communities in the project-impacted area. What we actually wanted to do was to go on a joy trip to the national park to view wildlife, while, of course, learning a lot in the process.

The expedition was approved, probably because everyone wanted the technical experts to at least stay busy while waiting for directions from the top-heavy project administrators on the OMVG and USAID sides. So off we went in our Chevy Blazer headed east toward Tambacounda in the middle of Senegal, the gateway to the park. We saw a lot of wildlife, conducted many interviews with locals, and generally got excited and optimistic about the work ahead.

We would drive slowly and observe up close all the wildlife we encountered inside the park. On one particular occasion we had stopped to observe a group of baboons about fifty yards to our left down by a stream. Andre was driving, so I stepped out and walked in front of the vehicle onto the left side to get a clearer view. The baboons all of a sudden got very excited, shrieking and flailing about; this gave me some concern because they were pretty close. Andre looked uncharacteristically concerned and told me to get back in the vehicle. I quickly ran in front of the vehicle to get to the passenger side and got back inside.

When safely there, Andre slowly put the car in gear and drove forward a couple of yards. And then he stopped and quietly said, "Do you see what I see?" "Where?" I said. "Over there to the left," he said, "in the tall grass." And there it was — the biggest female lion I had ever seen, crouching down in the tall grass intently fixing her eyes on us. I quickly estimated that when I crossed in front of the car twice, first to get out and second to get back in, I had been no more than three or four yards from this lion, fully exposed and vulnerable to being attacked. I could easily have been lion lunch and Andre didn't have any gun with which to protect me. Come to think of it, he probably would have taken the lion on with his bare hands. I have always wondered if the baboons' shrieking and carrying on had been intended as a warning to me that a lion was about to eat me, or if they were telling the lion to have me for lunch rather than one of them.

The smoldering feud between OMVG and USAID heated up, and the political realities incrementally grew into a massive tumor affecting the entire project. We — the technical experts — prepared well-researched and elegant solutions on where to locate the anti-salinity dams, the hydroelectric dams, and the irrigated perimeters. For political reasons, however, none of these solutions were adopted by either USAID or OMVG. And so it went for one whole year with the OMVG project. In the end, taxpayer money had been grossly misspent. A very tiring and long year in Senegal ended and we moved on to a much happier situation in Burkina Faso.

BURKINA FASO
Coup d'État

Moving from Senegal to Burkina Faso (known as Upper Volta then) was an easy decision after the USAID debacle with OMVG in Senegal. It all began with a short-term assignment to Ouagadougou (Ouaga for short), the capital, and Bobo Dioulasso (Bobo for short), the project headquarters located some 220 miles southwest of Ouaga. I worked with a team of experts, including Fred Weber, to evaluate the Forestry Education and Development Project (FEDP) and recommend changes in the project for the next several years. Phase 1 had been successfully run and completed by COP Bob Winterbottom. The funding for Phase 2 was already assured; our job was to simply document successes and failures of the past several years and recommend changes, if any.

I won't dwell on many specifics about this project, on USAID, or on many of the people involved, but suffice it to say that this project was one of those rare success stories. Things actually worked. We didn't have much political contention between USAID and the local government. All of the expats loved working in this country. All of that was soon to change, however, as I tell in the story that follows. It all happened on my first evaluation trip to Upper Volta, working with Fred. I was still based in Senegal at the time, getting ready to move somewhere (I just didn't know where yet).

"Wow, what was that?" I asked.

"What?" George said from the office next door.

"It sounded like fire crackers — didn't you hear it?"

"Yeah, I heard something … probably an early start to the Independence Day celebrations."

It was around 9 p.m. and George Taylor (a USAID-employee based in Bamako, Mali) and I had just returned from dinner at a local restaurant to the USAID offices located in the embassy compound in Ouaga. It was August 4, 1983, and we were working late that night on our report before our scheduled departure the next day. I was returning to Dakar, Senegal where Judi and the kids were, and George was to return to Bamako.

"Boom … boom" — there it was again, this time a lot closer. Uhhh … oh, that didn't sound like firecrackers — more like heavy artillery. And then, once again, quick bursts of what sounded like firecrackers punctuated the quiet of the evening. Something was up, that's for sure, I thought. This was no celebration. George had the same thought and came out of his office with a worried look on his face and joined me by the window to try to see what was happening. We were the only ones in the USAID building, and we felt sort of exposed and vulnerable, although we couldn't be sure yet what this was all about.

All of a sudden cacophony broke out all around us. The sky lit up overhead, not with fireworks, but with tracer bullets. We knew instantaneously that something really bad was happening, and it wasn't friendly fire. Both of us said it at the same time: coup d'état. Yep, one was very much underway, and George and I were right in the center of it. Not just in the city of Ouaga where this was happening, but truly in the middle of where all of the shooting was going on. Worse, we were inside the US Embassy compound, probably representing, by this time, the most universally hated country on earth.

Our knees buckled as we sank down by the window peering over the windowsill only to see chaos in the streets, people running in every direction and tracer bullets flying overhead. Outside the embassy compound we saw military trucks racing to and fro with soldiers in the back, shooting their rifles seemingly in the air as they went by. What to do? Our brains were in denial mode for some time, but finally sanity kicked in.

We knew we were alone in the USAID building, and inside the US Embassy compound. We also knew that this was not a good place to be when violence anywhere outside the US breaks out. This was a particularly intense thought since 1983 was just on the heels of the Iranian hostage crisis followed by the infamous 444 days in captivity for the embassy personnel there. So here we were, George and I, probably in the absolutely worst spot on the planet at that very moment. We had no way of knowing if what was going on outside the compound was directed at US property or not. It sure seemed like it since the action was taking place in our immediate neighborhood.

Our thoughts were racing. *Is there a place we can hide until this blows over?* We began to roam around the building looking for obscure bucket closets, any kind of closets, crawl spaces, under desks … anywhere. Then the thought came to mind that perhaps hiding wouldn't help if crowds were to breach the compound and set fire to it. What would we do then? Conflicting thoughts all demanded attention and we weren't sure which ones were valid and which weren't. One quick action that actually was good was to switch off all of the lamps to forestall any wanton curiosity by American-hating looters outside the compound.

Second, food and water came to mind. We had had dinner, so hunger wasn't an issue there and then. But, our fertile minds told us we might have to be there for quite some time, so food and water could eventually become an issue. There was an old refrigerator at the US-AID guard station we thought would be full of snack food. It was locked with an old padlock and so we rummaged around for keys in the nearby desk and finally found one that worked. In it was nothing but soft drinks … no food. Maybe we would have some time later to ransack each office in the building for private food stashes. But not now — we had other immediate survival things to do.

The mayhem continued outside, and George and I began to formulate our strategies should we be captured and held hostage. The Embassy compound wasn't under attack yet, although it seemed imminent from our perspective. After all, we were right in the middle of everything and what's to stop people from targeting anything American in the heat of the action? Scenarios pounded our brains and none were too pleasing. They all conjured up images of being tortured or killed by angry mobs, or being held as hostages. We just didn't know how this would all play out.

In the moment, we were too stunned to be frightened so we cracked jokes as we looked for hiding places, food, and a radio so we could listen to the news. We finally found a radio and turned it on. Sure enough, a coup d'état was underway and people were exhorted to remain indoors.

George and I had by now settled down a bit. Nobody had breached the compound and we began to feel some hope that perhaps we would survive and live to tell stories after all of this was behind us. We stayed away from the windows, kept all lights off, kept quiet, and prepared to settle in for the night. Getting back to the hotel was obviously out of the question.

The phone by the guard station in the USAID building startled us as it rang out loudly — our first connection to the outside. Calling out hadn't been an option during this adrenalin-producing time since we didn't have any numbers to call, nor was there a phone book in sight.

"Hullo …?" I said tentatively.

"You guys ok?" said a calm voice on the other end.

"Yes," I said, "who is this?"

"It's the Gunny—we know you're there and we're coming to get you out."

The Gunny is short for the Gunnery Sergeant in the Marines—they had arrived in the compound just minutes earlier, all five marines assigned to protect the embassy in Ouagadougou. As soon as the shooting had started they had all piled into the marine van and were driven at full speed to the embassy, hugging the floor in the van while receiving incoming fire. Arriving at the compound they checked the log book and found out that two civilians were inside the compound.

We waited by the exit door in the USAID building for the Marines to come and rescue us. The thought returned to me—"I really don't want to be here." My adrenalin production was in overdrive, hands were trembling, bullets outside were flying overhead, and there we stood clutching our briefcases as we waited for the Marines.

Then we saw three of the Marines charging toward us at full speed across the lawn between the Chancery and the USAID building. They were decked out in helmets, flak jackets, assault rifles, and other miscellaneous military hardware, very intent on protecting the civilians and the embassy. They quickly stepped into the hallway with us and gave rapid-fire instructions on what to do when outside and under their protection. We were to stay "in the pocket," just like a quarterback, with the Marines flanking us on all sides. We were to run at full speed with them across the lawn and until we reached the Chancery.

We just nodded our heads in agreement as our lives flashed before us in our minds. They opened the door and we were off, staying in the pocket and clutching our briefcases to our chests while crossing the fairly short distance in the open in record time. Safely on the Chancery side of the compound, two of the Marines took up their positions by the door, pointing their guns in the air as the third Marine ran over to lower the flag. My most vivid memory from that night is about one of the Marines, who couldn't have been more than twenty years old. I clearly remember his silhouette with his too-large helmet precariously balanced on his head, a huge M16 in his hands, turning to me with a calm smile, saying: "You didn't know it could be so much fun in Ouagadougou, did you?" Here I was in the middle of a war zone sure to die at any moment, almost wetting my pants, with this kid standing next to me seemingly without a worry in his head, cracking a joke.

I don't know how to say this any other way than I love the Marines: these guys are my true heroes. They are fearless, well prepared for anything, and respectful of civilians and country in extraordinary ways. We spent the next nine memorable hours with them inside the Chancery. The Marine who lowered the flag asked us if we knew how to fold it and we said "Yes," tentatively. "No," he said. "Do you *know* how to fold the flag?" "Well, we're probably a little rusty ..." we mumbled. "That's OK," they said, and proceeded immediately and carefully to fold the flag as per procedure into the shape of a tri-cornered hat with the red and white stripes folded into the blue with no part of it ever touching the ground. That was the last act before we all stepped into the Chancery.

George and I, in the middle of the Chancery office complex were for now out of harm's way with an army of five Marines bent upon protecting their house. The Marines took up their positions in the different offices and communicated with each other by yelling back and forth. George and I were tasked with listening to the radio and translating the news as we heard it.

By now the coup had been declared a success and one of the primary targets, the radio station, had been successfully taken. The inevitable martial music was playing incessantly, punctuated only by communiqués issued by the new rulers every now and then. The communiqués were wide-ranging, including the totally mundane as well as threats and short speeches heralding the fortunes to be bestowed on everyone by the incoming saviors. All of the communiqués were in French, and George and I translated them all for the Marines.

I particularly remember communiqués 41 and 43. Communiqué 41 was a short one: "We are declaring a curfew; any civilian seen on the streets after midnight will be shot on sight." OK, we thought, people would stay indoors and wait it out—this is what happens in every coup in Africa. Well and good—things had quieted down outside. There was only sporadic gunfire now, probably shots fired by soldiers who didn't have a watch and thought it was already past midnight.

Our breathing began to approach normal as quietness slowly deepened. The adrenalin had abated, and we began to relax ever so little.

The martial music stopped, communiqué 42 was innocuous and followed by more martial music, and then there was communiqué 43: "Would Amadou — the keeper of the keys to the storage shed at the Maison de la Radio [the radio station] — please come down immediately to unlock the storage shed." So picture this: poor and frightened Amadou on his bicycle holding a stick with a white cloth hastily affixed to it, key in his pocket, pedaling down to the radio station through streets patrolled by trigger-happy soldiers who probably had no idea what a white flag meant. I don't know what ever happened to Amadou, but I was praying for him.

By now things had truly quieted down and we were all a bit more relaxed. The Marines were at their stations cracking jokes but keeping a keen eye on the streets outside the compound. Suddenly overhead we heard the roar of jet engines as a large plane landed at the nearby international airport. We were puzzled because no commercial flights would have been allowed to land during a coup d'état. So we waited and listened to the radio. After a while we began to hear faint voices, yells coming from the direction of the airport. We strained to listen and could begin to make out distinct words after a while. A large crowd was approaching the embassy compound, it seemed. The Gunny called us in to listen to what they were yelling, and we strained to hear: "Vive la revolution … Vive la revolution." So we said, they are yelling "Vive la revolution." The Gunny looked at us quizzically and, being linguistically challenged, he said, "Yeah, I can hear that, but what does that mean?"

With the translation in hand — long live the revolution — and a large crowd approaching the embassy compound, we were certain we had now become targets. The Gunny began to issue rapid-fire orders: "Stay alert," "Fire only on my command," and then what I remember most vividly: "Where are the keys to the vault?" The vault is the fireproof safe haven of last resort in any embassy. Under attack, personnel can escape into the vault, and from there they can make their way to the roof for an eventual helicopter extraction. This was getting worse by the minute.

We waited, and listened, and translated. The crowd kept approaching and getting louder, but after a while the noise began to abate. The crowd was apparently no longer heading for the embassy but rather to the nearby downtown area. Gradually, we began to realize that we weren't the targets. The relief experienced by George and me was immense. We went back to listening to martial music and translating the communiqués. One of the bits of news we learned from the radio was that the plane which had landed about an hour ago was a Libyan plane bringing in supplies and dignitaries. Obviously, Colonel Gadhafi had been a conspirator in the coup, not exactly stellar news for Americans. And so, the adrenalin began to flow again.

It was now 2 a.m. and things had quieted down to an eerie silence broken only by occasional small arms fire. All of the important buildings had been seized, some twenty people had been killed, and Upper Volta was now under new management. We were still alive, we hadn't been taken hostage, and George and I began looking forward to daylight and some semblance of normalcy.

The Chancery phone rang. The Gunny picked it up and listened:

"This is the ambassador. Are you being fired upon?"

"No sir," said the Gunny, standing at ramrod attention.

"If fired upon, you are not to return fire, is that clear?"

"Yes sir, if fired upon we are not to return fire, sir," said the Gunny.

Some small talk about the general welfare of the Marines and the civilians ensued, and that was end of the phone conversation. Pause ... the Gunny looked at the phone, the Marines looked quizzically at the Gunny, who then said:

"You heard me, that's what the ambassador wants, but I don't have to like it. I'll be $%/**#@ if I will die in this #**/>>* country and if they shoot at me I will sure as ^&##@ fire back at them sons-of-*(%$##."

He was livid, which stirred up the other Marines as well. Strings of eloquent profanities ensued, all seemingly about the wide chasm between the politics of appeasement and action as demanded by the situation in the field.

Now it was 3 a.m. and we kept listening to absolutely horrid martial music and translating communiqués while all was quiet outside.

The shooting had all but died down, and we began to nod off. Then the phone rang again. The Gunny picked it up and again stood at attention:

"US Embassy, Ouagadougou, Gunnery Sargent speaking."

"This is the Washington Post in D.C., we understand a coup d'état is underway there."

"I can't comment on that, ma'am."

"Are you being fired upon?"

"I can't divulge that information, ma'am," the Gunny said.

"How do you feel about being in the middle of a coup d'état?"

"I can't divulge any information to you ..." the Gunny informed the pesky reporter. Click.

He hung up and we all sat back and had a good laugh. We were all more relaxed; things were eerily quiet outside, and the martial music playing on the radio had subsided some. Now 4 a.m. and the phone rang again.

"Hello, it's the Washington Post again, any information you can give us on the coup d'état?" This time it was a male reporter.

"No sir," the Gunny said.

"Any more hostilities going on? Has the embassy been under any attack?"

Three of the Marines were now in the same room with us and they had had enough. Everyone was tired and hungry, and we had been waiting for the daylight to come which would bring the end of the curfew. Many off-color jokes had been told and the Marines were loose. One of them let out a big yelp and cried out at the top of his lungs: "They're coming! Quick, pass me a grenade." Another one: "Oh no, I'm hit ... watch out, pass me another grenade." The Gunny quickly hung up the phone. I have always wondered if the Washington Post reporter heard all of this and what he did with the information.

At 6 a.m. the communiqué stated that the curfew was lifted and that we could go out on the streets again. George and I packed up our briefcases, piled into the van with the Marines, and headed for the Marine house. There we were treated to cheesecake, beer, and beds to sleep in for a couple of hours. Later that day we finally navigated our way through huge crowds celebrating in the streets. They were euphoric about their new regime, which lurched heavily to the left.

There was no chance to leave the country that day since the airport was closed. It remained closed for a full week, although we weren't told so, and every day we headed for the airport expecting to get out, only to be told to come back the next day. Every day on our way to the airport we had to pass through several checkpoints manned by fully armed and menacing-looking soldiers with bazookas that they pointed straight at our faces as the soldiers leaned into the car window to check our papers. We had many nerve-wracking moments and I was very glad to finally get out of there.

Judi and the kids had some anxious moments at home in Dakar, Senegal, waiting for me to return during this time. Communication between embassies and USAID missions back then was always flavored by the latest rumors, which did little but add to their worries. The rumors ranged from "all foreigners to be detained indefinitely" to "normal air traffic to resume soon" to "counter-coup rumored." The kids passed the time playing with their Lego towns and Fisher-Price airplanes, and created the newest Lego game called: "Let's play the airport is closed."

President Sankara, Ambassador Neher

As fate would have it, the project report that George, Fred, and I had evaluated during the coup d'état was precisely the project for which I became the Chief-of-Party (COP) a little later. So back to Ouagadougou I went after the new president, Thomas Sankara, had settled in and things were quiet again.

President Sankara was young, pro-military, and anti-American. In fact, most of us believed he was a communist. He had a governing style which seriously antagonized the US, and he instilled such fear into the general populace that citizens obeyed his every whim. During every public meeting he would require the participants to recite: "La patrie ou la mort, nous vaincrons" or "The fatherland or death, we shall overcome." We heard this phrase constantly. Our twenty-six project employees were obliged to cite it several times a day. One of his first decrees as president was to change the name of the country from Upper Volta to Burkina Faso. That was a mouthful, to be sure. It means "land of upright or honest people."

Now we had to learn how to bureaucratically oppose any move the president made that could be construed as being anti-US. Our government told us to not authorize any expenditure of funds for project purposes. If the project vehicles, for example, were requisitioned by the Burkinabe administration to be in pro-government demonstrations in Bobo Dioulasso or Ouagadougou, we were to refuse. In my capacity as project COP I had daily battles with my Burkinabe counterpart by refusing to let our vehicles be used for what always morphed into anti-US demonstrations. They took them anyway, despite my strenuous objections, which I carefully documented and passed on to US-AID in Ougadougou. There, they were dutifully noted, and passed on to Washington, D.C. along with similar messages from the other USAID-funded project in the country at that time.

Sankara was a very charismatic fellow. Good looking and very buff, he was soon admired by many of the American expats who actually met him—especially the Embassy and USAID contract staff wives in Ougadougou, who found him extremely charming and intelligent and probably fell under his spell. I remember one time when a delegation of American women—wives of embassy personnel and other expats—had an audience with Sankara. They came back gushing praise and adoration.

But, the US government is humorless—nobody criticizes the US in the public square and gets away with it (at least it was that way back then). In the official circles, Sankara was a socialist, or a communist with close ties to Libya, a hater of America, and generally considered a very bad guy. The US government quickly recalled the current ambassador—the one who had called the Gunny and admonished him not to fire—and replaced him with a new ambassador, Mr. Leonardo Neher. Ambassador Neher was perceived to be a lot tougher and one who could deal resolutely with Sankara. The Burkinabes referred to the new ambassador as the "cowboy" in the local press, which obviously didn't help matters.

After settling into his job as president, Sankara made his first over-seas trip—to the UN in New York where he was to participate in one of those highly diplomatic get-togethers, make a speech on the floor, and then fly home again. He commandeered the entire fleet of Air Burkina (one small commercial jet plane) for the trip and took with him an entourage of newly minted ministers and bodyguards. En route, they made the fatal mistake of making a brief stopover in Havana to meet with Castro, which definitely didn't sit well with the US authorities. From Havana they flew on to New York.

By now, the Americans were hopping mad, especially Jeane Kirk-patrick, our then-ambassador to the UN. Despite Sankara's diplomatic (Castro) faux pas on this trip, however, he did manage to set up a meeting with her to discuss the situation with the USAID programs in Burkina. Sankara showed up for the meeting with his ministers (one of whom later became a good friend) and told Kirkpatrick that he was well aware of the fact that his rhetoric and public persona had alien-ated the US. "But," he had said, "there's a huge difference between public relations and private relations in Africa." And he was right on that point, as I will get to later. "So," Sankara had said, "I do under-stand that you might want to cut some of the USAID-funded projects, but please don't cut two projects, because they work so well," —our forestry project was one of these. The result of the meeting with Jeane Kirkpatrick was definitely not one of softening her resolve. They had had a very cordial meeting with smiles and handshakes as they always do in the UN, but inside she had apparently been fuming.

Ambassador Neher had now arrived on the scene in Ouagadou-gou. One of his first marching orders was from Jeane Kirkpatrick: cut all USAID funding for all projects in Burkina, and begin with the for-estry project. She wanted to cut where it would hurt the most. I was summoned to the ambassador's office (a place I knew very well after spending an entire night there during the coup d'état). As soon as I arrived I was ushered in to meet Neher. He really did look like a cow-boy—rugged features, deep voice, definitely sure of himself. I liked him instantly, but obviously not what he said. The message was clear: I was to lay off all twenty-six project employees, stop implementing all project activities, transport all of the vehicles up to Ouagadougou to be stored at USAID's headquarters, and be prepared to vacate the project headquarters and leave the country ourselves, all within the short time span of one month if not sooner.

"Good Lord," I thought. "This is Africa. Nothing, and I mean nothing will/can happen at that speed." I went back to Bobo — the project HQ — and informed all of my counterparts who became very dejected. Our work had been an unmitigated success, many of Fred's ideas had been integrated in the activities we undertook, and many good things were happening. We had established excellent relationships with our Burkinabe counterparts, and now, because of all of the good things, we were the ones to be punished first and most severely. What kind of message did that send? Nevertheless, my marching orders were clear and we began making the preparations to close the project.

Meanwhile, in Ouaga, Ambassador Neher had completed his first meetings with Sankara. Lo and behold, Cowboy Neher and Communist Sankara hit it off — there was no tension, they mutually respected each other instantaneously, and over the following several weeks, they became good friends. Neher was still hardline — those were his marching orders — but he did learn from Sankara that in Africa there is a huge chasm between what is public and what is private. The public rhetoric wasn't at all related to how Sankara governed. He, in fact, wanted desperately to wean Burkina off of the country's deep dependence on foreign aid by becoming more self-reliant. That was precisely what had been my quest as a consultant for as long as I had been in this business, so I was in full agreement with him. All of this permeated Neher's consciousness as he started working with Sankara to achieve the unavoidable: closing all of USAID's activities. But he proceeded in a much slower and meticulous fashion in order to salvage many of the development lessons learned.

Instead of an immediate one-month project closure, we finally closed everything after nine months, and we all left on very friendly terms with our project counterparts. A sad end note to this story: Thomas Sankara was killed only a few years later, in 1987, in a brutal coup d'état perpetrated by his earlier best friend and military colleague, Blaise Compaore. They had had a growing disagreement about governing since the first coup, with the end result that Blaise assumed power by killing Sankara and thirteen of his closest confidants and bodyguards. Blaise remained president until 2014.

Next stop, Côte d'Ivoire.

COTE D'IVOIRE
Asif

After the Burkina Faso experience, all roads were again leading back to the one alternative still on the books: professing at the University of Idaho. The UI, however, was still not out of the financial woods, so returning was a depressing prospect since we really wanted to remain in Africa and be tapped to work on a different project somewhere.

As we were in the process of packing up during our final days in Burkina we decided to take the kids to Bamako, Mali for some R & R. We made a reservation at the Hotel Amitié in downtown Bamako, packed up the car, and started out on our adventure. Bamako is one of my favorite cities in West Africa, so I was very much looking forward to the trip. Bamako at that time had a big international community, including many long-termers whom we knew well. In addition, visiting consultants from the US whom we knew would also most likely be there. It would be a grand time, and we looked forward to it.

We arrived in Bamako and immediately reconnected with friends and colleagues. During the first afternoon in Bamako, as the kids were frolicking in the Amitié pool and getting seriously sunburned, Asif Shaikh appeared. He was at that time with Energy/Development International (E/DI) — a Washington, D.C. consulting firm soon to become the International Resources Group (IRG). Asif was based in Abidjan, Côte d'Ivoire where he was the COP on the Energy Initiatives for Africa (EIA) project funded by USAID. EIA was a regional project with a mission to deal with energy issues over all of West Africa, provide technical assistance where needed, launch small-scale energy projects, and to function as quick in and out technical resources to supplement other energy-related efforts in West Africa.

Asif happened to be in Bamako on a short TDY (temporary duty) and was scheduled to return to Abidjan the next day. What a providential meeting this turned out to be. Asif had been called back to Washington, D.C. to assume the role of Executive Vice President of E/DI and they were engaged in looking for his replacement at EIA in Abidjan. Well ... I couldn't believe this. Here I was, about to reluctantly return to the US after closing the Burkina Forestry project, and he was looking for someone to replace him in Abidjan. The replacement needed to have: a) the requisite biomass energy qualifications (obviously, that was me), b) the language skills (me again), and c) the willingness to live in Abidjan, Côte d'Ivoire (me once again). It was ideal. To make a long story short, one thing led to another with cables going back and forth to E/DI in D.C., and I was soon hired permanently by E/DI.

As is usual with USAID, however, things move at a snail's pace or slower. We had hopes that we could just move directly to Abidjan from Burkina, which would have been a relatively easy trip in the car, but there was no chance. Time ran out and only our three cats got to move to Abidjan directly to live temporarily with Asif and his family. We had to move back to the US for at least three months before everything was ready for us to settle in with the EIA project in Abidjan.

Mme Folleroux

Our EIA stint was a good experience, although I had to do a great deal of travel in the West Africa region on a variety of assignments. We lived in Asif's house until we found a large house—6,000 square feet—with marble floors, lovely tile bathrooms, large windows and balconies, a beautiful garden with banana, ylang ylang, and mango trees, bird of paradise flowers, cannas, and passion fruit vines climbing up to the balcony railings. The realtor put new carpets of our color choices in the bedrooms and installed powerful air conditioners.

Our realtor was Mme Dominique Folleroux, an elegant French lady. She was divorced, attractive, and moved about with ease in Abidjan's high society. She became our friend and, as it turned out, our close neighbor. Her daughter, Natalie, was the same age as our oldest daughter, Kari, and so they became friends and attended the same private French school in Abidjan.

Years after we had left Abidjan, we learned that Mme Folleroux had married a certain up-and-coming politician named Allasane Ouattara. Yes, that Ouattara — the one who became the president of Côte d'Ivoire in 2015 after a long and violent battle bordering on civil war to remove the old president. So now Mme Folleroux is the First Lady of Côte d'Ivoire — quite a jump from where she was when we knew her as our real estate agent, friend, and neighbor.

Robbed Again

The robbery in Dakar, Senegal wasn't the only one we experienced. It happened in Burkina Faso and Côte d'Ivoire as well. In Burkina it was small scale. Judi confronted a thief in our home, told him to leave, and he did. She was lucky. A few weeks later in another American's home, he knifed the guard. In Abidjan, however, we did indeed have a very serious incident. Abidjan is a large city with rampant crime in the suburbs as well as downtown. People were murdered for not obeying a thief quickly enough. It didn't help that when the pope scheduled a visit to Abidjan, President Felix Houphuet Boigny decided as a gesture of goodwill and forgiveness to release 8,000 criminals from prison. The entire expatriate population braced for the consequences, which hit us hard almost immediately. The pope came and went and we were left with the aftermath of having an additional 8,000 potentially violent criminals running loose.

I was in Rome when they hit our house. While there I received a cable from USAID in Abidjan that said: "Your house was robbed last night; family was not harmed; robbers fled before they could take much." There had been 14 of them. They had targeted three houses in a row on the same side of the street so they could scale the walls between the houses without being detected from the street. I was shocked beyond belief, and relieved at the same time, because Judi and kids were apparently intact. I called home and got the full story. That was the only time in six years that Judi told me she wanted to move back home. By the time I got back from Rome, however, she was okay again.

The first place they broke into was two houses up the street—they were in and out of there fairly quickly without incident. The next house—our immediate neighbor—wasn't so incident free. She was rudely awakened to discover fourteen robbers in her home while her husband, a Swiss African Development Bank employee, was away. They made her undress, tied her up, and put a gun to her temple and a knife to her throat and asked her which way she preferred to die. For some reason they didn't rape her or kill her, but they did manage to frighten her to the point where she literally lost her sanity, at least temporarily. Just a few weeks later she left Abidjan, never to return.

At about 3:30 a.m. they came to our house. We believe they had an accomplice there—our guard—a surly guy we had inherited from Asif. We suspect he was in on it, because before locking up and barring herself and the kids in upstairs, Judi went out to give him his cup of strong coffee. She locked all four doors of our car. He was angry about that and told her that it was not necessary. She had never done that before, and he must have intended it to be the getaway vehicle.

Once inside the compound the thieves used box cutters to remove the putty around a huge rectangular sliding window on our lower back terrace. Judi and the kids were all sound asleep upstairs, securely locked in behind bolted doors and iron bars, and a 2x4 to the wall, bracing the door. Every night we locked ourselves in to prevent would-be robbers from gaining access to the upstairs.

Once the window had been removed, they leaned it up against the wall. Now inside my office area, they must have headed first for the refrigerator and the pantry. There they helped themselves to whatever food we had. Thieves must eat too, and we were happy to oblige in that respect, because this took additional time. They found the liquor stash, and helped themselves to that as well.

Now well-fed and slightly inebriated, I can only conclude that these guys weren't the smartest dudes in the world. One of them must have decided he needed to cool off after so much work, so he opened the front door of the house to let in some air. Air he got on that very breezy night! This created a strong draft all the way through the house, and the large piece of glass they had balanced against the wall fell to the marble floor, smashing it into a thousand pieces and punctuating the night silence with something akin to a loud gunshot.

They must have fled immediately, taking with them nothing but our supply of canned cat food and international coffees (from America). A tablecloth containing a jumble of other small items was found abandoned close to the house. Yes, that's all they managed to steal, except for the food and the booze.

I made a serious request to USAID — either we were put on the Embassy guard service that provided protection with two guards, not just one, additional security measures, and a roving vehicle checking in on all of the clients several times during the night, or I would leave the project. The service also came with the installation of flood lights and an alarm system complete with a remote control device that would set off a loud wailing sound when activated. They agreed and we ended up staying for another two years in Abidjan without incident.

Attempted robberies were commonplace, and even humorous sometimes. An incident occurred on a visit to the local market when Judi and Annike, six years old at the time, were walking hand in hand. One young man walked toward them and bumped into Judi in such a way as to break the hold on Annike. Another man, behind them, at the same time, reached into Judi's pocket to relieve her of cash or money he would surely find there since she wasn't carrying a bag. Judi grabbed Annike and the thief's hand at the same time, pried the thief's fingers open and retrieved her treasured color swatch. That was the only thing that was in her pocket. She still has the swatch – it's her favorite color.

Project Counterpart And The US Ambassador

The EIA project placed us front and center on all things even remotely touching the biomass for energy question. This was *the* question of consequence in West Africa, and expert consultants were flooding the region. All roads led to Abidjan and the EIA project. It was as though we were a force to be reckoned with, which actually wasn't a bad feeling at all.

The major fly in the ointment (and these are unavoidable if you work with USAID) was our Ivorian counterpart. His name was Agnissan Kouassi, the true personification of African greed and corruption. It all began fairly innocently. He didn't ask for much, just the use of project resources such as secretaries, stationery, office space, etc. to conduct all of his personal business. He also got himself elected to the Ivorian Assembly as a regional representative (akin to a House member in the US Congress), which made him insufferably bolder in draining our project resources for his own personal affairs.

I confronted him and told him to stop. He didn't, and so I took the steps I needed to sever the relationship with him as a counterpart. I documented what was going on to USAID and wrote up my recommended action. I had my home office behind me so I eventually fired Mr. Kouassi because the project funding level could no longer justify the continued theft by a counterpart, especially one like him, who contributed absolutely nothing of professional value.

The meeting we had about this was ... well ... highly unpleasant. Mr. Kouassi yelled at me, told me he would destroy the project, told me I was a racist and that he knew where we lived and where my children went to school, and he succeeded in leaving me with a lively vision of potential sinister actions he could perpetrate upon us. He also told me he had very powerful friends who could arrange for (unspoken) things to be done and that I wouldn't know until after the deed (whatever deed he was referring to) had hit me, or my family. He also had the power to prevent me from leaving the country — after all he was a powerful assemblyman and had unlimited powers.

It went on and on, and I was literally in awe of the vast measure of havoc he had already contemplated foisting upon my person and my family if he were let go. I was also worried, naturally, because it wasn't beyond him to actually act on any of his sinister plots. So, through some friends who had friends in high places, notably the chief of police in Abidjan, I reported what had happened to the authorities in order to have it on record should something come to pass. We also notified the school that under no circumstances was anybody to be allowed to remove our children from the school except Judi or me.

But that wasn't all. I was told by USAID that, as a matter of courtesy, I also needed to notify the US Ambassador of the action taken, since Mr. Kouassi was an elected official. I did so and sat back, breathing a sigh of relief for finally getting rid of this useless blowhard (and that's the best I can say about Mr. Kouassi).

And then the phone rang.

"Hello, this is the EIA project."

"This is the US Ambassador's office. The ambassador requests your presence in his office immediately."

"Wh ... wha ... what is this about?" I asked tentatively.

"It's about your project counterpart, Mr. Kuoassi—please come to the embassy immediately."

I instantly knew something was amiss and quickly called the US-AID Director in Abidjan who had stood behind me our decision to fire Mr. Kouassi. The director decided to come along with me, so we hopped into the car and headed for the embassy. Upon arrival we were immediately ushered into the ambassador's office for the meeting. I will always remember the scene: the ambassador was ensconced in his chair behind his desk, glaring at us as we entered. He didn't shake hands, but directed us over to the sofa and chairs away from his desk.

So there we were, the USAID Director, the deputy chief of mission, the ambassador, and me. He was new in Abidjan so I guess he wanted to make an impression. And that he did—he launched right into one of the strongest tirades I've ever heard a diplomat deliver to an underling. Not only was it loud, it was profane at times, bordering on the mildly insane, I think. "How dare you? ... Mr. Kouassi is an elected official ... you are jeopardizing international relations ... are you tone deaf?" I think this went on for at least 10 minutes. I was asked to defend my actions, but at every attempt to do so I was interrupted and yelled at once again.

Wow. Twice now in that many days I had been yelled at by two powerful people. Was I wrong? Should I have let this overt graft and corruption go on? So many conflicting thoughts occupied my mind as all of this was going on. At first I was as intimidated as anyone would be, but then it became increasingly clear to me that I really wasn't an underling of the ambassador even though he treated me as one. I was from the private sector under contract to manage a USAID project in Abidjan, and I had taken all of the required steps before firing this counterpart. Furthermore, every step had been clearly documented, including Mr. Kouassi's outright theft of project resources.

But none of this mattered one whit to the ambassador, and I was told in no uncertain terms to reverse what I had done. The USAID Director was sitting in the sofa with his eyes wide open just absorbing the incredulity of what was happening before him right then, and I ended up not saying anything beyond my aborted attempts to defend myself.

Then the meeting was over — the ambassador had said his thing, and by golly, he had made some decisions. That's what ambassadors are supposed to do, isn't it? By this time, the ambassador had managed to stir up some hefty anger in me, and I no longer was intimidated. It didn't take me very long to decide that I would rather leave the project and Côte d'Ivoire than grovel to Agnissan Kouassi and let him back in. That's what I told the USAID Director as well.

So I didn't heed the ambassador's decrees and just waited ... and waited ... and waited for my walking papers. At the same time we also developed an acute awareness of our surroundings in order to prevent Mr. Kouassi's goons from harming our family. Nothing happened, and we continued on with the project for at least another six months. I suspect it was because the friends who had arranged for us to meet with the chief of police made separate and very convincing arrangements with Kouassi's goons to leave us be.

I never saw the ambassador again, but I heard nobody liked him during his tenure in Abidjan. Maybe he developed a close friendship with Mr. Kouassi — they certainly were kindred spirits.

Rising To The Occasion

While living in Côte d'Ivoire I visited and worked in the country of Guinea many times. The best I can say about this country is that it probably is the armpit of the world. Conakry, the capital, is a fairly large, dirty, crime-ridden, and immensely dysfunctional city located on the Atlantic Coast. Conakry is also the only place in that country where there is some semblance of paved roads. Everywhere else there are only dirt roads which are largely impassable during the rainy season. If any roads outside Conakry ever did receive a thin layer of paving, they reverted to pothole nightmares within one year. Trucks and other vehicles were always heavily overloaded. The wearing of the pavement begins with deep tire ruts followed by small and then large potholes which, when sufficiently large, cause spectacular vehicular accidents.

USAID and the World Bank were quite active in Guinea, funding several different kinds of natural resource management (NRM) projects—biomass for energy in particular. Our EIA project in Abidjan was often called upon to provide technical assistance as a part of the planning for new donor-funded NRM activities. On one occasion, I was asked to go to Conakry to participate in a UNDP-sponsored conference on NRM issues in Guinea. This turned out be a trip I will never forget.

The first obstacle in my way was simply getting to Conakry from Abidjan. I had booked a flight on Air Zaire, which was without doubt the worst airline in the entire world. We didn't have a choice of carriers while living in Africa—we had to accept whatever arrangements we could make to get from point A to point B. I did so much travel in and out of Abidjan that I can safely say that God must have worked overtime to shield me from many different travel hazards. I showed up at the airport on time, the flight had arrived, and soon the boarding announcement was made. We lined up and headed for the aircraft, only to be stopped halfway. "Please return to the waiting hall (with no functioning air conditioning) to await further announcements." So there we were again waiting for not one, not two, but four hours before the "technical difficulties" announcement was made. We were now five hours delayed ... groan.

From the waiting hall we watched the work on our airplane. Four or five mechanics were occupied with affixing an entire jet engine onto the right wing, the chief mechanic sitting on the wing holding a manual open to a page which I hope was labeled: "Affixing engine to wing." Engine parts were scattered on the ground and soaking up water while

the rain was coming down in sheets. When the engine was firmly affixed and the mechanic closed the manual and wiped the grease off the
wing, he gave the "all clear" signal. The announcement soon followed:
"Air Zaire flight 340 to Conakry is ready to board." We all lined up
again, trekked across the tarmac, and boarded. Firmly strapped in, I
looked at the decrepit interior of the aircraft and silently prayed for
a safe trip, vowing never again to fly Air Zaire if I survived this trip.

The engines started. We remained in the same spot while the pilot kept revving both engines to the point where the aircraft trembled
and shook. Then he switched everything off, keyed his mike and made
the announcement that the mechanical problem hadn't been fixed and
would we please return to the waiting lounge. We all let out a vocal
groan, but probably this time out of relief that our lives had been spared.

I headed to the ticket desk to look for alternative flights. Lo and
behold—I found one on Air Afrique scheduled to depart at 3 a.m. I
said—"Yes, book me." "Do you have any luggage?" "Yes, it is on Air
Zaire over there," as I indicated the plane on the tarmac where the
mechanics were taking the engine apart again. It was now 9 p.m., but
miracles do happen. With some appropriate bribing I got one airport
official to accompany me out to the plane and climb into the baggage
hold with me to retrieve my suitcase.

It was too late to go home, so I checked into a hotel near the airport
and got one hour of sleep before it was time to head back to the airport.
We took off on time—3 a.m. As we took off I saw the Air Zaire plane still
in pieces as the drizzling rain soaked all of the scattered engine parts.

Conakry finally. I got through customs and headed for the hotel.
The convention was scheduled to start at 9 a.m. and it was now 8 a.m.,
so I had one hour. I checked in, managed to get a quick shower and
dress appropriately, and I headed for the convention center to arrive
only a half hour late. No problem, I thought. I'll take my seat in the
back and try to stay awake through the morning session speeches. The
hall was full of about 500 African and expatriate participants, and the
first speech was already underway.

As I sat down in the rear of the room, someone from USAID/Guin-
ea spotted me and quickly came to see me. "Glad you made it, you're

on soon." "What?" I exclaimed. "Come with me," he said and escorted me to an empty seat at the head table where all of the dignitaries were sitting — ministers and cabinet chiefs from several countries. I was dumbfounded; somehow I had missed the slightly important tidbit of information that I was to be one of the presenters. I knew what the conference was about and I knew the details of USAID/Guinea's ongoing and proposed portfolio of activities, but I hadn't prepared anything, certainly not a speech … in French.

The current speaker droned on in typical African fashion and went at least ten minutes over his allotted time. Good, that meant less for me to say if we were to stay on schedule, I thought. The Guinean Minister in charge of the opening session then turned to me to welcome me and to lament the difficulties of air travel in Africa, and said that he was really looking forward to hearing my presentation. "But before getting to that, the next speaker is …" and he proceeded to introduce the minister who was to do the next presentation. This one launched into a long-winded and detailed speech about what was going on in his country in natural resource management. I was in a state of near panic at this point, since I was the next one to be on that podium.

I asked my neighbor for a few pages from his yellow pad and proceeded to frantically write down some notes. What to say? What to say? First things first — say thanks for the invitation to speak here to such a distinguished audience, apologize for being late, crack a joke about the plane engine being on the tarmac in the rain, hope for some comic relief. Then, briefly talk about what the EIA project was doing in fuelwood economics, biodiversity, and natural resource management in general and in which countries. Then finally conclude with the Guinea ongoing and proposed USAID project portfolio to stay within the confines of the convention mission statement. I was shaking in my boots, because all of my notes were literally plucked from thin air in the span of twenty minutes — all I needed to do now was deliver this speech before this dignified audience of expatriates all dressed up in suits and ties and the Africans in their fine African garb and to make it sound as if I really had something important to say.

The speaker finished, the applause was polite, and I was introduced next. There I was, facing this audience, dead tired from lack of sleep, hot but not able to remove my jacket because of protocol. I looked down at my notes and began … in French.

Well … there really is something to the saying "rise to the occasion." Every now and then, very rarely, people do rise to the occasion, and I did on this day. My French all of a sudden became fully fluent. A welcoming sense of quiet and confidence permeated my being, which meant that my notes worked. A plane engine on the tarmac with worried passengers looking on was apparently hilariously funny and I got the comic relief I had so desperately wanted. All of the things I said about EIA weren't just informative; they were also pertinent to the conference mission. When I got to the Guinea project portfolio the audience was all ears. I don't think anyone even napped.

I returned to my place at the table of dignitaries, and our session chairman announced a fifteen-minute break. I was suddenly surrounded by participants asking questions, and then, I saw Guinea Television powering through the crowd toward me with their entourage of camera technicians, cord bearers, television personalities, urging me to come outside for an interview. I ended up being interviewed twice by different TV crews.

I have often wondered why it is I did so well on this particular day. Perhaps it is because God wanted to show me that He is the controller of all things, and that worry and panic don't help any situation.

I had at least eight separate missions to Guinea for USAID and the World Bank, each one associated with stories I may tell some other day.

MALI
The Legend Of Angel Togo

Like so many other countries in West Africa, Mali is a chaotic place where things don't always work, the heat is overbearing, the dust clogs up computers, and the roads are either non-existent or impassable outside of Bamako, the capital city. This is especially during the rainy season. But aside from all of this, sipping that cold beer in the shade of a massive tree after a long day of work, exchanging stories with friends and colleagues as the sun sets, just can't be beat. The people of Mali are vibrant and full of life, and all are engaged in some sort of economic pursuit to make ends meet.

So many things happened in Mali, little things really, that made working there fascinating. I often traveled to Mopti, about a day's drive northeast of Bamako. Mopti is the gateway to the Dogon country and the staging ground for many different projects I visited frequently. We soon became regulars at Mopti's best hotel, from which we made long day trips.

One of our regular site visits was to Angel Togo, a farmer living a couple of hours' drive from Mopti. Mr. Togo was a legend; a unique individual who had the entire development community in Washington, D.C. — USAID and the World Bank alike — abuzz with excitement. He had been anointed as *the* farmer in West Africa who got it, the one all farmers should emulate, and the one who provided justification for donors spending literally millions of dollars on field activities.

Mr. Togo did everything the technical experts recommended: he established windbreaks to protect against the predominant winds and wind erosion; built contour dikes to retain as much water as possible from very little annual rainfall; planted live fences rather than building "dead" fences; practiced agroforestry; and on and on. Among the development experts in D.C., acquaintance with Mr. Togo was the contact that counted and the key to obtaining respect and authority in high places. If you knew Mr. Togo, whatever you said at the many meetings we attended would be received as gospel, and you would gain immediate gravitas. Angel Togo could do no wrong.

I visited Mr. Togo many times and signed his visitor books (of which he has many). My purpose was to interview him and learn applications that could be replicated elsewhere. It was fascinating to visit him and to tour his farm. It became a rich oasis in a barren and non-productive area characterized by extensive livestock grazing and little farming. Angel Togo had managed to transform this kind of land into a very productive farming operation, and this served to strongly confirm everything we — the economic development professionals — had preached for many years. Angel Togo and a few others were to us proof positive that our solutions for Africa's natural resource management problems had merit, and consequently the donor money kept flowing, perpetuating our involvement.

The Blanket Flasher

Mopti is located on the banks of the confluence of the Niger and Bani Rivers in Mali. It is a city full of activity and intensive river-oriented trade. The heavily laden pirogues travel up and down river with goods to be traded wherever markets were located. This is how things have been done in this region for centuries. Right at the confluence of the two rivers there's a restaurant where we would enjoy our evening meals and watch the frantic activity in the harbor area. It was great theater.

One remarkable aspect of the restaurant-by-the-river experience was the blanket salesmen. Mopti has the distinction of producing very unique, intricately designed, and colorful Fulani wool blankets. These are in high demand with tourists and will fetch up to $1,500 in the US. They are great gifts, and people cherish them, even if they should never be washed or even dry cleaned.

Unfortunately, I am a sucker for good salesmanship, and these guys knew they had a potential customer. While having dinner and drinking that cold beer on the restaurant terrace, surveilling the chaotic life in the harbor area, I would invariably spot a blanket salesman intently watching me from far away. If I shifted my gaze in his direction even for only a brief moment he would notice and immediately do a flashing move—spread the blanket out to display it in all its glory, lift his eyebrows, and beckon for an invitation to come see you on the terrace. There were many blanket salesmen around the terrace vying for your attention, and the moment you nodded your head, even in the general manner of normal conversation with your colleagues, they took it as an invitation to rush to your side with blankets flapping in their wake and to inundate you with their sales pitches, unfold their blankets and point out all of the very attractive and authentically cultural features. The frantic activity of six or seven blanket salesmen fighting for our attention, the frenzied harbor commotion, and the enjoyable cameradrie with fellow consultants at the end of a busy day is a priceless memory.

I ended up paying more than I should have for blankets we still have, which I bought from a particularly compelling blanket salesman in Mopti.

Train From Kayes To Bamako

Other trips took us deep into the Mali interior where travel was possible only during the dry season and only with four-wheel drive vehicles. The roads were rendered impassable during the rainy season. On one occasion our team decided to avoid wear and tear on the project vehicles (and on us). In order to get from Bamako to Kayes, deep into the Mali interior, we decided to fly to Kayes and take the train back to Bamako.

The flying experience was unique in itself. We flew an eight-seat dilapidated Russian air craft of unknown vintage with an equally dilapidated Russian pilot at the controls. But the real adventure was the return trip on the train. We had three days in Kayes doing our thing and lodging at the town's only hotel which provided no air conditioning, no running water, no mosquito nets, but plenty of unknown critters in every crevice of the room. Needless to say, I didn't sleep even for a minute.

We had reserved the entire first class car for the return trip to Bamako, figuring that after our three grueling and sleepless days in Kayes we needed some R & R in first-class comfort on the way back. Well, first class on trains in West Africa has many different meanings, as we soon discovered. In this case, first class was roughly equal to worst class. Whereas we had hoped for at least an air-conditioned car, no such thing was even remotely possible. They may have had air conditioning on the train at one time, but it had died at least fifteen years earlier, never replaced.

The heat was a blistering 115 degrees Fahrenheit in the shade, and no breeze. For air, the only option was opening all windows in the car. The car hadn't been cleaned in at least ten years—it was caked with old dirt and grime; the seats were only halfway affixed to the floor; the cushion springs were exposed, and the inside padding had long since been removed; there were no "facilities" in the car except for a half-way enclosed space at the very rear end of the car where there was a simple hole in the floor. The odor was overwhelming.

As we left the station in Kayes, we were looking forward to a seventeen-hour ride back to Bamako if the train managed to stay on schedule. And it never ... never ... did. We sat on the decrepit seats and just looked at each other, all feeling panic gathering momentum in the pits of our stomachs. This too shall pass, we said to ourselves over and over again as we settled in and tried to find some semblance of comfort either sitting or standing.

After about one hour of travel, we discovered another major problem—the first class car placed at the very end of the train had more side to side and up and down motion than cars closer to the locomotive. This little tidbit contributed immensely to our discomfort. Not only were we nauseous from the smells of the "facilities," we now had to control our natural tendencies to descend into the abyss of motion sickness. So we all stood by the windows, staring straight ahead desperately holding back breakfast which came up and out with every twist and turn on the tracks.

But it didn't end there; the last car on the train is also the car where all of the dust, grit, and grime collected in the train's wake as we traveled at the blazing speed of thirty miles per hour. If we closed the windows, we would suffocate from the heat; if we kept them open, we would suffocate from the dust and odors entering the car as we traveled. Pick your poison—we kept the windows open and proceeded to pick through our clothing in our suitcases to fashion breathing filters over our noses and mouths. I think I had one pair of clean socks left that did the job somewhat.

Such was our existence for the first ten hours. We stopped at every possible small village en route to pick up passengers and freight. Out of nowhere appeared people bearing trays of fruits and vegetables, live chickens, and other unidentifiable foods and drinks to sell to the passengers. They gravitated to the "first class" car because that's where the money would be—with the white foreigners. We took turns standing our ground by the doors to block the vendors (if allowed in they would have immediately overwhelmed us, and fights would eventually have broken out) and to prevent other passengers from entering our reserved haven. We wanted to keep our misery all to ourselves because we had paid for it.

The next five hours was more of the same, except by now the resolve to protect our territory had weakened. We noticed that the other cars had rapidly filled with passengers — they were beginning to climb up on the roof, and some were just hanging onto the sides with their hands. As we traveled down the track we began to give in to the reality that we could no longer keep the last car to ourselves — there were too many stops remaining before we reached Bamako.

I think we silently thought of administering last rites to each other because our habitual standards of western comfort had been incredibly violated. We were now in our twentieth hour of train travel (yes, behind schedule), nauseous, sleep deprived, and totally irritable with no hope of keeping the misery at even that level. We had to accept a deeper level of misery as hordes of new passengers would enter our blessed first-class car.

After twenty-three hours of travel on this train we finally arrived in Bamako, fully broken in body and spirit. I had no idea how I was going to recover from that trip, although somehow we eventually regained our strength and dignity and managed to carry on. I can only look at the Africans with great admiration because they endure this kind of hardship any time they travel anywhere, in bush taxis from the city to their villages, or on trains.

Why I Love Africa

Finally, there's a little story that makes me love West Africa forever. I was on an extended field trip in the Mali interior, traveling with an entourage of Malian counterparts and some expatriate consultants. We were doing the usual — interviewing local farmers and documenting their activities to create farm budget databases. Every night we would stay at some local hotel, or wherever possible, secure an invitation to stay at the village's guest house built for the president in case he decided to grace the village with a personal visit, usually during an election year. Many villages build and maintain such presidential guest houses because they have no hotel, let alone any hotel with a presidential suite.

The guest houses are, of course, supposed to be luxurious. And in some strange African way, they are. Luxury, however, is a relative thing. The living room is cluttered with way too much locally made overstuffed furniture arranged, along all four walls to accommodate as many visiting dignitaries as possible. The bedrooms are sparsely furnished with locally produced bed frames, straw mattresses, wooden chairs, and an armoire with warped doors that won't close. There is typically no air conditioning in these houses because that would be far too costly to install and operate.

One night we had permission to stay overnight at one of these guest houses in a very remote village in Mali. Although it was very spartan compared to western standards, it was a huge improvement over some of the hotels where we had been staying. After dinner we settled down on the balcony for an evening cup of tea and a chat before turning in to get some sleep. It was a cool evening with a refreshing breeze. The darkness of the night had overtaken us, and the only light we had was from our flashlights and from the fire lit for brewing the tea. The village had a few lanterns burning here and there, but the village was devoid of electricity. I remember sitting on that balcony and looking out over the village, seeing only the faint glow of kerosene lamps in the individual homes and courtyards and hearing small snippets of music, dogs barking, singing crickets, and accompanying frogs. African nights are not quiet. The chorus of crickets and frogs comprise a soothing and peaceful lullaby. Overhead, the vast expanse of stars provided a magnificent spectacle of the universe that left us speechless and in complete awe.

As we enjoyed this very special moment, we were suddenly jarred into reality by a knock on the metal front gate of the compound. We looked at each other not quite knowing what to do, so we called out to inquire who was there. We received a muffled response from the other side of the gate, which didn't help much, so we trekked out with a flashlight. I stood on my tiptoes to look over the top. I could see nothing but a vague outline of two people. Suddenly out of the pitch black, two brilliant Cheshire Cat grins gleamed at me, followed by the exclamation: "Eeehhhh, Christophersen!!!!!!"

I had no idea who they were. Here we were in the middle of absolutely nowhere, and I was being greeted by two people who apparently knew me. They were forest guards who had seen activity in the presidential guest house and wanted to check it out, because they knew the president was not in town. We opened the gate to let them in. They were excited to have this unscheduled grand reunion with me. I pretended to be just as enthusiastic about this as they were, but I was actually frantically searching the nether regions of my brain to recall where I had met these guys.

As their reunion enthusiasm gained momentum, I finally connected the dots from things they said and concluded that they had been Malian participants in a two-week course on farmer perspective economic feasibility of field activities which we had hosted near Bamako some three years earlier. Yes, it all came back to me and it was great seeing them again. We brewed another pot of tea and sat and talked long into the night.

NIGER
FLUP

Niger is another one of my favorite West African countries. There was a USAID project there called the FLUP project—Forest and Land Use Project—that became quite well known among the donors. The project was considered exceedingly successful. For several years, literally millions of dollars were spent on projects in other countries mimicking the FLUP activities.

The success was largely attributable to the management of one of my colleagues, John Heermans, who is a development professional par excellence. He is the personification of a "field man," not unlike Fred Weber—the same no-nonsense approach to dealing with local people, never condescending to them, always well liked, and most importantly, very firm with his employer, USAID. He had a vast amount of experience, and he knew how to motivate local farmers without relying on handouts and subsidies. We were all in awe of what happened around the Guesselbodi village project headquarters (near Niamey, Niger), where the condition of the natural forests actually improved significantly, and the villagers prospered as they were handed the responsibility to sustainably manage these forests around their village to their profit. The project was very much responsible for the birth of the movement to decentralize the management authority of natural resources to the local people.

But this was Africa. While the project was up and running the economy thrived, people enthusiastically adopted the management techniques taught by the experts, and training was offered in everything ranging from how to manage the natural forests to book-keeping and setting up rural markets for fuelwood, charcoal, and natural forest products/bush medicines, etc. The people who received the training learned well and became quite adept at their jobs. All of the desperately sought-after indicators of improved well-being in development aid were present, and so the activities were emulated everywhere.

USAID funding continued for a full eight years before the project closed. One year after closure I was tapped to work on a team to evaluate the aftermath of the project. Our task was to document what had happened in the area after the project ended. What had happened was an eye-opener. Not only had the natural forest surrounding the Guesselbodi village degraded to an even worse condition than it was in before the project had started, none of the management expertise had remained intact, the vehicles that had been left behind were no longer functioning, and the rural fuelwood/charcoal markets were nonexistent.

The erosion had begun on a small scale. Once the project resources were withdrawn, things continued for a while until the bookkeepers who collected the money from the sales in the rural markets caved to the temptations of actually having money in their possession, even though it wasn't their money. The opportunity was there for them to enrich themselves just a little ... a temporary loan perhaps, to cover some immediate need, with every intention of paying it back. Then the next time perhaps the need was a little greater, so they borrowed again. After several iterations of this, all self-discipline and control were abandoned and the well had run dry. Things began to fall apart.

The vehicles were increasingly used for personal purposes until they broke down from lack of maintenance and spare parts. Meanwhile, the forest degraded because the active management had stopped, so the villagers had unhindered access to whatever the forests offered. The degradation accelerated because the Nigerien Forest Service was no longer in charge of this particular natural forest, thanks to the management charter provided under the USAID FLUP activity.

I vividly remember a village meeting in Guesselbodi with thirty to forty of the village elders, where we asked the question over and over again: "What happened?" Their response was simple—"Well, the project left." I would say, "But that was the purpose—the project was here for eight years, you learned how to manage not only the forests, but also the money and how to reinvest so that the system could continue on a sustainable basis. All of the investments made were intended to equip you to easily continue without any further outside assistance." So I asked again, "What happened?" It didn't go anywhere. Their answer was always: "The project left. When will a new project come here?"

And that's the problem of Africa in a nutshell. Without the cover of an outside mechanism—USAID, World Bank, an NGO—the culture destroys just about any discipline individuals may want to exercise in the quest for improving their economic well-being. If someone does well, others in the village notice, and unless he shares everything with them generously he can even be in danger. Not only can jealous neighbors come during the night and destroy the very thing responsible for his economic improvement, they can be even more vicious and perpetrate violence against him, even murder with poisons or by other sinister means.

The few that have succeeded have done so by keeping their success very secret. A man will typically not tell his wife that he has a bank account, and he will certainly not tell any of his relatives or neighbors. If the secret gets out, he will be expected to foot a large part of the bill for baptisms, marriages, funerals, and many other feasts that rural Africans host during the year, not only for his extended family but for the village in general. An African who has "made it" can avoid perpetual poverty only by moving away and severing his ties with the village structure. Even if he shows boundless generosity, jealousy and envy may still cause some to destroy whatever brought the success in the first place. It is extremely difficult to break out of the vicious cycle of poverty, so most efforts undertaken by donors intending to improve the economic well-being in the rural areas rarely succeed once the donor presence has ended.

Traveling To Diffa

One of my short-term assignments in Niger took us far into the interior — to Diffa and beyond — almost all the way to Lake Chad, a road distance of some 1,500 kilometers east from Niamey. We had to hug the southern part of the country and avoid the north, because the Tuaregs (Berber nomadic pastoral people), were stopping travelers, taking their possessions, including vehicles, and sometimes harming them. Presumably the east/west southern part of the country was safe, so we were told to stay there. How USAID deemed that area X was safe and area Y was not is beyond me, but we took their word for it and set out on our trip.

Our task was to visit rural code offices in the region and document how well the code worked with respect to the management of natural resources: how the local people responded to code guidelines, what were the problems, and what were the needs. Each administrative district had a rural code office, which, in some cases, consisted of a hut made out of mud bricks with one termite-ridden and rickety desk inside, two rickety metal chairs, no electricity, no paper or pens, no filing cabinets, and piles of paper records/files stored on warped and sagging wood shelves. These records were covered with thick layers and obviously hadn't been touched in decades.

Occupying the single desk was the rural code officer. His job was to travel throughout his district to talk with the local villagers about the code, what they could and could not do, and provide whatever assistance he could. Often he had no means of transportation — no vehicle, no motorcycle, no mobylette, no bicycle. There was no way he could do his job thoroughly, so the rural code office had no effective purpose other than to remain on paper as a key government institution for which the donors were more than welcome to provide funding.

Our main headquarters on this trip was an almost-functioning hotel in Zinder, a large city of some 200,000 people about 900 km east of Niamey. From there we would take daylong excursions to different field offices to conduct our interviews and then at night return to write our reports.

It wasn't until we had to leave Zinder and travel much further east—deep into the interior, to Diffa and beyond—that the real fun began. There is no way to adequately describe the conditions in eastern Niger (or in any part of rural West Africa for that matter)—the heat, the dust, the wind, the poverty, the occasional mass starvation, and the near total absence of anything that could conceivably provide some creature comfort. We had to bring everything we needed—water, food, gas, flashlights and batteries, soap, mosquito repellent—everything.

There were small villages en route where we would find a dilapidated hotel of sorts with a bed and straw mattress for each of the team members. But sleep would escape us—it simply wasn't possible. The heat was suffocating and there was no electricity to power fans. The mosquitos were abundant, and with the windows open to catch even the smallest hint of any night breeze, they were free to come and go at will.

Such was our lot during the second half of this field trip to eastern Niger. No sleep, adrenalin-fueled field trips to rural code offices during the day, and then serious attempts to do some writing at night. The only comfort that we all eagerly anticipated was sitting in the shade of sunset at some local watering hole, sipping that all-important cold beer plucked from coolers filled with ice from some mysterious place. How they procured ice in an area almost devoid of electricity is still a mystery to me.

When we reached Diffa (near Lake Chad), as far east as you can travel in Niger, our luck changed. We desperately needed sleep, and we weren't looking forward to checking into another "hotel" to live through another night with no shower and little sleep. Then our local contact told us about a house vacated by European expatriates who had been there on a recently closed long-term project. The house still had electricity, air conditioning, running water, and furniture. You could stay there. "Yes, yes," we all said in unison, salivating at the mere thought of a shower, a real bed, and most importantly, air conditioning, and mosquito nets. Could it be possible? Could it be possible to find such pure luxury this far from Niamey? Niamey now loomed in our consciousness as the most modern and comfortable city in the entire world, and we couldn't wait to return there to find some creature comforts.

Our contact led us to this house, located just outside the village. It was in a wooded area, so shade was plentiful. Good. Then we noticed it had a compound with a perimeter fence. Even better. Guards were still there, so that meant we could sleep through the night and not be worried about intruders. So far so good. We entered the house and flipped the light switch—it worked. The naked bulb in the hallway actually lit up, as did the lights in all of the bedrooms. We were delirious with happiness and quickly claimed our individual bedrooms, where we checked the air conditioning and the presence of mosquito nets. Next, we met in the living room where we had furniture—overstuffed sofas and chairs and a coffee table. Luxury upon luxury. There were four of us and we drew lots on who should get the first shower. I didn't win. Our Danish sociologist type team member quickly headed for the bathroom to get his first shower in a week.

We sat down to wait our turn. We heard running water sounds coming from the bathroom. This was going to be special, we all thought. Our pleasant thoughts, however, were rudely cut short by what sounded like a big explosion in the vicinity of the bathroom, and subsequent incessant hammering. We rushed to the scene and looked in—there was the Dane in his birthday suit frantically trying to turn off the water which now gushed and sprayed from burst pipes everywhere in the bathroom—the tub, the sink, every exposed pipe connection, and directly through some cracked tiles in the wall. The entire bathroom had in a fraction of a second transformed into a gigantic mess of broken pipes with water gushing out of every conceivable opening. We just stood there in total disbelief and watched this, wondering where the master turnoff valve was. Then, in unison, we broke out in hysterical laughter.

Now it was decision time. Fixing the plumbing was obviously a high priority, but a shower was an even higher priority. So we chose to the latter, forgot about the tub, and proceeded to shower using the exposed pipes. It wasn't until we had all finished that we called out to the guards to set things in motion with plumbers and fix-it people — whoever they could scrounge up from the town. The bathroom had quickly become a hazard zone with water and soap flooding everywhere, but we were all blissfully clean. Now it was up to the plumbers to repair the damage.

They came, four plumbers, hand-carrying all sorts of pipes, glue, soldering tools, and on and on. Others were mobilized inside the house to mop up the flood and soapy waters, while we quietly retired to the living room for a "team meeting." It was almost bedtime by then and we were all dead tired, but we luxuriated in our now clean selves relaxing on comfortable furniture while we waited for the last of the workers to leave.

It was then that the last insult hit us — our Danish team member felt something crawling up his leg, obviously a critter that had exited from the nether regions of the overstuffed furniture. Yep, sure enough, as soon as he stood and frantically hopped around shaking his clothes, he exposed a very confused and agile scorpion. Well, needless to say, we all did our own bit of hopping and shaking and tearing clothes off. We gingerly removed cushions to expose yet another three or four scorpions awakened from their slumber by this team of expatriate consultants squirming on the furniture to maximize their individual comfort.

We proceeded to kill all the scorpions with the heels of our shoes and then sprayed all of the furniture and all crevices and cracks in the room with heavy insecticides. Then we did the same in all of the bedrooms after we carefully inspected under the bed covers to see if other critters had taken refuge there. After that, we were off to bed with the air conditioning blasting at full throttle. Finally, we all had a good night's sleep before waking up to another day of work around the great village of Diffa.

The USAID Driver

Another close encounter with a lion occurred in Park W in south Niger. Park W is a large national park encompassing areas in Niger, Burkina Faso, and Benin. This was truly a bizarre experience. I was attending a three-day conference on a wildlife-related USAID project at the main lodge in Park W and was utterly bored to tears. There were two other consultants with me who were equally bored. We were shut in a conference hall listening to excruciatingly boring presentations while outside the weather was beautiful with wildlife viewing beckoning. The conference was, in our minds, a complete waste of time and money, so we decided to skip out of the last session of the day to do some wildlife viewing in the park during the last few hours of daylight. We figured we had about two hours before we would have to head back to the lodge.

We quickly located the USAID driver and headed out into the park, delighted to escape the presentations and the stifling conference room, eager to see some real wildlife rather than just talking about it. As we traveled along the rutted dirt roads inside the park I noticed that the USAID driver was abnormally tense. He was usually an engaging fellow with lots of stories to tell, and we regarded him as a part of the team. At first, he was quiet, but then he became increasingly tense with every animal we saw. Then, as we came around a bend in the road, we suddenly confronted five fully grown but young female lions who were obviously on the hunt. The driver stopped the car abruptly and we just sat there as the lions approached, heading straight toward us at a slow pace. We were fascinated by what was in front of us, grabbing cameras to make sure we got pictures.

Our driver, however, had different ideas. From my peripheral view, I noticed he was now sweating profusely and had a very pained look in his face. As the lions ambled ever closer to our vehicle, he transitioned from a pained look to one of total panic, which by now, overwhelmed him. He was frantically looking for solutions to his imaginary problem of being attacked by a pack of hungry lions — his worst nightmare. He

tried to do the worst thing possible—bolting out of the car to climb a
nearby tree. I had kept an eye on him, and as soon as the panic over-
took him I grabbed him and held him back. My colleagues caught on
to what was happening and helped me keep him inside the vehicle. He
quieted down after a while, so we gradually lessened our grip on him
just a bit. Bad mistake. Now back in the control of the vehicle, but still
uncontrollably panicked, he quickly put the car in reverse and stepped
on it without looking where he was going. We traveled in reverse at
full speed with no control over the vehicle. I can only thank God for
the wide open space behind us with no trees, large termite mounds, or
other obtrusions that would have either seriously damaged our vehicle or caused us to flip over, not exactly a pleasant thought with five
hungry lions still approaching us.

In just a few seconds, he stopped the vehicle and stared intently at
the lions. They didn't miss a beat and kept coming toward us. For the
driver, this meant he had run out of options to escape. Panic time—he
had to get out of there. The only thing left to do was to gun the engine
and charge the five lions at full speed trying to mow them down. And
that's exactly what he did. He floored it and headed for the first lion at
top speed—it just barely escaped being mowed down as did the others. After this was over we finally managed to subdue our driver, who
was now foaming at the mouth with raw fear. Someone else drove the
vehicle back to the lodge while we tried to calm him.

In retrospect, if the driver had killed any of the lions with his panicked maneuver, I would still be in jail somewhere in Niger along with
my consultant colleagues. Non-Africans accidentally killing protected
wildlife in any park in Africa results in a very serious charge involving
huge fines and possibly long prison sentences.

CHAPTER 5: OTHER AFRICAN COUNTRIES

ON THE HEELS OF THE GENOCIDE

Of all the countries where I have worked for USAID and the World Bank, Rwanda is in a class of its own. Everything about that country chills me to the bone. I interacted with both Hutus and Tutsis during my work in that country and know full and well that despite being civil to each other during peace times, they are mortal enemies in the long run. The Hutus maintain lists of Tutsis to kill when the time comes, and the Tutsis maintain their lists of Hutus to kill as well. It is all just under the surface as they live and work together in apparent harmony until some incident triggers another outbreak of unimaginable violence.

Although peace reigns today, I have no doubt the ethnic violence will flare up again. People do not forget. Every individual in Rwanda is either a predator or prey or both; no one is exempt or allowed to stand on the sidelines and act as a neutral observer. Ethnic strife is probably more prevalent in Rwanda than elsewhere on the African continent. Grudges are held forever, and fifty-year-old unsettled feuds over some minor incident often cause killing sprees.

My first trip to Rwanda was with Fred Weber on a forestry project evaluation just a few years before the outbreak of the last civil war, when nearly one million Rwandan Tutsis were slaughtered in just a few months. We were assigned a couple of FSNs (Foreign Service Nationals) from the USAID Mission to help us set up meetings, do some field trip excursions, collect data, and write up the reports. The assignment was routine, we submitted our reports and fulfilled one task among many in the life of an ongoing project.

A few short years later war broke out in Rwanda and the nearly one million people were killed brutally over the span of just a few months. Almost everyone remembers this—it even rose to front-page news in the US (which is rare for African tragedies), and President Clinton later apologized for not having intervened when the genocide was taking place. A couple of years after this tragedy, I was asked by the World Bank to lead a major biomass for energy survey effort in Rwanda as a prelude to a large project there. My task was to document the current fuelwood and charcoal energy supply and demand situation in the country, the consumption patterns, and determine what could be done to increase supplies on a sustainable basis without depleting the existing natural forests. This was a major task, and I looked forward to a full month of survey work with some seventy enumerators strategically dispersed at main entry points to cities throughout the country, and collecting questionnaires relating to biomass or energy supplies and consumption patterns.

I was well prepared and looking forward to the assignment as I boarded the plane. For reading on the trip I had bought a book by Philip Gourevitch entitled *We Wish to Inform You That Tomorrow We Will be Killed With Our Families: Stories from Rwanda*. The war had ended but the aftermath was very much in my mind, and I needed to learn whatever I could about how to deal with Hutus and Tutsis in light of the worst human tragedy in recent history.

The book chronicled in detail the events of the war—what had caused what, how the UN had been rendered impotent, and how the killings had escalated. The book also documented the ordeals of several individuals who had barely escaped death not only once but several times during the war. One was the hotelier Paul Rusesabagina at Hotel des Milles Collines in Kigali, the same hotel where I was booked for my stay in Rwanda for this assignment. The other war survivor was His Excellency, the Minister of Industry and Commerce, Mr. Bonaventure Nyibizi — a Tutsi — with whom I already had a meeting scheduled.

I read the book from cover to cover and learned the details about the role of the Hotel des Milles Collines (Hotel of a Thousand Hills) as a sanctuary for nearly a thousand Tutsis. The lucky ones who made it to the hotel grounds congregated around the pool area, in the rooms, the lobby, and in the hallways. Paul Rusesabagina led this effort and is credited with having saved more than a thousand lives while every day putting his own life at considerable risk. He managed to procure food and water (using the pool water for drinking) and kept people alive until the end of the killing sprees. A movie was later made documenting his efforts.

I remember sitting by the pool after each workday, thinking about all of this and trying to visualize more than a thousand souls assembled in the relatively small area. I could only imagine what this heroic man accomplished as he kept the lid on the palpable fear among those inside the compound, while resisting the pressures from the Hutus outside to come in and kill every Tutsi on the inside. What an enormously compelling story this was.

I was looking forward to my meeting with Minister Bonaventure Nyibizi. The book had also chronicled in detail — a horrific story — his experiences during the war and described his near death moments. We had been given a full hour to meet with the Minister, an indication that this project was considered important. I put on my suit and tie and joined my Rwandan colleagues, and off we went. Once there, we were asked to wait in the office ante room, where we sat on comfortable couches drinking tea and coffee and conversing. Meetings with ministers in Rwanda are sort of a big deal and my entourage was slightly nervous; they wanted to make sure that what we had to say would meet with the Minister's approval.

Time passed and we began to worry if we wouldn't get that one full hour we had been promised. After about an hour's wait, however, the Minister's assistant opened the heavy doors and ushered us in to the waiting Minister Nyibizi. I approached his desk with my hand outstretched for a handshake. The Minister shook my hand, and then looked at me quizzically "Mais, on se connait, non?" (But we know each other, don't we?) he said. I said, "No, I don't think so."

"Have you been to Rwanda before?"

"Yes, once before, working on a forestry project," I said, "with USAID."

"I knew it," he exclaimed. "We have worked together before—I was the FSN at USAID who arranged all of the appointments for you and Fred the last time you were here—we traveled together on field trips and had many beers together during those trips."

I don't think I have been more embarrassed in my life than I was at that very moment. It all came back to me like a raging torrent—the last trip to Rwanda we had indeed spent a lot of time with the FSNs, who were indispensable in getting the work done, clearing the obstacles to meetings, making sure we stayed on schedule, and using their contacts to allow us to get the inside track to get all of the work accomplished on time. Every USAID field mission employs many FSNs, who are invaluable to incoming short-term consultants. Over the years I have worked with dozens of them. Unfortunately, because we worked in so many different countries every year, the individual FSNs became a blur, and we quickly forgot who were in which countries and their expertise. Some were administratively brilliant, others were professionally very competent.

Bonaventure Nyibizi, I remembered, had been a true professional, very effective, and we had hit it off very well the last time we worked together. And here he was, now a Minister. I had been reading about him in Philip Gourevitch's book, been fascinated with his story, and completely failed to connect the dots that I had known him all along. He remembered me, and I had not remembered him. I truly was embarrassed.

All of this happened over the span of two minutes while we shook hands. All formality was immediately suspended and the minister began to address me with the informal "tu" instead of "vous." It was like old times and we began to reminisce about the old USAID days. I told him I had just read about him in Gourevitch's book and he told me he was the only surviving FSN. All had been brutally killed during the first days of the war. The other FSN we had worked with back then – Dr. Diab – had been killed along with his entire family on the very first day. Dr. Diab was a highly competent professional and wonderful human being, now dead. His only crime was that he was a Tutsi.

It was wonderful to see Bonaventure again after all of those years. My entourage was flabbergasted at our conversation, which ended up with zero business conducted. Yet it was one of the most meaningful meetings I've ever had with anyone in my lifetime.

MONKEYS AND BIRDS

Kenya is best known for its wildlife and beautiful national parks. I worked there on many occasions for USAID and had the privilege of visiting all of the major wildlife parks. The entrance fees were waived for us and we traveled around in park vehicles on official business. We would mingle with tourists asking questions and gathering data, but were also permitted to travel to remote corners of the parks where tourists weren't allowed.

Consider the following couple of short stories a small warning to prospective safari travelers anywhere in Africa. On this trip, there were two of us and a driver covering all corners of the parks to meet with officials and gather data on visitors, wildlife species in the park, hunting concessions, and poaching problems. Along the way we saw amazing wildlife and had spectacular experiences ... except for a couple of small incidents, both involving food.

Consultants and drivers get hungry from all of that driving around and meeting people, so we often stopped to buy street food such as fruits, small bags of peanuts, and bread in small rural markets. Better to be well supplied at all times than to risk going hungry if we had to camp out. So, our car was laden with fruits and food stuffs as we traveled about. On one occasion we stopped at a rural market where we saw the most wonderful looking bananas – ripe, sweet, delicious, and just harvested. We couldn't resist it and we bought several hands of bananas, probably a total of at least 40 individual bananas. It was overkill, I know, but they were ridiculously cheap and the saleswoman was very insistent.

Driving up to the entrance of a park (I can't remember which one) we had to stop and check in with the gate-keeper, show him our official documents, and enjoy the moment of not having to buy the entrance tickets. As usual, any pit stop like this was welcome for other reasons as well, so we got out, stretched our legs, and used the facilities before moving on. Huge mistake. We had become accustomed to the immense richness of wildlife, both inside and outside the parks, and hadn't at all noticed the entirely ordinary monkeys that loitered around the park entrance. There were several of them, and they were acclimatized to the coming and going of park visitors. They were just part of the landscape and we paid no attention to them.

The driver had left both the driver side and passenger side windows open, which must have been a huge temptation for the monkeys. I can see them in my mind, casting furtive glances at each other and then heading at full speed for our vehicle, because they most certainly smelled our food stash. They scrambled up the side through the windows, at least seven or eight of them, and in seconds found themselves inside enjoying the food treasure—particularly the bananas.

They must have lost every sense of discipline and organization—what they should have done was grab the entire food stash and repair to a safer place to enjoy the loot. But no … it was all about eating everything, eating it quickly and raising as much havoc as possible during the little time they knew they had. The bananas were the first victims. While there must be tomes of scientific documentation out there about how many bananas monkeys can consume in a limited span of time, this I'm sure would have been a world record. But that wasn't all; nothing was sacred. The bread, the peanuts, the water—any food item they could get their hands on fell victim to their ravenous appetites. Then they went for the plastic bags full of laundry, throwing our clothes out and mixing them thoroughly with half-eaten bananas, banana peels, broken water bottles, bread crumbs, and half-eaten peanuts.

All of this took place in a time span of no more than four minutes—the time it took to get our papers in order inside the ranger office. As we approached the vehicle we noticed some commotion inside and quickened our step. At that moment, the monkeys realized they were confined inside an enclosed space with limited possibilities for an easy exit, so they followed what I would guess is their instinct — complete and unhinged panic. Imagine eight monkeys all trying to exit through two small windows at the exact same time, with their hands still full of bananas and other food items. It was total chaos that will forever be firmly imprinted on my memory. We spent the next two hours trying to clean up the mess before we could continue with our trip.

******

The other incident involving food took place on the same trip. This happened on the day after the monkey incident, so we should have learned our lesson. But alas, we hadn't learned yet about the birds. This was a much milder incident, but still amusing; particularly since it occurred on the heels of the traumatic monkey incident the day before.

We had managed to resupply ourselves with food and vowed to keep all the car windows closed whenever we stopped, in order to prevent further monkey business. And so we did when we arrived at an idyllic place where we had gone to enjoy our lunch sandwiches. It was close to a fresh water lake which was home to some hippos; giraffes paraded before our eyes in the distance; the temperature was fairly cool, and a slight breeze was blowing. It was perfect. There were other people there — park officials — enjoying lunch too, but they stayed inside their vehicles. How ludicrous, we thought, on such a perfect day who wouldn't want to be outside?

We grabbed our lunch packs, closed the car windows, and left the vehicles. Ah ... life was good, the sandwiches made by the hotel staff were excellent, and we were truly hungry. We noticed we were the only ones outside, but didn't even consider why. All seemed normal so we didn't think any more about it. Lunch boxes came out, drinks were poured, and we settled in for a most welcome lunch break. What we hadn't noticed was the gathering number of large birds hovering over us. We were talking about the day, our past meetings and upcoming meetings, and we were planning the rest of the day.

My first bite was rudely interrupted as a huge bird dive-bombed me with flawless precision and grabbed my sandwich with outstretched talons while in full flight. A fraction of a second later another bird made off with my colleague's sandwich in a similar fashion, and likewise a third bird grabbed the driver's sandwich before either one of us could get even a bite.

We were dumbfounded and sheepish at the same time, because now we understood why everyone else stayed inside their cars to eat their lunches. Looking around, we noticed they were all snickering because they had all seen this before. I think they all came to this very spot to have lunch every day just for the theater.

GHION HOTEL, HARRI AND UNTO

In Ethiopia I worked on biomass energy assignments for the World Bank on several occasions. The experts on the teams were from different countries and had entirely different backgrounds, which meant that the work environment was interesting, to say the least. Many different languages were spoken, and we were all expected to understand each other. The requirement, however, was that the reports had to be written in English, which unduly burdened the American and English team members. Having French consultants write their reports in English, for example, would have been an absolute nightmare.

When the assignment was for the World Bank, the work dynamic changed entirely. The taskmasters were very serious, borderline workaholics, and they expected no less from the consultants they hired. We were expected to work at least twelve to fifteen hours a day and if we needed to sleep some, we should at least dream about our work so we could get a headstart the next morning. There was less camaraderie among the team members than there was in USAID projects; there was no light banter between colleagues, and everything had an air of being very important. In meetings with the taskmaster (usually a WB direct hire) he quickly took the lead and dictated how things would evolve, even if the person with whom we were meeting was a very important minister.

This Ethiopian assignment was no exception. Our leader was a Swede—very bright, somewhat arrogant, with little sense of humor, and he expected us to work hard. Our team members included two Finns—Harri and Unto—who were both competent in their respective disciplines: forestry and sawmilling, and paper and pulp manufacturing. But none had any significant developing country experience. Another team member was a Brit, an expert in management, and yet another one was a Swedish sociologist. I was the economist. Our task was to put together some gigantic forestry project with an emphasis on addressing the biomass for energy question in meaningful ways.

I won't elaborate on this particular assignment here because it ended up being a fairly standard one—moving the project down the pipeline to the point of actual implementation. The work itself was the usual run-of-the-mill World Bank approach—very intense with too much to do and not nearly enough time. Ethiopia, however, is politically tense a lot of the time, often to the point of barring any travel by technical teams any farther than the outskirts of the city. We were even discouraged from venturing far from the hotel. This was unfortunate because the team needed to visit the proposed field sites to get a feel for logistics, soil conditions, and available infrastructure. But that was not to be this time, we had to make do while cooling our heels in Addis. The city was completely overrun by the conquering soldiers, many of them 16 years old or younger. There is something frightening about young battle-hardened trigger-happy boys laden with automatic weaponry and roaming the streets. They are mostly illiterate, and I suspect many of them became soldiers after being brainwashed by drugs from childhood and on.

The Ghion Hotel in the center of Addis Ababa was our headquarters—an old and worn hotel but popular among the expatriate consultants. It was not without some charms we all learned to appreciate: It had a large swimming pool, tennis courts which we used after hours, and also a terrific and authentic Ethiopian restaurant. The hotel was always bustling with the coming and going of expatriate consultants, so it was the happening place in Addis at the time. Perhaps that's why it was the target of a terrorist bomb, in between two of my several trips there. Although the bomb had taken out at least a fourth of the hotel and killed many guests and staff at the time, it had re-opened just a few weeks later when our team arrived for another in-country visit.

Knowing about the terror attack and seeing the carnage it had wrought, I quickly became disenchanted with my room. It was a suite reserved for frequent Ghion Hotel guests, a privileged group of which I now was a member. The problem was not a lack of creature comforts; it was the view of the heavily fortified machine gun nest installed just outside my balcony. The sandbags, large guns, and cases of ammunition by themselves were menacing enough, although not nearly as menacing as the soldiers manning the nest. Sleep was impossible because I knew that just about five meters outside my bedroom window there were at least three boy soldiers with huge afro hairdos, probably illiterate, sitting there with their fingers on the trigger waiting for the next attack.

After the first sleepless night I went to the front desk to request a change of rooms.

"Why?" they asked.

"Well, there is a machine gun nest manned by sixteen-year-old boys just outside my window — I'm not sure I like that."

"But they are there for your protection — their task is to protect the hotel guests."

"Oh," I said, "I'm so relieved to hear that, but that's not alleviating my concern. Although I'm sure these boys are serious about protecting the hotel guests, I'm less sure about the enemies who want to hurt the hotel guests. If they fire at the hotel, they'll aim first at the defensive installations, and this means, Mr. Concierge, that my bedroom is a bull's-eye target for any incoming fire."

The Concierge wasn't getting it, and — the hotel was full, so no, I couldn't have another room. I had no choice but to keep the room and put my mattress on the floor to get out of the line of fire at least some. Sleep didn't come easily — some nights not at all — so I compensated by taking clandestine catnaps during meetings and relying on adrenalin to get through the day.

******

Because of the tense political situation this time, we rarely left the hotel to try different restaurants. The hotel restaurant, however, was actually pretty good for authentic Ethiopian food, which is something you might normally choose once or twice a year. It is very spicy and, although very tasty at the moment, it usually wakes you up at 3 a.m. when the havoc it does to your system is peaking.

Our team would congregate at a large table in this restaurant just about every night to enjoy the spicy dinner, drink some atrocious local wine or some cold beers, eat Ethiopian food, and reconvene every morning to tell war stories about our 3 a.m. bouts. The first meal in this restaurant was the most memorable. There were two fairly corpulent Finns on the team—Harri and Unto, the pulp and sawlog specialists—who liked to get thoroughly tanked on vodka and other alcohol-laden liquids every evening, in order to take the edge off the intense work during the day. These guys were fairly possessive of their work and how their component should fit in with the overall forestry project being planned. But they weren't very culturally sensitive and brushed off any talk about local field realities that might negate their planned schemes. If we talked about sociological phenomena (which you have to in all African countries), they would get somewhat agitated and dismiss them as irrelevant. They were interesting to work with at the very least.

Save for Harri and Unto, we were all seated for our first Ethiopian culinary experience sipping our cold beers as the waiter explained the process of eating Ethiopian food. Before us on the table was a large tray covered with one huge crepe-like pancake called injera, the unique Ethiopian staple bread made from a grain called teff. On the injera they place little dabs of very spicy meats and vegetables and sauces. The food is eaten by tearing off pieces of the extra injera served on the side and scooping up mouthfuls of the different treats. That's the process. There are no knives or forks. Simple enough.

Just after we had been educated by the waiter, here come Harri and Unto. They were both in fine form and tanked on vodka. They loudly asked the head waiter where our table was and then walked rather unsteadily toward us. Arriving at our table they greeted everyone jovially and sat down in the remaining two vacant chairs. Ready for some cold beer, they got the attention of the waiter and ordered two each so they would be sure to have enough.

Before us was the large tray covered with the injera, but without the meats, sauces, and vegetables which we had just ordered. Being slightly inebriated, Harri proceeded to spill some beer on Unto and some on himself, and noticed he didn't have a napkin. Trying unsuccessfully to get the waiter's attention, he got frustrated because he needed to dry it off. He promptly grabbed the large grayish-looking "napkin" on the tray before him and began to vigorously brush off his and Unto's shirts and dry his hands. Of course, the injera immediately disintegrated, producing an incredulous look on Harri's face as he looked down at his hands and the mess of injera now all over his and Unto's laps.

"This is not towel," he exclaimed vocifereslly in his heavy Finnish accent.

Waiters stopped in their tracks.

Other guests stopped eating and looked over at our table where Harri was holding court with pieces of injera dripping from his fingers, loudly uttering Finnish profanities.

After we had completed our work in Addis, I never saw Harri or Unto again. I doubt, however, if Harri will even remember this little incident at the Ghion because it was his nature to repeat this kind of experience many times over, wherever he traveled.

CLOSE ENCOUNTERS

Working in Francophone countries (as I did for most of my time overseas) meant I had to do a lot of the writing because the French and Swiss team members couldn't write their reports in English. That task always fell to the English speakers. But Tanzania was different. The official language there is English, so that made it a favorite country for me in the Southern Africa region.

I worked for USAID in Tanzania on many wildlife-related economic assignments, and every single time it was a pleasure. Our Tanzanian counterparts were competent and enjoyable people, and our work consisted largely of visiting the several rich and diverse wildlife parks. There we interviewed local people—the Masai and other ethnic groups, village chiefs, wildlife poachers, and many others as we encountered them on our travels. Most of all, however, we very much enjoyed the wildlife viewing we experienced (and for which the safari tourists all around us had to pay).

One of our trips took us to Momella Lodge, close to Arusha National Park. The Lodge was our home for several days. It was also the temporary home of John Wayne and Hardy Krueger while filming the famous movie *Hatari* in 1960. I happened to stay in John Wayne's room—which of course gave me the Duke swagger while staying there. I saw the movie several times and cherish the memory of having "been on the set," albeit many years later. Judging from what I saw in the movie, little had changed at the lodge.

My most vivid memories from the national wildlife parks are of the elephants—the most spectacular of the African creatures, and also one of the most fearsome (second only to the buffaloes). Unlike viewing lions or most other predators from the safety of a car, no such safety exists with the elephants. They can upend a Toyota Land Cruiser with a flip of their trunk, so wisdom dictated that it would be unwise to irritate them … which is precisely what we did on one occasion.

We were inside one of the parks away from the tourist spots when we saw an elephant by the side of the narrow dirt road we were traveling. We told the driver to stop, because we had a great close-up view. We sat there for a long time watching this huge animal go about her feeding routine until, as it appeared to our driver, she became a bit too jittery. And there was good reason. Just then, appearing from behind the big elephant we saw a small calf tagging alongside, apparently without a care in the world. Our driver was on alert immediately, watching the elephant intently as he began to rev up the engine ever so slightly.

Without any warning at all, the elephant let out a fierce trumpet blast, flared and flapped her huge ears, and then charged the vehicle at full speed. It was truly amazing to see how an animal that size could gather speed and momentum so quickly. The driver, bless him, knew what was about to happen. That's why he had begun to rev up the engine. The elephant crossed half of the distance in about a second, at which point the driver reacted. He gunned the engine already running at a fairly high RPM, so we immediately gained just enough speed to barely escape annihilation by the crazed elephant intent on protecting her calf. Safely down the road, we saw in the rear-view mirror the elephant arrogantly blowing the "trumpet" again and returning to her feeding routine. I can honestly say I have been chased by a huge elephant and lived to tell about it.

******

The other elephant incident happened on the same trip, just a day later. It was only what could have happened that still makes me break out in a cold sweat. It was late in the day, the sun was setting, and we were heading back to the lodge anticipating a cold beer, some food, and then some sleep. We didn't pay a lot of attention to the road, so we were a bit shaken as the driver slammed on the brakes. Directly in front of us to the right a huge elephant was about to cross the road. It ambled slowly across in front of our vehicle, was soon followed by a second, and then a third elephant. I'm sure they were aware of our presence, although they must not have considered us a threat.

Nevertheless, we held our collective breath and slowly closed our windows so they wouldn't get our scent and become curious. The driver slowly put the gear into reverse to back up just a little as a fourth elephant appeared in front of us. Again, however, he had to slam on the brakes, because right behind us we saw another six or seven elephants crossing or about to cross the road. We were caught smack dab in the middle of a sizable herd of elephants where each and every one of them could do irreparable damage to our vehicle and its passengers.

I clearly remember the driver very quietly asking us if all of the windows were closed and telling us to sit perfectly still until the herd had passed. I think my heart was about to explode from beating so fast. I don't think I have ever felt so vulnerable in my life, except when I was with Mme Jamar and the chimps in the Congo (see below). There was absolutely nothing we could do except sit perfectly still, pray, and hope for the best. That's one of the few times I felt like I had literally "dodged a bullet."

CHIMPS

The Republic of Congo, or perhaps more commonly known as Congo-Brazzaville, is located in central Africa, bordered by Gabon, Cameroon, the Central African Republic, and the Democratic Republic of Congo (known earlier as Zaire). In other words, Congo-Brazzaville is right in the middle of some chaotic countries rife with extreme poverty and perpetual political unrest. Brazzaville, the capital city, is located on the banks of the Congo River from where you can actually see Kinshasa, the capital of the Democratic Republic located on the opposite bank a bit farther down.

When I made the trek to this God-forsaken country, Brazzaville was a ghost town ravaged by numerous wars. Businesses were shuttered, all buildings downtown were peppered with large and small bullet holes, and in some places entire sections of walls and roofs were reduced to rubble. A large luxury hotel in the downtown area had been severely damaged and apparently closed forever. Bullets had cracked the concrete floor in the lobby and exposed bare dirt. Fast-growing trees had sprouted in the dirt, and by the time I made my visit to this fine city, the branches had, in the quest for sunlight, popped out of the high windows in the hotel lobby. It was a surreal experience to see this and to move about in a large city virtually devoid of any life or commercial activity.

We stayed in the one hotel in the downtown area which was open and functioning. The hotel restaurant occasionally had food, even some wine and beer. The rooms were comfortable when the air conditioning worked, but the power was interrupted several times during the day and night, which made working in the room or attempting to sleep unbearable. In the gardens there was an outside bar where guests could be cooled by the shade of a tent awning. The tent canvas, however, was riddled with bullet holes that made the sunlight patterns on the floor and tables very interesting. The hotel lobby itself was so damaged that attempts to repair it had not yet been made.

So there I was in Brazzaville on a World Bank assignment with a French WB staffer and a Canadian sociologist. The Bank was financing a GEF (Global Environment Facility) project and our task was to travel up country to the project sites to do some sort of evaluation of the project and determine future course changes if needed. This was a fascinating experience, not only from a work perspective, but also from a life perspective. I found it completely amazing that people could manage to survive when war, cruelty, brutality, and extreme poverty are the norm. People were obliged to settle into an existence saturated with constant fear and uncertainty, perpetually on the lookout for the next meal and focusing on self-preservation from violent crime and economic disaster.

Both of the project sites were up country, far from Brazzaville. Off we went in a four-wheel drive project vehicle. It was good to finally get out of Brazzaville and away from the palpable undercurrent of tension permeating everything in that city. After many hours of driving at an average speed of less than five kilometers per hour on virtually non-existent roads or on roads with four- to five-foot deep ruts, we finally arrived dead tired at the first project headquarters. This was home to one very crusty old francophone Canadian consultant named Denis Allaire. I knew Denis from a Canadian forestry project in Burkina Faso, so we had a great reunion.

The project HQ was in an enclosed compound with several small buildings intended for housing incoming consultants. These buildings were so very, very, very ... spartan. There were bunk beds, mosquito nets, and minimal furniture. Nothing had been cleaned for ages, and linen was either non-existent or too dirty. Lighting was provided by gas lanterns and/or outside bonfires. It was blazing hot and very humid even in the middle of the night—no breeze whatsoever—so sleeping was impossible. The team decided to stay in Denis' house, which had an extra room and was reasonably clean, but without luxuries such as sheets or blankets. I guess the project wasn't visited by many consultants; our presence there must have been a major event. This was confirmed by the crowd of villagers who appeared just outside the compound to stare at the pale-faced visitors.

While we had dinner Denis enthralled us with many stories. Some of them made me a bit anxious, particularly in light of my keen awareness of the staring villagers just outside the compound. Several of the stories were about the project we were to visit—the Tchimpounga Chimpanzee Rehabilitation Center located up-river several kilometers. This project was managed by one of those folkloric chimp rehabilitation women (like Jane Goodall), Mme Aliette Jamar, and it had a questionable reputation in the surrounding villages. Mme Jamar was French, had been in the Congo-Brazzaville for years, and had successfully rehabilitated many chimpanzees back into the wild.

To set the stage for the story that follows and place Denis' recounting of his stories in some context, it is important to understand first why the chimp rehabilitation project had a questionable reputation. These kinds of efforts in Africa were perceived as a work of mercy by westerners but much less so by the local villagers. Chimpanzees are a source of food, heavily hunted all over Africa. The presence of a donor-funded rehabilitation project in an area, therefore, created an unintended and perverse incentive for the local villagers. As they hunted the chimps they killed the parents for the meat, but not the babies. They trapped the babies and sold them to the rehabilitation centers to be rehabilitated. Under this system, they got both—meat from the hunt, and cash for the babies. All to the good for them.

However, rehabilitation of the babies was a long-term process. An important part of this effort was that each animal was first assigned a human "baby-sitter" with whom the animals would bond. This relationship continued for a fairly long time until the chimps are ready to be on their own but not yet in the wild. In that time period, they lived on an island (on a lake close to Denis' compound) where they were fed daily and visited by the project people whom they knew and with whom they had bonded. The chimps could not escape the island be-cause they could not swim.

The lake that was home to the chimp island was also where the villagers fish. The villagers had been compensated some with project funds for having given up the use of the island for the benefit of the chimps, but one could also say that the relationship between the proj-ect and the locals was anything but warm and fuzzy. This lack of be-nevolence was exacerbated by the many slightly unhibited, scantily clad female volunteers living out their dreams of doing good in the world by rehabilitating orphaned chimps. Their presence stirred up lust among the villagers and the possibility of forcible rape had oc-curred to Denis, not only as a question of if, but when.

So what happened, as told by Denis? A few weeks before we ar-rived in the compound, a local villager had gone fishing in his small dugout canoe with his four-year-old son, and had ventured too close to the chimp island. The chimps were getting agitated because they hated any human other than their handlers. Chimps have a keen mem-ory and remember if their parents were killed by people with black skins. And that essentially made them racists, hating blacks except for their Congolese "babysitter" handlers plus the European (white) peo-ple who worked on the project and with whom they had bonded.

You can guess the rest of the story. One particularly agile chimp sitting on a branch overhanging the water managed to reach down and snatch the little boy in a nano- second and the chimps quickly and brutally killed him. In the aftermath of this incident, the local villagers thirsted for revenge — a life for a life was their considered pronounce-ment. Their targets became the young women, who now justifiably feared for their lives. They all fled to Denis in the compound because that was the only place they could go. The villagers showed up en masse, and a very tense confrontation between Denis and the village spokesman ensued. Denis himself was certain this would be his last day on earth based on how the negotiations went in the beginning. But he didn't back down, and finally talk of large sums of money began to resonate with the locals. Money always resonates, and it confirms the basic economic principle that everyone has a price. In this case the incident was settled with a transfer of a substantial amount of money to the villagers. The girls were allowed to live, and a major crisis didn't materialize; there was a happy ending for all except the poor family that lost a son.

But the villagers were still suspicious about the project and displayed a surly attitude toward the project staff among them. The tension was palpable, and it didn't make me look forward to the long trip up-river with Mme Jamar and her staff the next day. Nor was I at peace with the group of villagers who had congregated just outside our compound to gawk at us from a distance while Denis told the story.

Mme Jamar showed up at dawn with the boat, prepared to head up-river. The trip would take two to three hours and it was, at least in my mind, fraught with dangers. The jungle on both sides was very dense, and I wondered what would happen to us if the rickety outboard engine broke down and we were stranded up-river in excruciating heat with dozens of potential calamities awaiting us. Worse, there were stretches of river where the tree canopies had closed overhead and thick overhanging branches forced us to duck, sometimes lie down in the boat, in order to give it unencumbered passage. These branches, Mme Jamar informed us, were often resting places for large and small snakes that could kill you in many imaginative ways. People had received snake bites in these stretches, some had died and others had jumped out of the boat to avoid the snakes when they fell into the boat, but had then been vulnerable to whatever dangers the water held.

In spite of my lively imagination nothing happened to us, and we proceeded without incident. We arrived at the project site located in the middle of a mosquito-infested swampy area where very simple project dwellings had been built on stilts high enough to keep them dry when the swamp waters rose during the rainy season. The main danger for the permanent staff was the herds of elephants roaming about in the neighborhood and often passing by the dwellings. I just couldn't imagine waking up at 3 a.m. in my stilt house staring eyeball-to-eyeball with a huge elephant. A sneeze from an elephant that close could bring the entire house down. No wonder the permanent project staff, mostly young Canadian and European volunteer women and some young men, plus all of their Congolese counterparts, seemed slightly odd. They must have spent the time there in perpetual fear of not only the soon-to-be rehabilitated chimps, but also of the elephants and the mosquitos, of the snakes, and of the … I don't know what.

This particular camp is the last stop for the orphaned chimps before their release back into the wild. We were there to document for our World Bank masters the processes involved, if they were working, and if there was any sort of economic feasibility to the project. They had a group of chimps being prepared for release, and had already released another group of some twenty-five chimps just a week earlier. We were met and greeted by the soon-to-be-released group and then set out to find the already released group in the wild out there somewhere. Tracking devices had been fitted on some of the chimps in this group, so they knew where they were. Mme. Jamar, the team, and three from the Congolese project staff set off in the boat again along with the tracking equipment. On the way, we received instructions:

a.) The chimps don't know you, so don't make any sudden moves when we encounter them.
b.) Good thing you're white because the chimps hate blacks except for the Congolese project staff. Whites are OK because they will be "counted" as part of the European or Canadian project staff.
c.) Leave anything loose or semi loose — glasses, hats, papers, watches, belts — on the boat before we begin our tracking on foot. The chimps will take it from you, whatever it is.
d.) Stay close together and don't look the chimps in the eyes.
e.) Don't be nervous. The chimps will pick up on that immediately.

Needless to say, none of these instructions eased any of the anxiety I felt at that particular moment, as I proceeded to empty my pockets of absolutely everything, even the pocket fuzz. I determined to stay as close to Mme. Jamar as I possibly could because I figured she would be the one most loved by the chimps. If I were closest to her, chances of my survival would increase. I know my teammates had similar levels of anxiety they were dealing with as we prepared, plus we all had gallons of adrenalin coursing through our systems.

Finally, pockets empty, boat parked, we were on the trail working our way to our rendezvous with the chimps. It was an overgrown and barely discernible trail that I would easily have completely lost if I hadn't been with people who knew where they were and could find their way out again. What if, I thought, something happened and we had to scatter? It's funny how the mind works when you are completely at someone else's mercy. I have to admit I felt really vulnerable that day.

We stayed on the trail for a good forty minutes working our way inland. The heat and humidity were oppressive, even in the shade of the thick vegetation. I was sweating profusely and I think my heart was beating a good 160 beats a minute. It wasn't because of the exertion — it was probably from what I knew was about to happen. We stopped on several occasions and took our bearings. The tracking system worked and the project staff declared we were close.

My adrenalin pumped furiously as we arrived at a small clearing of relatively less dense jungle. We stopped, stood still, and just listened.

Nothing.

The Congolese tracker waved the antenna in every direction and nodded silently. We had found them — the chimps were here.

Still nothing.

I stood there for what seemed an eternity, stiff as a board silently praying for safety, as, I think, did my fellow team members. And then all of a sudden, total cacophony broke out as twenty-five chimps leaped out from the dense tree canopy overhead and landed all around us, screeching and running around expressing great joy in being reunited with their human "family." I was there in their midst and within a split second I had two chimps latching onto each of my hands and a third one climbing up my body to look for loose stuff in all crevices of my clothing. My heart was literally racing, my breathing was labored, and my adrenal glands operated as if they were commercial producers.

Finding nothing in my pockets, the chimp jumped down and climbed up on the next victim. Finally, they found treasure with the Congolese staffers who had left some loose items in their pockets intentionally for the chimps to find. They grabbed the stuff and screeched with joy, jumped down, and scattered up a tree to study their newfound treasure.

My two chimp friends who had latched on to my hands didn't let go. I was theirs for as long as they wanted to hold on to me. My teammates also had chimps all over them. So there we were, affectionate chimps holding on to us, with another fifteen or twenty adult and juvenile chimps all around us running between our legs, jumping up and down, screeching with the joy and excitement of being reunited with their human benefactors.

I was totally preoccupied with my two hand-holding chimps, talking a blue streak to them in a very friendly and loving tone of voice. In fact, my voice was perfectly pitched to be a true personification of someone totally friendly to chimps and their cause, while the real reason was to mask my, by now, raw fear. It was at this moment my memory harkened back to one of Denis's stories that rehabilitated chimps in the wild were in fact much more dangerous than wild chimps naturally. This was because, as Denis had said, the chimps have a keen memory and they remember when people had killed their parents. So, hatred for people becomes a natural disposition, except for the people who had subsequently raised them and essentially replaced their parents. So there I was completely surrounded by rehabilitated chimps, all man haters, all naturally three times stronger than humans, completely at their mercy. Needless to say, I was petrified.

Mme. Jamar spent most of her time with one particular chimp with whom she had been particularly close. This was a fascinating thing to observe. She literally became one of them, squatting down to the chimp's level where they began the ritual of ridding each other's hair of real and imaginary bugs. They did this for a long time while she talked softly to the chimp and the chimp cooed softly back. It really was a touching thing to see.

Then, without missing a beat, Mme. Jamar said quietly we needed to leave soon because the chimps should have less and less contact with humans as part of the release process. She slowly stood up and motioned to us to begin walking away. On cue, the Congolese staffers followed her, as did my team members who had jockeyed more successfully than me for a position nearest to Mme. Jamar and the Congolese staffers. I, on the other hand, was in the rear with my two close chimp friends holding on tightly to my hands, slowing my progress. Soon I saw Mme. Jamar and everyone in our group disappear around a corner on the trail and now I had my two chimp friends holding on to me with now another twenty or so chimps filling the void between me and my now-vanished human team members.

This was serious, really serious. I tried to increase my speed to catch up with my group, but the chimps held me back. Panic began to set in as I began to call after Mme. Jamar and my team members still employing that same loving and tranquil voice pitch, clearly remembering the instructions we had been given — don't make any sudden moves, and don't appear nervous.

This experience was probably fairly short in duration, but to me it seemed like an eternity I will never forget. Mme. Jamar and the team quickly figured out they were missing one of their own and turned back to find me. My two chimp friends finally released me to rejoin my human friends. I think my knees buckled ever so slightly when I knew I had been restored to life with a reasonable chance of surviving this experience. Now, thinking and writing about this unique experience in the wilds of Congo-Brazzaville, I know I wouldn't want to change anything and I thank God for giving me such incredible life-changing moments.

GORILLAS

Gorillas also roam the jungles of Congo-Brazzaville, and they, too, often meet the same fate as the chimpanzees. Adults are hunted for meat and the babies are captured and sold ("rescued") by the gorilla rehabilitation people. The gorilla rehabilitation reserves are set up and staffed, as with the chimps, by slightly weird and wonderful Europeans who also aspire to folklore status of the kind featured on *60 Minutes*, in airplane magazine articles, and on wildlife TV shows. One such project funded through the World Bank and staffed by these Europeans and Congolese was on our schedule to be reviewed.

Two days after we had recovered from the visit to the chimp release project, we were ready to visit the gorilla project. This time, however, no middle-of-the-woods meetings with recently released gorillas had been planned, so I was secretly very relieved. I don't think my capacity to produce adrenalin had been fully restored by then.

As with the chimps, young orphaned gorillas were assigned human surrogate mothers who raised them, fed them, and took care of them all the way through adolescence. During our visit with the staff, little baby gorillas were climbing all over them and us as we tried to take notes. What we learned was that gorillas weren't released in groups, but as individuals. Few make it in the wild, and they are dangerous for the same reasons that the rehabilitated and released chimps are. They hate all people, except project staff. Several of the gorillas they had released had to be returned to captivity after they had attacked or sometimes killed humans.

Just beyond the compound, the project had funded and built a large area approximately 20-by-40 meters in size, completely enclosing its own jungle and housing in perpetuity a particular adult silverback that had been released and recaptured twice. This one was particularly nasty and passionately hated people of all colors. He had killed at least one individual while on the outside. We were invited to visit the enclosure to have a look at the silverback. The trail to the enclosure was on a narrow track through thick vegetation where the soon-to-be-released gorillas liked to hang out, socialize, lounge, eat breakfast, lunch, and dinner. There they mingled with each other and with the project staff as if it was perfectly normal. Being that close to adolescent gorillas, however, didn't exactly place me in my comfort zone — that feeling of vulnerability began to raise its ugly head once again.

Once we arrived at the enclosure, the silverback sat there looking at us with intense and hateful eyes for a long while. He clearly didn't like any of us and he probably was bored. So he decided to do something which he knew would scare the daylights out of all of us. He decided to mount a ferocious attack, even though he knew it would be to no avail. And ferocious it was, from one side of the enclosure to our side he covered the distance in full charge in just a couple of seconds at maximum speed and threw his considerably heavy body against the fence about two meters from the place where we stood. Oh, how well I remember the panic I felt in the pit of my stomach as the fence bulged and stretched to its limits upon impact, followed by this huge silver-back falling down in a heap, scrambling to his feet, and letting out a fierce roar that chilled me to the bone.

ESCAPING WAR

That trip to Congo-Brazzaville is forever seared into my memory. In the short span of three weeks, I had nearly died of fright from exposure to man-hating chimps and gorillas, lived in a ghost town with most of the buildings boarded up and pockmarked by bullet holes, slept in a hotel where the lobby and rooms had been severely damaged by bullets and grenades, and generally felt very vulnerable every minute I was there.

The day the team was to leave the country on an evening Air France flight we held a meeting at the hotel with the entire government structure — some twenty ministers and their staff — to discuss our findings. We went through the motions and presentations, but noted that the ministers really didn't pay much attention. This was unusual because any time the World Bank is in town, money — more of it — is all they can think about. This time, however, our World Bank leader commented to me quietly, "Something is going on."

Indeed, something was going on as we quickly learned when the meeting was over. There was an underlying tense atmosphere building up around us. Back at the hotel we noticed that the staff was very nervous. Our driver told us he couldn't take us to the airport but that someone else from a different tribe would. And we had better pack our stuff and meet in the lobby as soon as possible. Apparently, there was a large and well-armed group of soldiers and semi-soldiers, many of them drugged up and trigger-happy, amassed just outside the city limit ready to enter and kill whatever and whoever would cross their path. All of our team members had confirmed tickets on the evening Air France flight except for our World Bank team leader. He was to

stay a few days longer for some extra meetings. His face was a bit ash-
en as he urged us to get our stuff and head for the airport.

Our route to the airport was circuitous in order to avoid the trigger-happy soldiers. We finally arrived at the dilapidated airport to a
chaotic scene. The airport was jammed with people scrambling to get
out, and Air France was the only remaining flight scheduled to leave
the country that night. The tension was palpable. Somehow, with
much prodding and authoritative commentary, our expediter managed to get us inside the building, where he muscled his way with us
in tow to one of the Air France agents. We flashed our passports and
our confirmed tickets and then we were led to the counter in front of
dozens of stand-by passengers all trying to get the attention of anyone
looking like an official.

Breathing deeply and focusing on controlling emotions, I think we
all prayed that there would be no paperwork glitches, so we could get
our boarding passes. The process took forever—the ticket agent was
practically illiterate and misspelled my name as he wrote it excruciatingly slowly on the boarding pass, so I had to have him do it again. He
first didn't want to do it, but I knew that a boarding pass that didn't cor-
respond exactly to the passport information would be sufficient cause
to prevent me from getting through security. So I insisted very firmly,
and he finally relented. Again excruciatingly slowly, he wrote each letter exactly as I spelled it out for him. It was nerve-racking, indeed.

Finally through security and safely on the inside, our next tension
generator was the fact that the Air France plane had not yet arrived. It
was delayed, but en route we were told. "How late?" we asked, but no
one seemed to know. Our expediter summoned us and led us to the
VIP lounge that was a haven—the air conditioner worked. And there
we joined nearly all of the ministers with whom we had just met and
debriefed at the hotel. They had all bribed their way to get a seat on the
Air France flight and were scrambling to get out of the country.

The sound of Air France arriving was one of the most welcome
sounds I had heard in a long time. It quickly refueled and we were
told to board the flight. Walking out on the tarmac towards the plane
was another sweet feeling, although I freely admit it was also mixed

with lots of anxiety for our remaining World Bank leader and all of the Congolese people we had met and with whom we had worked – the drivers, the hotel staff, the expediters, etc.

Safely strapped in my seat and ready to take off, there was only one remaining fear – and it was strong. I wasn't the only one harboring this fear; all of my team member colleagues had also thought of it. The plane carried nearly twenty Congolese ministers who would be prime targets in any political upheaval. What better opportunity to take them all out than with one single Stinger missile as the plane took off? As the plane took off, every second without incident was considered a blessing. We arrived in Paris early the next morning as tired as I have ever been in my life, not from the work but from all the tension during the past three weeks.

About two hours after we had taken off the war broke out. Our World Bank leader had to lay low in the hotel for three days – the electricity had been shut off, there was no food or water, and finally, on the third day, he was evacuated by helicopter to Kinshasa on the other side of the river where he finally caught a flight to begin his journey back home.

I don't think I would want to go back to Congo-Brazzaville again: it is a country richly endowed with diamonds, but this exacerbates ethnic strife to the point that wars break out far too often. Well, perhaps I wouldn't mind seeing my chimp friends again. An experience like that is a life-changer, and sort of makes me think I should take up extreme sports just to feel the intense adrenalin rush once again.

HASSAN

While I was teaching at the University of Idaho I was tapped as a consultant to go to Morocco with a forestry professor colleague to survey what USAID could do in the forestry sector. I was invited because I had indicated that my French was functional, which at that time it wasn't. It was latent … very latent in fact. Some twenty-five years had passed since I had last sat in a French class back in Norway. It wasn't until 1982 when preparing to go to Senegal on a long-term assignment that I took an intensive course in French in order to become reasonably fluent. But I must have convinced them that my French expertise would be sufficient for this assignment, so off we went, Dave Adams and I, two professors from the University of Idaho with little knowledge of forestry issues and field realities in North Africa, and virtually no skill in French. There it is … your taxpayer dollars at work.

I quickly learned to like Morocco, the people, the USAID folks there, and the Moroccan counterparts. Of all the North African and Near and Middle Eastern countries where I have worked, Morocco is by far the best. When we arrived in Rabat we were met by Hassan Mazzoudi, a Moroccan Forest Service field agent who spoke fluent English. He was the spitting image of Fidel Castro, complete with the beard, the uniform, and the large cigar. Hassan and several other Forest Service officials were to be our field guides for the entire three weeks. We were to go on a number of field trips to all corners of the country. Hassan quickly became a close friend, a life-long friend in fact. He has an incredible sense of humor, his English is excellent, and his professional competence is impeccable. I soon found out that I didn't really need my limited French at the time because Hassan's English was perfectly fine.

After about a week on the road, our US/Moroccan team had gelled, and we were having a marvelous time together. We learned about Moroccan forestry rapidly, and our report began to take shape. One evening after a long day on the road we had a nightcap with Hassan and talked about everything under the sun. Hassan talked about his interest in statistics and his desire to come to the US as a student and to pursue a Ph.D. in forestry and biometrics. Could we do something? So we did the usual: "Let us have your curriculum vitae to take it back with us, and we'll see what we can do." Only 1 in 1,000 of these actually pan out because of a lack of scholarships, language difficulties, and educational background gaps.

Hassan gave us all of the papers we asked for, and then he never gave up. He sent letters, made phone calls, followed up with requests to USAID for scholarship money and on and on. The hoops he had to jump through were endless. But Hassan did manage to get USAID funding for his masters at the University of Texas, and off he went. He continued to pursue his desire to come to the University of Idaho where his friends were. After just one semester in Texas, he managed to get himself accepted at the University of Idaho in the Ph.D. program. He arrived with a big smile on his face, we had our reunion, and he began his studies. It turned out that he not only became legendary at the university as an excellent student, he was also the first of many Moroccan students to study forestry at the University of Idaho for years to come.

Hassan earned his Ph.D. and landed choice jobs with the UN in Senegal, earning about twenty to thirty times his salary as a field agent in Morocco. I worked with him on several assignments in Senegal. I still stay in touch with Hassan, who is back in Morocco now working in the private sector as a successful entrepreneur and a local politician. He is an elected official serving on the Rabat City Council.

THE MOTHER OF ALL LUNCHES

While Dave Adams and I were in Rabat getting acquainted with Hassan and our Moroccan counterparts, we met with many high-ranking Moroccan forestry officials. One of these officials was the Chief of the Forest Service, Mr. Tamri. We met in his office for an hour early in the morning one day, whereupon he invited us and the team for lunch at his home. We accepted his invitation and showed up at his beautiful home on the outskirts of Rabat at the appointed hour, 1 p.m.

Small talk about our work ensued in the living room until the cook arrived to say that lunch was ready. We were positively starving, having had the foresight to not spoil our appetites in anticipation of this lunch. Besides, Moroccan food is out of this world. We sat down, grabbed our napkins, and the cook entered with a huge platter full of couscous and meat. Dave and I were in heaven—it was fantastic. We had first, second, and third helpings until we could eat no more.

As the cook and some helpers scooped the entire platter and the tablecloth off with practiced hands, they exposed a perfectly clean tablecloth underneath. In they came again, this time with an even larger platter of couscous and, this time, chicken. I looked at Hassan and our teammates with some despair, as I began to understand why they had eaten so little of the first couscous platter. They were pacing themselves.

We didn't want to appear rube (which we probably did), so we loaded up on the chicken couscous. This time we only had one helping. By now both Dave and I were painfully full. Hassan and the other Moroccans were in fine form and were carrying on animated conversations. The cook and helpers came in once again, scooped up the remains and the tablecloth, and again, exposed another clean tablecloth.

I groaned.

Dave groaned.

We both looked at each other with despair in our eyes realizing we were in the midst of learning a valuable lesson: when sitting down in a Moroccan home for any meal, count the tablecloths — then pace yourself. We had three tablecloths and that meant three different varieties of couscous. Sure enough, a third platter arrived on the scene, full of couscous and another meat topping. It was time to dig in again. And we did — but this time with much pain and discomfort.

When it was all over two hours later, I had never felt so stuffed in my entire life. The urge to assume the horizontal and go to sleep was overwhelming and was exacerbated by jet lag. Mr. Tamri continued to talk about forestry in Morocco. After all, this was a business lunch. I saw pity in Hassan's eyes as if he were saying "Sorry I forgot to tell you to count the tablecloths." Mr. Tamri then had chocolates, whiskey, and Moroccan tea brought out for his guests. It took another full hour before we could gracefully leave this most extraordinary lunch. It took a full two days to recover from this experience.

BECHAR

I had the dubious pleasure of working in Algeria only once. I don't think I would want to go back there again. Algeria, as it seemed to me, was a socialist, repressive, and backward country. This was early in my international career. The purpose of the project identification trips we made for the FMC was to locate possible sites for large-scale vegetable production so we could eventually sell vegetable processing plants. We traveled by car to meet and greet officials, visit other projects, and document how things worked. Our last potential project site on the schedule was a two-hour flight from Algiers to Bechar near the Moroccan border. There were four of us who showed up at the airport to catch our flight on an old DC3, probably built in the '30s. The plane had definitely seen better days.

We arrived in Bechar without incident and settled into our very old, non-functioning, and uncomfortable two-star hotel — the best the town had to offer at that time — for an extended stay of one week. Our meetings went reasonably well, followed by (not-very-good) dinners at the hotel, sleepless nights, and more field trips and meetings during the rest of the week. The time stood still — we were insanely bored; there was absolutely nothing to do there — and we very much looked forward to our departure.

The day finally arrived. At that point we were so anxious to leave that we hailed a taxi early, just to get the feeling that departure was a real and compelling upcoming event. Arriving at the small Bechar airport, however, we saw that it was full of people crowding around our check-in gate. We got the initial feeling in the pits of our stomachs that something was amiss. So we asked an official-looking Air Algiers agent what was up. He said that the flight from Bechar to Algiers was a once-a-week event, and that the flight was always oversold to the tune of at least 200 percent. "You might already be too late," he said.

We looked at each other, and, as if on cue, we decided to step into the fray. We muscled our way up to the head of the queue waving our confirmed tickets and called out to any official-looking agent to render assistance. Maybe it was our obvious VIP look that did it, but we finally did manage to get to the head of the line to state our case. Our team leader handed over some cash, and we finally got our boarding passes and were led into a waiting hall of sorts.

The incoming plane hadn't arrived yet so we settled in for a long wait. Forget about food — airport restaurants there were non-existent. Behind us at the check-in gate the chaos continued, bribes were handed out, and the lucky passengers began to trickle into the waiting hall. An hour passed, and then another, before the incoming flight arrived.

Sure enough, it was that same old DC 3 that had ferried us to Bechar a week earlier.

All four of us looked around the waiting hall and noticed that the number of passengers let into the waiting hall far exceeded the passenger capacity of the plane. It became abundantly clear that the agents had sold far too many boarding passes and we were now on our own. Our objective now was to get onto the plane and strap ourselves in. We sat in our chairs for about a minute to strategize and then moved as near as we could to the exit gate. There we strategized some more, deciding to link arms and run out on the tarmac when the flight was called.

It was like the start of a running event; everyone had lined up as close to the starting gate as possible and were jockeying for the best starting position. The flight was called, and an immediate traffic jam by the door was created by people yelling, pushing, and pulling. It was reminiscent of the monkeys trying to get out of the car through two small windows (see Chapter 5). We had our arms solidly locked, which allowed no one to pass us. The agent took his half of our boarding passes and we ran out onto the tarmac, arms still locked heading at full speed toward the plane. By the time we reached it and climbed in, it was already two-thirds full. We found four seats and sat down, breathing heavily, and buckled ourselves in. No one was to unseat us, we had determined — we were ready to fight to keep our seats.

The plane quickly filled up — eventually no seats were left. Outside there were at least another thirty or forty passengers with confirmed boarding passes yelling and screaming and getting into fights. Some were inside the plane trying to remove already seated passengers, leading to scuffles inside as well, though these were quickly subdued. Things eventually began to quiet down, and our spirits began to lift just a little, since it looked as if we had made the flight after all.

When the mayhem was over, the flight agents came around to check off all of the passengers already seated so they could unload the luggage belonging to the passengers who didn't make it. We asked them if the scene we had just witnessed was normal, and they said this had been a relatively mild one.

By now the plane was completely loaded with passengers, luggage, and freight. It felt very heavy as we taxied down the runway to prepare for takeoff. We taxied the entire length of the runway and then continued taxiing on a wide dirt road far beyond the end of the runway. Finally we turned around and stopped. We sat there for a long time as the pilot checked everything, flaps, rudder, windshield wipers, oil pressure ... everything.

Then he started to rev up the engines to a feverish pitch while stepping hard on the breaks, until the entire aircraft and all the passengers inside trembled violently. I sat there with white knuckles, as I was gripping my seat and shaking along with the plane until the pilot let go of the brakes and we leaped forward. As we were gathering speed on the dirt road we suddenly hit the seam between the dirt road and the asphalt tarmac with a loud and violent bump. The plane continued to build speed, but didn't lift off for the entire length of the runway. It wasn't until we hit the seam between the end of the tarmac and the dirt road on the other side that the pilot got the plane off the ground, just barely. About one foot up in the air he sucked the wheels up to minimize the drag ... and we were air borne.

That's my one brief story from Algeria. I don't think I'll make it back to Bechar again anytime soon. They probably still have that old DC 3 in service on the Bechar run, complete with the chaos at the airport, the fights, and the bribes.

CHAPTER 6: RUSSIAN FAR EAST

TIME WARP

It was 1994 and Russia was in an economic funk. The value of the ruble was all over the map, crime was rampant, and anarchy reigned. It was also the period when I made several trips to the Russian Far East (RFE) on short-term USAID assignments, trying to make some economic sense out of the RFE forestry and potential ecotourism sectors. My challenges were to convince the Russians in charge that market economics applied to forestry would be far preferable to Marxist "economics," and to prepare an economic analysis of the eco-tourism potential in the RFE based on the presence of some 170 Siberian tigers still roaming the area. The Russians we worked with were in charge of the RFE forestry sector, or they were members of international NGOs seeking to preserve the habitat for the Siberian tigers and other near extinct wildlife species.

The trips to the RFE were eye-openers. The infrastructure was worn and restaurants (if you could find any) had menus several pages long (all in Russian), but there was nothing to serve except one or two dishes. The lines at the bread store were still insufferably long, and it was risky to line up at the end of the queue without first gauging the remaining supply of bread on the shelf and mentally calculating if there still would be anything left for you at the end of the line.

Shopping in Khabarovsk was a major time warp for me. The Russian stores looked and smelled exactly like stores looked and smelled back home in Oslo in the '40s and '50s. Of course, there were major differences between the two countries. In Norway we always had more to buy; in the RFE hardly anything was available.

The typical store itself consisted of a counter made out of wood. Behind it there were floor-to-ceiling wooden shelves, just like there were at home. In Khabarovsk, the store shelves contained a sorry collection of unidentifiable products that, based on the dust accumulation, had been there for at least ten years. Behind the counter was the quintessential rotund "babushka," who, I believe, hadn't cracked a smile since the commodities on her shelves arrived ten years earlier. When it was my turn to be served I pointed to the most promising-looking food item I could see on the shelf, hoping to quell my hunger pangs after a dinner at some restaurant with inedible food. This was followed by an attempt to secure my newfound treasure by producing my rubles.

But "nyet": I couldn't have my items just yet, I was handed a slip of paper and then directed to queue up with the people on the other side of the room waiting for their turn with the cashier. Only one cashier sat in a small cage with a tiny slot through which we handed our slips of paper along with our rubles. The woman in the cage would also typically have the same disaffection for smiling. Once at the head of the line I was liberated from my rubles (if the inflation rate hadn't already caught up in the time it took to complete the transaction), received another piece of paper, and was then redirected to the first counter to receive the merchandise — the third line.

Whew … done! Finally, I had succeeded in acquiring the much-needed additional calories to supplement the inadequacies of what the hotels or restaurants could serve. Once I found out which unidentifiable food items I could actually tolerate, I would buy in quantity to avoid having to repeat the experience.

ACCOMMODATIONS

My experience with the Intourist Hotel chain can be summed up in the familiar Russian phrase: nye rabotayet ("it doesn't work").

"Hello, reception?"

"Da ... vot du yu vant?"

"I don't have any water in my room."

"Vot rum r'yu in?"

"356"

"Da, 356, vater nye rabotayet."

"May I have a different room, please?"

"Nyet, hotel full."

And that was that. Since I haven't spent any time in European Russia—Moscow, St. Petersburg, and the like—I can only speak to the charms of the hotels in Khabarovsk and Vladivostok in the RFE. And these were the decent ones when compared to the "hotels" found outside of these major cities.

In the '90s, the availability of water in hotels was not a given, and hot water was a luxury. Only very rarely would it mercifully arrive through the pipes, usually along with healthy doses of rust and dirt, while making loud and strange noises. The elevators didn't work, or if they did work and there was a power outage while one was between floors, chances were slim to none that any occupants would be extricated in time for dinner if they became stranded around noon. Then there was the issue of temperature control in the guest rooms, or the complete lack thereof. I would usually be in the RFE around October, a time of the year that can see either extreme hot or extreme cold weather. The problem was this: before October 15 (I think that was the date) neither the hotels nor any other buildings in the city were authorized to access the heat (which traveled through huge pipes from the heating plant far across town) even if it was ten degrees below zero outside. That's precisely what I experienced in October. I had no heat in my room, just a ton of scratchy blankets to get me through the night. Or conversely, after October 15 even if it was blazing hot outside, the hotel room was blessed with enough heat to compete with the lower levels of Hades itself, and there was no chance of opening any of the windows. Layers and layers of paint had firmly and permanently fused the windows shut.

The field trips were adventurous because they were punctuated with vehicle and other equipment failures, usually in places where no services existed. On more than one occasion the choice was either to succumb to mild panic as we faced the prospect of spending a very uncomfortable night in the vehicle in the hope that someone would pass by the next day to rescue us. Or, the driver would rise to the task and cobble together some hare-brained technical solution that would get the car started again and eventually get us back to civilization where mechanics could occasionally be found and maybe, just maybe, spare parts. On our field trips, the driver somehow figured out temporary solutions on several occasions, and we would make it to some semblance of civilization to find a mechanic and bed somewhere.

RUSSIANS IN THE US

The Russians reciprocated and two groups came at different times to the US to receive short-term training. The first time they came, we had twenty-five foresters from the RFE staying in Pullman, Washington at Washington State University for two weeks. They were here to learn about the concept of ecosystems management, the cutting edge of forest management at the time. Naturally, this concept has since fallen by the wayside and has been replaced by something with a new catchy phrase or word, but at that time, it was the "in" thing.

To a Russian forester, however, these environmental lectures didn't make a lot of sense — trees are to be harvested and turned into lumber, and that's that. We also failed miserably in our attempts to convert them to market economics. The Russians weren't ready to even begin to appreciate the concept of markets, of fundamental economic principles such as supply and demand, or the rationale behind transparency in production, commerce, and trade, be it in the forestry sector or in realizing their eco-tourism potential.

In the RFE, however, the forestry sector had largely been hijacked by the local mafia (it wasn't the only thing they controlled), and massive log exports to Japan and other Asian countries ruled the day. Some of

our twenty-five Russian foresters were bona fide members of that organization. The forests had almost become a fugitive resource—the officials with management authority who didn't get on the bandwagon
to harvest and export as fast as they could failed to pocket a substantial
percentage of the proceeds. Somebody else would step in to harvest
whatever was available. Rules of the game were almost non-existent.
It was not unlike the gold rush in California during the 1800s, or so it
seemed.

While in the US, the Russians were always eager to compare their
management prowess with ours. One such incident occurred during a
meeting we had with a Boise Cascade forest manager in Kellogg, Idaho. Here's an approximate paraphrase of a conversation between Sam
and the Russian, Igor:

Igor: "How many hectares do you manage?"

Sam: "75,000 or so" (after he was coached on how to convert acres
into hectares).

Igor (bristling): "Da ...I manage 16 million hectares" (implication: I
am so much more important than you). "How many people work for
you?"

Sam: "Four—there's Joe over there, Pete, John, and me, our office is
this old beat up truck."

Igor (bristling some more): "I have 10,000 people working for me
and we have helicopters" (implication: I am so much more important
than you).

Sam (who finally caught on): "That's interesting. I made $20 million
in profits last year, how did you do?"

Well, Igor had no comeback comment this time; he had just been
exposed to the term profit in the classroom and knew what it was in
theory. Perhaps this particular lesson took somehow—do I detect the
sweet taste of a small victory at last?

******

On another field trip we went to Elk River, a small logging community of 200 or so, nestled in a remote area of north Idaho. It was the

middle of December 1994 during bitterly cold weather. The Elk River region is blessed with a rich and diversified forest resource and the whole community depends on the logging industry for its economic well-being. This trip, indeed, was a cultural experience to behold. All of us — some thirty strong, twenty-five Russians plus the US team herding them around — checked into the Huckleberry Heaven Lodge in the mid-afternoon, the only motel in town, after a day in the woods which had begun early in that morning. The Russians had been deprived of their usual quota of vodka during the day in the field and so were ready for the evening to start.

Next on the agenda before the evening would start in earnest was a short snowmobile ride in and around the Elk River forests using the twelve or so rental snowmobiles available in town. Picture the following: twenty-five rotund Russians, all with fur hats, black leather jackets, and gold teeth, doubling or tripling up for their first-ever snowmobile ride. While the Russians deafeningly revved their engines, the Huckleberry Heaven manager in the lead snowmobile tried to give instructions on how to operate the machines, admonishing everyone to "… please follow me and stay at least sixty feet apart." That was all duly translated into Russian and yelled by the translator as he attempted to out-shout the revving engines.

Nobody paid any attention. Adrenalin visibly coursed through their veins, and all eyes were intently fixed on the undisturbed snowy terrain ahead. The moment the leader took off on the lead snowmobile, the Russians took off in all different directions at full speed, fur hats bobbing up and down all over the terrain. Within a matter of minutes we had lost three snowmobiles. I was thinking international incident — "Six Russians on short-term training in the US lost in the woods in sub-zero temperatures because of snowmobile snafu, presumed dead …" I suffered an anxiety attack then and there.

An hour later, however, they were found in different corners of the woods in reasonably good shape, stuck in deep snow and needing to be pulled out. That hour was probably the longest I have ever experienced. I was sure our next move would have been to send out a helicopter rescue team, since the night was already setting in and it was bitterly cold.

Safely back in town, the Russians thawed out at the Huckleberry Heaven Lodge and were more than ready for some heart-warming vodka, wine, and even some food. In typical US fashion, we had evening presentations on the forest resources all lined up with slides and guest speakers and gravitas, but the Russians wanted no part of that—they were done for the day and it was time to party. We struggled through half of the presentations until we finally gave up and yielded to the incessant pressure to receive toasts and dispense them on just about everything conceivable, all of which contributed vastly to the rapidly improving international relations between our two countries, to be sure.

After a very long dinner and many, many, many toasts, the Russians by now were fairly inebriated and wanted to interact with the Elk River locals—mostly loggers. So we were talked into taking them to the local tavern—the Elk River hot spot. Feeling a not-so-subtle and rapidly developing panic in the pit of my stomach because of what I knew could happen in a tavern full of temporarily unemployed loggers, we walked over to this fine establishment, flung open the doors and loudly announced: "The Russians are coming." Given what I already knew about the Elk River tavern, I was, to put it mildly, paralyzed by pure and raw fear. I was certain that there would be fistfights. After all, Elk River is serious red neck country, communists are still the enemy, and here we were with twenty-five of Russia's finest communist ex-bosses and mafia members—they even looked like classic Russians with their leather jackets, fur hats, and gold teeth.

But fist fights didn't materialize. In fact, the Elk River loggers and the twenty-five feeling-no-pain Russians immediately hit it off. The beer flowed, it was standing room only, and deep intellectual conversations between the Russians and the loggers quickly ensued. The American loggers, I believe, discovered they had long lost relatives in the RFE and that at least two or three of the Russians thought they were related somehow to some of the Elk River elite. The Russians wanted to serenade the Americans, which they did with considerable gusto. The loggers responded in kind with drinking songs, and friendships developed to the point where I firmly believe this was, by far, the finest hour ever experienced in the otherwise complex relationship between the US and Russia.

******

And then there was the trip to Wal-Mart, in Moscow, Idaho. We traveled by bus from the WSU campus, a distance of nine miles, to take the Russians shopping. As we approached the end of our short trip, we drove by the sign announcing we were entering the City of Moscow. Of course we had to stop the bus so they could get some snapshots of the sign with them posing underneath. We obliged (because it was impossible not to do so) and they surged out of the bus and posed next to the sign, blocking traffic left and right, while we — the guilty group leaders and instructors — cast sidelong glances to detect any approaching presence of cops. We survived, however, piled back into the bus, and finally ended up at Wal-Mart.

Now picture the twenty-five Russians (the ever-present fur hats and black leather jackets), all carrying a fortune in gold teeth smiling and laughing their way into Wal-Mart with a visible zest for the upcoming shopping they had never before experienced at home. Once inside, they scattered to all corners of the store. We only had two translators with us and the Russians had a lot of questions, so we had to commandeer the store intercom to facilitate the translation. Russian and English questions and answers were broadcast all over the store for at least an hour or longer.

The jewelry counter was particularly popular. I think they cleaned out the inventory that day. Digital watches (the $10 to $20 Casio variety) were also big, as were the Walkmans. Some went to the gun section and purchased loads of ammunition for their guns at home, intending to pack it in their luggage for the trip back to Russia. We found out about this after the fact and tried to convince them that they wouldn't be allowed to board the airplane with any ammunition for guns, but they didn't listen. What problem or danger would there be with just the ammunition, they argued, and no guns? We counter argued as much as we could, but they prevailed, as we knew they would. But we won in the end at the airport, also as we knew we would, when they had to surrender every bullet and clip before being allowed to board.

The Wal-Mart experience had some other consequences, as well. For several of our participants this trip was their first ever outside Russia, and for a smaller subset, this was also their first trip outside the very remote region they called home. For them, the Wal-Mart experience was overwhelming. The range of choices available was immense, and it rendered them paralyzed. It became a profoundly unmanageable experience for them, and two of them actually went to psychiatric counseling sessions afterward — with translators.

AEROFLOT

If you've ever flown on Aeroflot you know you should probably avoid it in the future. Although by now it has probably improved, back in the '90s I heard many horror stories of Aeroflot crashes and near crashes. Flying from point A to point B without incident rarely happened. Delays, mechanical problems, turbulent air, drafts inside the planes from cracks in the fuselage, you name it — all happened routinely. Once you are in Russia and have to fly, you must agree to suspend all fears, put your life entirely in God's hands (as you always should anyway), and pray for safe deliverance to your destination, especially if you fly with Aeroflot's division of commuter planes.

I had the occasion to take one such flight from Vladivostok to Tierney, a small village located on the Japanese Seacoast in the Siberian Tiger habitat, a two-hour flight away. This one was a flight I will never forget. It all began at the Vladivostok Airport. Arriving there on time we were informed that the flight to Tierney had been delayed.

"For how long?" we asked.

"Delayed" was the answer.

Again I asked: "How long?"

"Flight delayed" was all we were told.

So we sat down obediently to wait along with the other hapless passengers who seemed to be perfectly resigned to this reality. One hour passed, and then another. We asked again and got the same answer:

"delayed." By now I was beginning to feel an urge to visit the Vlad-ivostok Airport restroom and began the long trek in that direction. Trying to enter it, however, was a problem. Standing in the doorway was a rotund Russian hammer-thrower woman demanding rubles for admittance to the restroom. I only had large denominations in my pocket and she was unable to give me any change, as were other ven-dors in the area. So I turned around and walked the equivalent of at least a kilometer back to the gate and asked my colleague to lend me some smaller denomination money. He only had large denominations as well, which he had been unable to change, so I was faced with the choice of losing all of my money for one bathroom trip or waiting until the flight boarded so I could use the restroom on board. I decided on the latter. Besides, a kilometer walk to the restroom might cause me to miss the flight if it boarded while I was away. The airport announce-ments were all in Russian so I wouldn't understand them anyway.

One hour later the flight was announced and we, along with all the other passengers, scrambled to get on board. We all walked to-ward what I had thought was our plane—a big one sure to have a restroom—but I was wrong. As we continued our trek across the tar-mac, I finally made out a much smaller propeller plane way off in the distance—a tail dragger kind of bush plane that looked like it had been built in the '30s.

At this moment I knew I was in real trouble, but the die had been cast. I was boarding a plane that couldn't possibly have a restroom, and I was sure to look forward to a two-hour flight without any relief. The horror. I frantically looked around the tarmac for some bushes, anything to hide behind, before boarding, but saw none. So I boarded and realized I had run out of options upon confirming that the plane had no restroom. The plane accommodated twenty passengers in ten rows. I was ushered all the way to the front right behind the pilot, where I thankfully sat down to take some of the urgent pressure off.

Soon all of the twenty seats or so were occupied. The pilot strutted down the aisle and sat down at the controls ... and waited. "Why aren't we leaving," I thought. My answer came quickly — they began to load cases of fruits and vegetables in all the seemingly vacant spaces. Right under my feet they placed a large case of fresh tomatoes. "Good," I thought, now we're ready to go.

The pilot finally started the engines, black smoke belching out of each one, and we taxied down the runway for takeoff. "Please, please, let this be a smooth and safe and quick flight with lots of tailwind," I silently prayed as I straddled the case of tomatoes and glanced at the passenger sitting in the aisle across from me. He didn't seem to have a care in the world and was happy to have caught the ride. We took off. Sure enough, the pilot obviously didn't intend to reach a high cruising altitude to avoid turbulence; instead he hugged the valleys and mountains while choppy air tossed us around like a beach ball. I glanced at the other passengers who were all sitting with closed eyes while their lips were moving. They probably were praying.

My urgent need for a restroom had now reached the critical stage, and I knew it would not be possible to wait until we reached Tierney. I was desperate and started to look around for any kind of container of sorts. None were available and I began to resign myself to my inevitable fate. But God is merciful. Our flight had a scheduled stop along the way at a small village, unbeknownst to me, where a few of the passengers and the boxes of vegetables would be unloaded. After several zigzag maneuvers down a narrow valley we finally touched down on a dirt landing strip and came to a stop. By now, I figured I had mere seconds before something had to happen. I was sitting at the very front of the plane and they were unloading in the back. First off were the boxes of vegetables. Next were the passengers in the back of the plane, but by then, I had reached the end of my rope, and decided it was now or never, so I yelled out at the top of my lungs something akin to "restroom emergency," stood up and forced my way through the passengers in the aisle, left the plane running as fast as I could while holding my knees together, to a spot behind a dilapidated hangar. There I joined a line of other passengers who had been in the same predicament, yet perhaps not as severe as mine.

Blessed and joyful was the rest of the flight to Tierney, turbulence and all. I was in an ebullient mood because I had avoided at the very last second the most embarrassing moment anyone could have, ever.

We landed in Tierney only three hours behind schedule, which was as close to perfection for Aeroflot as possible.

BANYA

Working with the Russians was a pleasure. They were eager to be friendly, and they liked to laugh, joke, party, and above all, drink vodka. The Russians who came to our training course at Washington State University had become our friends. They were all from the RFE, on the edge of the Siberian region where, during the winters, the temperatures often dip below -50° F. It is rugged country with few passable roads and very hardy people. I had already made several trips to this region as part of a USAID project before we hosted the training component in the US. So when I traveled to the RFE I was affectionately greeted with bear hugs, vodka, and Russian hospitality from our colleagues and friends.

On the schedule was a trip deep into the forested region near Khabarovsk. Our destination was a ranger station some fifty miles inside the forest on barely passable logging roads. I was loaded into a vehicle with five of my Russian ex-students/now friends, and we were off. After a very bumpy two-hour ride we arrived at the station and were greeted by the head ranger there. We sat down in front of the fireplace and began our discussions, which all funneled through a translator who, I suspected, embellished her translations with her own imagination.

After about an hour of discussion, our Russian leader said it was time for a banya—the Russian version of a sauna. I protested meekly because I hadn't prepared for that, which made them all laugh. In a Russian banya, they explained, you don't wear any clothing at all. Now picture this—here I was in the depths of the RFE forest region with five rotund Russians embellished with gold teeth, unable to speak any English, headed for a very hot experience without a stitch of clothing, and I had absolutely no say in whether or not I actually wanted to do this. Resistance was futile.

Inside the banya I soon realized that this was not the same thing as a sauna. A sauna is civilized (you can carry on a conversation while sweating); a banya is not. It is far too hot, and I literally could not breathe, only pant. The Russians sat on the top bench where the heat was most intense, motioning for me to climb up there and join them. The were chatting amiably without any difficulty whatsoever, and I, with sweat gushing out of every pore of my body, was panting and close to panicking. The Russians took some pity on me as they picked up some birch twigs that were lying around and began to beat me on my back and legs. This was a kind gesture I was told, because it ostensibly opens the pores so sweat can flow even more freely, making breathing easier.

After a few minutes on the top shelf, I simply couldn't handle it anymore and had to get out of there. I escaped and immediately dived into a small indoor pool of ice-cold water. Ahhhh ... relief. The Russians also came out and dived in, making it a bit crowded because of their considerable girths.

After frolicking in the water for a few seconds, they motioned to me again, and back into the banya we went for a second session. This one only lasted two or three minutes before I had to run out again and into the pool. After that they took mercy on me and didn't make me enter the banya a third time. Instead, they gave me a thin towel about 1½x1½ ' in size and steered me into another adjacent room with more benches. This was sort of a "recovery" room I surmised, because it felt so good to be back in a normal temperature room again. The small towel was the only piece of clothing we had in this room, which I used for modesty, being the good and prudent American/Norwegian I was. The Russians completely ignored any attempt at modesty, even when a stout Russian woman — probably the banya keeper — entered bearing a tray with five full glasses of what I thought was water. It wasn't: it was vodka, which I think is synonomous with water in Russian.

So there we sat, butt naked, sipping vodka with this stout woman busying herself with tidying up in the room and fetching our clothes. Our conversation was devoid of any understanding because their English was non-existent and my Russian was non-existent. But we did communicate some with sign language and by drawing pictures with our fingers.

Dressed again and feeling good, we headed back to the ranger building to have lunch. We were all very hungry and looking forward to it. This too became a unique experience because of all of the vodka consumed in the full two hours devoted to eating and drinking. There must have been twenty toasts and many refills of glasses (except mine—I only nursed one full glass of vodka during the entire meal, despite their efforts to persuade me to drink a lot more). After lunch, we all piled into the vehicle for our return trip to Khabarovsk, my five rotund and inebriated Russian friends singing Russian drinking songs the entire way back. It truly was a day to remember.

All in all, I will forever cherish the experiences I had with the Russians in the RFE and in the US. They were fun-loving folks, smart, not-at-all-polished in urbane ways, but definitely diamonds in the rough. They have a lot to learn about capitalism, markets, and what makes the US tick, but we, too, have much to learn from the can-do Russians. But that's for another time.

CHAPTER 7: EAST ASIA

A fter spending a fair amount of time in Far East Asia (Sri Lanka, Thailand, Indonesia, Nepal, Vietnam, Pakistan, and the Philippines), I was still much more comfortable in Africa. This had little to do with liking Africa more than Asia: it was my own ability to fit in. The heat, dust, and grit in Africa didn't bother me much because I knew the people, the culture, what worked and what didn't. In Asia, the dynamic was different. The heat and humidity in some of the Asian countries were just as oppressive as in Africa, but the people were more complex and difficult for me to understand. Reading between the cultural lines there was a necessity. Africa too had cultural realities which had to be respected, but I knew them — they had become second nature to me. In Asia, I felt that I had to be on my guard every moment. Perhaps the difference is that I spent a lot more time in Africa than I did in Asia.

Travel to Asia was exhausting, and the jet lag excruciatingly brutal. Getting to Africa would sometimes take just as long, but I would recover quickly and be able to function normally. In Africa, there were no language difficulties — English or French were the operative languages in all of the African countries where I worked. In Far East Asia, I never got over the jet lag and rarely had a moment of physical comfort. Food didn't taste good, sleep evaded me most of the time, and I had no knowledge of the languages spoken. We had to have interpreters with us on field trips, and I was never certain if they translated correctly.

EYE OPENER

In 1980 I went on one of my early trips to Sri Lanka, and it was an eye-opener. There were three of us from the University of Idaho, and our task was to plan a USAID forestry project focusing on fuelwood plantations. This was also when I first came face to face with the miseries characterizing so much of the Third World, seeing poverty in its raw form for the first time. I remember how this experience affected me and the difficulties I had reconciling my own standard of living with that of the people of Sri Lanka. Hordes of people were living on the streets or running to and fro in heavily polluted Colombo — the capital city — trying to scratch out a living peddling cigarettes, ointments, street food, all in intense daytime heat that didn't abate much during the night. Many were plagued by leprosy or other diseases, and beggars were everywhere.

At the time I actually became depressed by seeing what I then thought couldn't get any worse, at least compared to everything in my life which I had always taken for granted. The Sri Lanka experience gradually eased me into a deeper understanding of poverty and how it not only destroys the ability to provide, but also how it sucks the life out of souls. Poverty is debilitating and blocks any chance of breaking out of its vicious cycle: it saps energy, drive, and pride.

The eye-opening and disturbing discovery triggered by this trip to Sri Lanka was the sharply growing awareness of what I had and what they didn't. Never in my life have I known hunger. Sure I've been hungry (always am, come to think of it), but I haven't known persistent hunger or been unsure of where my next meal would be coming from. I've always had a well-built home with comfortable furniture, but they live in mud or straw huts and sleep on burlap bags filled with straw in the rural areas, and in the cities, many are homeless and sleep in doorways, on the sidewalk, behind bushes ... anywhere.

Seeing all of this in Sri Lanka and later in Africa brought on a sentiment best described as confusion. Where do you draw the line? How much of yours should you give up for them? For a staunch conservative like me, however, I should not have been confused even then in retrospect, because the difference is rooted in the question: should the government tax its citizens to provide for the poor, or should individuals be more generous? In my observations, the latter is far better than the former. When the government taxes its citizens to provide for the poor in other countries it relieves them from feeling the heart tugs—empathy—for the poor. Norway's contributions through taxes to alleviate world poverty is among the highest in the world, but Norwegians rarely feel the need to deeply care about this because they are "covered" through the taxes they pay. Likewise, they are "covered" when, as in Norway, everything from cradle to grave is cared for through the taxes levied. The unforeseen consequence is to absolve the younger generation from ever having to care for elderly parents. Instead, the parents are shipped off to nursing homes paid for through taxes.

On the trip to Sri Lanka I remember that my entire belief system was shaken, and I had a difficult time getting back into equilibrium. My "solution" while living in Africa was to be overly generous to a few of the beggars, but not to all. Even when giving to the few, the nagging thought haunted me that the amount I gave was only a mere pittance out of my abundance, and that I could afford to give a lot more.

THE QUEEN OF THAILAND

I was in and out of Thailand on week long teaching assignments at least seven times, teaching community forestry economics at the Regional Community Forestry Training Center (RECOFTC) in Bangkok to students from East Asian countries. Traveling to Thailand was difficult. Bangkok is the largest moving parking lot in the world—the traffic jams are insane. Even at 3 a.m. when planes from the US are landing, the traffic jams are impossible. The flying time from the US to Bangkok is about fourteen hours in addition to the time just to get to the airport to begin the trip. By the time you arrive in Bangkok you can count on having been up for at least forty to fifty hours, about half of that in cramped coach seats.

Sleeping on the plane is not even a remote possibility for me, so when I finally arrived in Bangkok at 3 a.m. and had got through the traffic jams to the hotel, it was time for breakfast followed immediately by one full day of teaching. One day of rest and recuperation before the teaching started was only a possibility if you arrived one day earlier and you didn't get paid for it. Eager to save money, I taught a full three hours in the morning and three hours in the afternoon with a two-hour lunch break in between for the entire week. It was brutal. It was always the same routine: severe jet lag, no sleep, and always contracting some disease or another, either a cold or laryngitis; not handy when you're on your feet teaching all day long. What was I thinking by repeating this routine seven years in a row?

Well, there was one year that stood out a bit more than the others. That was the year when the queen of Thailand was going to visit the center on the day after I was scheduled to leave the country. The preparations during the entire week were frenzied. People were cleaning and scrubbing, sprucing up, and decorating to get ready for the event. That particular year I was given the guest room at the center, which was very handy—it had a functioning air conditioner and a TV where I could get some news in English. It also let me take quick catnaps on my lunch breaks just to get me recharged for the afternoon session.

The preparation for the queen's visit included some construction in the lobby area to change the look and feel of the entrance door. On both sides of the entry door they installed huge floor-to-ceiling glass windows to give the lobby a light, airy, and modern feeling. Two days before my scheduled departure this construction effort was completed. On the evening before my scheduled departure I went out in search of a nearby restaurant to get some dinner. I was a wreck as usual—jet lagged, sleep deprived, looking like someone who had had one or two drinks too many. I found a restaurant and ordered the first thing on the menu, ate my dinner, and headed back to the center to hopefully get some sleep. My thoughts were focused on the glorious day tomorrow when I would be heading home, maybe even getting some sleep on the airplane despite all odds, and not having to worry about teaching the next day.

Arriving at the center I was completely lost in my thoughts, not paying any attention as I ascended the steps to the lobby. I had completely forgotten about the reconstruction, which had been finished earlier that very same day. The entry door had changed location, and, in my zombie-like stupor I walked right up to and through the newly installed floor-to-ceiling window where the old door was supposed to have been. The window shattered into a thousand pieces and some heavier ones fell down on the top of my head and shoulders. That, needless to say, rudely shook me out my reverie, only to be replaced by the sudden awareness that I may have been seriously hurt. I instinctively brought both hands up to my head and felt glass shards solidly embedded in my skull, my neck, and my shoulders, now with blood streaming out between my fingers and dripping to the ground.

The guards inside the center lobby freaked out as they came running out to render assistance to this bobbing lunatic. One of them got his wits about him and ran back inside to call for a taxi to take me to the hospital. To get an ambulance there would have taken too much time. One arrived just a couple of minutes later, and they loaded me in, equipped me with a towel to stop the bleeding somewhat, and told the taxi driver to take me to the emergency room.

At the hospital, the receptionist took one look at me and put me in the front of the queue. A doctor spent the next two hours patiently removing tiny bits, and some not so tiny bits of glass from my skull, and applying suture tape to the small wounds. I now personally know the literal meaning of the saying, "bleeding from a thousand wounds." It was a painful process, but he told me that I had been very lucky. If I had broken the window pane at a lower point, the shards above would have been larger and heavier and might have penetrated my skull and caused some real damage.

After two hours he had finished and given me a tetanus shot, and I was ready to be discharged. "Where do I pay?" I asked, and he directed me to the payment office. There I was handed a bill for approximately $10. On my way out, I stopped at the bathroom to have a look in the mirror—it wasn't a pretty sight. I looked like Frankenstein on a very bad day: suture tape ends protruded from everywhere, dried blood was all over my shirt and pants, my face was a mess with long and short scratches, and I wasn't sure a taxi would take a chance on having me in the back seat.

One kind taxi driver did, however, and I was driven back to my bed at RECOFTC. The construction crew was already at work replacing the broken window. This time they placed a huge RECOFTC decal chest high on the window panes on both sides of the entrance door to make sure I wouldn't do it again. The lobby guards looked at me as if I were from Mars, but they kindly got me to my room and told me to get to bed. The next day I was back at it in the classroom, but I'm afraid the students didn't learn much about economics. Just looking at me and hearing my story again and again was much greater entertainment.

MOUNTAINS AROUND KATHMANDU

I went to Nepal only once for a forestry and reforestation project funded by USAID. Nepal is a beautiful and mountainous country with a fascinating culture. Kathmandu—the capital city—had the look and feel of a large village. There were domesticated elephants ambling up and down the streets right alongside cars and buses, and the revered cows were free to roam at will. Kathmandu was then also home to many drug-drenched "refugees" from the '60s who never grew out of those "glory" days.

A large percentage of Nepal's rural people lived in the mountains eking out a living growing rain-fed rice on man-made terraces clinging to the steep hillsides. As they built these terraces, they also permanently removed any woody vegetation, trading off one type of soil conservation for another. Over time, therefore, fuelwood and charcoal supplies—the only available energy resources—became increasingly scarce, and something had to be done. Enter USAID with suitcases full of money to solve the problem through reforestation of the mountain tops around Kathmandu in an effort to increase the supply of fuelwood for the mountain villages. This was our task: mobilize the villagers to establish and care for the tree nurseries and carry out the reforestation and plantation maintenance efforts.

One of the most memorable events of my trip to Nepal was the helicopter ride from Kathmandu to the mountain tops encircling the city. Along with my colleague and the forestry minister, we were supposed to participate in ceremonial tree planting efforts. This was a big deal for the villagers, who had gone to great lengths in preparing for the arrival of the minister and the other dignitaries — us. The helicopter ride was harrowing to say the least, with updrafts and downdrafts causing us to bounce in every which direction. But the pilot, who dressed and looked like one of the villagers himself, proved to be very capable as he guided the helicopter in its climb to our first stop.

As we approached the mountain top, we saw hundreds of people clustered around the landing watching our helicopter slowly descend. The authorities were scrambling to shoo them away so we could land without mishap. Off in the distance I saw that a band was getting ready to play. We touched down, the doors opened, and we were met by the village dignitaries, hordes of men, women, and wide-eyed children all wanting to shake hands.

Speeches were next — the forestry minister, the village mayor, the forest nursery chief, and the women leaders. Luckily, we didn't have to give any speeches, although we were treated as royalty. The perception was that we were the folks who had given the money so the trees could be planted. In reality, we were there simply to observe and write about what we saw and to do the analysis of the project components. Nevertheless, our reception in the village was very warm and welcoming.

Following the speeches, the ceremonial tree planting began. I saw that literally thousands of holes had already been neatly dug on the steep hillsides. The nursery people appeared with bags of seedlings which they distributed to the villagers … and to us. Time to plant, so off we went. TV cameras appeared out of nowhere and began filming my colleague and me as we planted seedlings while surrounded by hundreds of villagers cheering us on, the band playing, and the minister in the distance at a nearby planting site admonishing the villagers to remove the plastic bags around the roots before planting the seedlings.

After a full hour of planting trees to the accompaniment of cheering audiences and band music, it was time to eat. The villagers were now fully engaged in filling all of the holes with seedlings while we—the dignitaries—were ushered off to have some lunch. This too was very well prepared. The villagers had erected a tent to protect us from rain, which came in occasional torrents, and they had prepared an incredible feast. The table was groaning under the weight of the food, most of which I couldn't identify. But it tasted delicious so I didn't ask what it was. Knowing could easily have spoiled it for me if it had been rat, dog, snake, or anything outside our customary western diet. But we were hungry, and we ate and drank our fill before returning to the helicopter. We climbed on board, there were more speeches by the minister and village dignitaries, more handshaking, then we were off.

Instead of returning to Kathmandu for some much needed R & R and sleep after the physical labor and the huge meal, however, we flew to the next mountain top only to repeat the entire process there. By this time, we were mentally prepared for the day to be over. But recalling the lunch in Morocco, I braced myself for another session of tree planting and another overdose of Nepalese calories.

And so it was, tree planting, band playing, speeches, and another huge meal under a tent as hundreds of villagers peered at us partaking of the spread that had been placed before us. That day was memorable—I could only pray: "Please, God, not another mountain top village."

HEAD-HUNTERS

I made several journeys to the Philippines to do economic analyses for a USAID project, ranging from fuelwood production to natural forest management to agriculture. Everything relating to natural resource management was included in this project, so my plate was full. Much field-work was involved, so I traveled around the country with a Philippine entourage to meet and interview different local community groups and to collect field data on crop and wood yields, energy consumption patterns, sources of energy supplies, and cultural constraints to local development. I loved the work, especially getting out of Manila and into the rural areas to meet with different tribal groups and find out what they were like.

One of my trips took us to an area about a day's drive from Manila, where we were supposed to interview villagers just outside the project area about the activities in the neighboring project area and to determine if there had been any spillover (demonstration) effects. It was a hot day, the air conditioning in the car wasn't working, and the roads were miserable, so we were very glad when we finally arrived at our destination. Some twenty villagers had already congregated under a hangar and motioned to us to sit in the two chairs they had provided for us, the visiting dignitaries. Everything was formal. We were presented with drinks, and introductions were made. All of the village elders were squatting in a wide circle in the shady area under the hangar; my Filipino counterpart and I were the only ones sitting in chairs.

The interviews began. My counterpart was supposed to translate the dialogue, but his knowledge of the tribal language was poor, so that task was handed over to the local priest. He was elderly and had lived in the village for more than thirty-five years, but was not an ethnic member of the tribe. However, he was fluent in both the tribal language and English. It was clear that he was highly respected and had assumed a leadership role in the village. As he translated, he looked at the village elders in their eyes and smiled at them, reflecting total respect for his flock, and they revered him in return as their priest.

I got my usual questions in about crops, tree species, yields, farm-to-market roads, weekly markets, and so on. My notebook was filling up and I turned to cultural questions, which brought about a lot of fidgeting and casting sidelong glances. After a bit of agitated talking back and forth with no real sharp answers, the priest told me that my questions had touched a nerve. "This used to be a headhunting village," he said. "All villager elders you've met here were active head-hunters as late as the mid 1970s. I came here as a missionary in 1970, and an important part of the village culture then was to conduct war with neighboring villages, cut off people's heads, shrink them, and keep them as trophies."

"In fact," pointing at a small village elder squatting next to him, "this fellow right here tried to take my head in 1971 and in 1972. Somehow I talked him out of it, and we have since become friends, particularly after the entire village converted to Christianity in 1974 and renounced their old ways."

I was stunned at this revelation and looked around at the small group of some 20 elderly villagers squatting around us, all wiry and wrinkled, with gnarled hands, and looking at us kindly. They had been fidgety, the priest said, because they were ashamed of their past and didn't want to exhume the old memories. It was difficult to imagine that these were once fierce warriors raiding neighboring villages and cutting off heads to be kept as trophies.

I don't think many can say they've met and talked with actual headhunters, but I have had this dubious honor. What happened in this village in the heart of rural Phillippines – the conversion of an entire village to Christianity – happens in Africa too. While living in Africa, we nurtured strong relationships with several young people who went back to their villages to preach. In some cases, the entire village was subsequently converted.

A rabbit trail: In Africa headhunting is still taking place, particularly during election years. National political candidates in Ivory Coast, for example, who wear fancy western suits, speak perfect French, still practice voodoo against opposing candidates. They cast spells to have members of their own tribe cut off the heads of members of the opposing tribe. Often we would see reports in the newspapers about heads being harvested, and photographs of the headhunters posing with cloth bags containing the grisly evidence.

ALMOST KIDNAPPED

On another trip to the Philippines for USAID I was supposed to travel to Lake Sebu in the district of South Cotabato on the island of Mindanao. This particular area, however, had on-again off-again travel restrictions due to security concerns, particularly for Americans, because of active Muslim insurgencies by the infamous Abu Sayyaf group. This group had kidnapped a missionary couple in 2001, holding them captive for a full year, killing the husband and allowing the wife to escape in a rescue attempt.

I arrived in Manila when travel restrictions were in effect and had to cool my heels there for a couple of days. Then, the wise people at USAID in Manila lifted the restrictions after a couple of days, and I got my airline ticket. Off I went — a white American expatriate consultant along with an entourage of four Filipinos. I stuck out like a sore thumb. We arrived at our destination, checked into a hotel, and the anxiety of traveling to a restricted area slowly began to fade. Everything seemed normal and I began to look forward to the work scheduled to begin in Lake Sebu the next day.

We rented a Jeepney and a driver near the hotel for our travel to Lake Sebu, some two to three hours away on rough roads. When we got there we checked in at the local and only hotel, where we would be staying for the next three nights. I was given the best room in the hotel, a very basic one with no air conditioning and only occasional electricity to power an old rickety fan. Thankfully, there was a mosquito net covering the bed. Sleep was impossible because of the oppressive heat, so I reverted to the usual for all my Asian trips — rely on sheer will power and adrenalin to get through.

Day one was good: the work went well and notebooks filled up. About half-way through day two, however, my Filipino colleagues changed their demeanor and showed far less enthusiasm for the work. Instead, they spoke among themselves, exhibited quite a bit of edginess, and never let me go off on my own to talk to anyone. I was a bit frustrated because their behavior slowed down the work, they didn't make appointments with the local dignitaries, and they were always eager to get back to the hotel. We returned to the hotel far earlier that day than normal. They claimed they were super tired and didn't want to go out to eat that night, so instead they would send someone out to a restaurant to bring back dinner to the hotel. I protested, but to no avail. They brought the food back and we had an early dinner. Then at 8 p.m. it was lights out and off to bed for another sleepless night.

Early on day three I was ready to get started; we needed to recapture some of the time we had lost the previous day. When we met at breakfast, however, my Filipino colleagues were adamant that we already had more than enough information and it was time to leave. There was none of the usual banter or camaraderie we had developed while together. Now they were all serious and very eager to leave Lake Sebu. So we loaded up the Jeepney and headed down the mountain toward civilization. No one talked — they were all paying attention to the road, the people along the road, and denying rides to anyone who asked along the way, a very unusual behavior.

I had realized for some time now that something was going on, and I was feeling a bit anxious. I assumed it had to do with the on-again off-again travel restrictions, but no one had told me anything. I decided to stay quiet and close to my colleagues and to give up on completing the data gathering on the Lake Sebu region. We finally arrived back in the city without incident and checked into the hotel in town, this time one that had its own restaurant. Once again we didn't venture out but ate at the hotel and then went to bed for another sleepless night.

Early the next day we caught our flight back to Manila. After take-off I noticed that my colleagues were once again relaxed, and the bantering had increased. I had asked them several times about what was going on, but they only had very vague answers that didn't explain anything. Now, however, they were ready to talk. Early on day two in Lake Sebu, the leader of my Filipino colleagues had taken off by himself to run an errand with the Jeepney and the driver, leaving the rest of us to conduct an interview. While away, he had run into a group of six people who asked him for a ride. Being gracious and having plenty of room in the vehicle, he had let the six climb on board. They were talking among themselves in their local tribal language, which they were certain no one in Lake Sebu knew. My Filipino colleague did know it, however, although he didn't let on. The six were probably members of the Abu Sayyaf terrorist group he surmised, and they were talking about me, the only white American person in the Lake Sebu region, and a prime target for kidnapping.

My Filipino colleague listened intently while feigning sleep. Finally, the six were let off at their destination, and he immediately turned around and headed back up the mountain to reconnect with us. There he conferred with his Filipino colleagues about the situation and they collectively decided not to tell me about it in order to protect me from worrying (and that, needless to say, was probably a very wise move). It was too late to leave that day, which is why they brought food to the hotel and provided protection for me until we all went to bed that night early.

For two and a half days in Lake Sebu, I had been in danger. Nobody knew the first day, they found out on the second day, and we left on the third. I have often since reflected on the fate of the missionaries who were kidnapped by the same group just a few months later. I think I may have been close to the same fate, and I was very glad my colleagues took matters into their own hands and gently ushered me out of there before anything happened, and that I knew nothing about what could have happened until after it was all over.

ORDERING BEER

In the early '80s I was pulled out of West Africa for two-and-a-half weeks to go to Pakistan as a candidate for Chief-of-Party (COP) of a large USAID-funded forestry project based in Islamabad. This ongoing project had already destroyed two COPs so I experienced quite a bit of trepidation in even considering it. Nevertheless, I was in the middle of closing the Burkina Faso project so the timing was right. I decided to make the trip just to learn more — no commitments.

Arriving in Islamabad in January was an experience I wasn't prepared for. The internet wasn't widespread and we certainly didn't have Google or anything like that, so I thought, rather naively ... Asia, it must be hot. After all, my previous Asian experiences had all been hot and muggy, why should this be any different? Surprise, it was sub-zero when I arrived, in my best short sleeve African safari suit. It was cold!!! The taxi, of course, didn't have a functioning heater, so the ride to the hotel was a rather uncomfortable and teeth-chattering experience.

We thawed out a bit and decided to have a team meeting to plan for the following day. "Hey, how about ordering some beer," exclaimed one of our team members, and we all agreed without any arm-twisting. We were in my room so I called room service:

"Hello, room service. What can I do for you?"

"We would like four beers delivered to room 315, please," pause … pause … and I said, "… you still there?"

"Yes, you said beer? One moment please."

"Hello, this is the hotel room service manager. Did you just order four beers?"

"Yes," I said, slightly exasperated.

"Please, I will come to your room right away."

We thought he would bring the beer so we waited, continuing with the meeting. Thirty minutes passed and finally, a knock on the door. The beer had arrived, or so we thought. The hotel room service manager arrived with a rather grim face, clutching several sheets of paper. "You need to fill these out," he said as he gave us each a form. It was a long form with many questions like name, address, gender, age, phone number, reasons for being in Pakistan, and reasons for ordering the beer. In essence, the form, properly filled out, would be tantamount to officially declaring publicly that we were infidels.

So, because thirst trumped the business meeting, we sat down and dutifully filled out the form for the next twenty minutes. The manager stood there with his hands clasped and waited. Finally done, he gathered up all of the forms, scanned them, told us to complete some undone questions and he was off. A half hour later, four lukewarm beers arrived along with four glasses. Needless to say, the experience left us far from satisfied, so we mentally prepared ourselves to drink Cokes or bottled water for the next two weeks.

SHOPPING IN PESHAWAR

The trip to Pakistan also took us to Peshawar on a harrowing drive from Islamabad, which included dodging oncoming traffic, looking out for livestock crossing the road, squeezing through street vendors and crowds of people. We stayed in Peshawar for four days at a hotel heavily guarded by uniformed men carrying menacing weapons, uninterested in greeting, smiling, or speaking. It was comforting to have the guards there just in case there was an attack of sorts but also a bit unnerving because their presence was a strong reminder that the hotel was a likely target. All the foreigners stayed there, and from our windows we could see the Afghan refugee camps just down the road. We didn't feel particularly safe in this part of the world so we were pretty anxious to get out of there.

My fondest memory from Peshawar, however, is my carpet-buying experience. We didn't sample Peshawar's "nightlife" or restaurants because of the tense political situation there, and besides, the only way you could get from point A to point B back then was with horse-drawn taxis. You could get to your destination okay, but getting back was not always easy. So we took all our meals at the hotel and also checked out the hotel stores for local handicrafts. One such store was the ubiquitous carpet store. Fine carpets are sold everywhere in Pakistan. The carpets are expensive and the business is highly competitive. The salesmen are very aggressive and very good at their jobs.

One afternoon after lunch I was walking past the hotel carpet store and cast a brief glance at the display carpets in the window. A brief glance was all it took. The store manager spotted me … an American … someone with money … a likely target. He was comfortably overweight and had an engaging smile. When he saw me perusing his wares he caught my eye, lifted his eyebrows, and motioned to me to enter his store. I shook my head, but hesitated — something I should not have done. Hesitation is all a carpet salesman needs. Despite his considerable girth, he appeared next to me in a fraction of a second, grabbed my elbow and pulled me into his store.

As if on cue, all the lights went on and the store immediately shone with brilliant illumination. From nowhere there appeared two young men who busied themselves pulling carpets out from the huge rolls stacked next to all four walls. I was gently lowered into a comfortable chair in the middle of it all with the manager standing next to me, smiling and directing the traffic of the two hard-working young men.

They removed carpet after carpet until they found, deep in the stack, one of the same color and size as the carpet upon which I had cast my sidelong glance. This one they unrolled before me, looking at me as if it was time I said something. At this point I was at a loss. I really didn't want to look at carpets, but here I was. The two young men were panting from their work, and sweat had broken out on their foreheads. The manager motioned quickly with his hands, said something, and the two went back to work. They tore down nearly all of the carpets on a different wall until they reached another low-lying carpet that they pulled out and unrolled. This process was repeated several times.

What was I doing here? I only wanted to kill some time after lunch by looking at the shops near the lobby, and now I was sitting here in this brightly lit store looking at carpets I didn't want to buy and was desperately trying to think of a graceful way out and back to the safety of my room. I began to feel a bit anxious. These guys had by now invested a lot of labor to show me carpets. They were panting and sweating, and the manager kept egging them on to show me more carpets. They unrolled them on top of each other, and by now the flattened unrolled carpets stacked on top of each other had reached at least four or five inches.

What to do? What to do? And so I did the first thing you should never do in a situation like this: I shortlisted the carpets by pointing out likes and dislikes, color choices, and so on. The manager was delighted. He told the two workers to remove several carpets, which they did by rolling them up and stacking them up by the walls again—now panting and sweating even more.

By this time I was pretty desperate since I realized I had taken the process a fateful step too far. Before me were at least five shortlisted (and beautiful) carpets, which I would not under any circumstance be buying. So I made the second mistake—I told the manager that I was traveling back to Africa after this trip and I didn't have any means to transport a carpet this large on the plane, and on and on. "I'm really sorry," I said, "but I like this carpet in particular; do you have a card so I can get in touch with you when I get back to the states in a month or so? I really wish you had a smaller version of this particular carpet."

That last part was the clincher. The manager barked out orders to his men and they went back to work, now appearing to be exhausted. They hauled out carpet after carpet, and finally found a small one that they unrolled—yep, it was the same one I had shortlisted but in a much smaller version. It was a beautiful carpet to be sure, but I wasn't in the market for one. I had just wanted to take a look.

I was now resigned to my fate, so I made fatal mistake number three; I asked how much he wanted for the small carpet. Oh, the manager knew he had me by then. I, on the other hand, had frantically thought about how to regain the strategic advantage. I had to get out of there, so I tried to come up with something quick. Here's how it went down:

"This carpet is one of the finest—it comes from a special region in Pakistan, and it has at least 350 knots per square inch. It is the absolute best quality. But, woe to me, I have large family and I have not made sale for one week. I need to sell today or my family will suffer. For you, therefore, I will sell below cost—only $2,500 for this carpet."

I gulped. You kidding me? "You can't be serious, $2,500 is so way out of the realm of even the remotest possibility," I said, thinking I was maybe getting some of the control back. The manager wrung his hands, got a really worried look on his face, and exhibited pain in his body language because he was really thinking about his family and his (in)ability to feed them.

"For you I do special favor, please no tell to anyone, but you can have carpet for only $2,200," he whispered in my ear. I now knew I had regained at least some measure of control—so I made mistake number 3. I counteroffered. "I tell you what," I said, "I am going to give one offer for this carpet, and one offer only," thinking that my offer would be so low that he would never consider it. "I will pay $400 US for that carpet," I said and waited for his reaction. He just stared at me. Silence …. more silence … and then I started to squirm. I swear I saw a tear in his eye and he just shook his head in disbelief. It was a very uncomfortable moment. The two helpers were off in a corner with incredulous looks on their faces, shaking their heads in disbelief as well. The manager finally broke the spell. "Please, the very lowest I can go is $1,900. I have already paid the rug makers more than $2,000 for this carpet."

I steeled my resolve and said, "No, $400 is my one and only offer. I will not negotiate." The manager stared at me in silence, again with pained looks. He shook his head again and told me thanks for visiting his humble store, but that was, essentially, an unacceptable counteroffer. I stood up and finally got out of there with some of my dignity intact.

This was day two. We had another two days to go. The carpet store was located in the lobby and every time I went out or came in I had to pass his store. He was always on the lookout for me. I noticed that my carpet was now proudly displayed in the window so I couldn't avoid looking at it every time I passed by. Once when I was on my way out he came rushing after me and said, "Please, I think it over, price now is $1,700. Final offer, please." I responded, "$400, final offer." This was repeated at least three times and final price dropped to $1,200. Every time I said, "$400, final offer," he just stood there dejected with a pained look on his face.

Day three came and went, and day four arrived. It was time to leave. I packed my bags and headed for the lobby to check out. And there he was, the manager and his two helpers. He rushed back into the shop and came back with a package and paperwork. He was all smiles, opened the package and, yep, it was the carpet all right. He resealed the package and handed it to me saying: "Pay the money." "What?" I said, "My final offer was $400, not a penny more." "That's my final offer too," he said. "Pay the money."

After all of the haggling with this brilliant salesman I finally realized I had lost and I dug out my credit card and purchased the darned thing. I had no idea how I would transport this back to Africa and then on to the US, but nevertheless, I was now the proud owner of a small Pakistani carpet with at least 350 knots per square inch purchased for the princely sum of $400. Ah, I thought, this will be worth at least double that in the US.

Fast forward several years; we were back in Idaho and in the midst of doing some redecorating of our home. This involved making several visits to Spokane, Washington, some 90 miles to the north, to check out some Persian carpets that would be a perfect fit for our living room. Hey, I thought, vividly remembering my Peshawar experience with a certain rotund carpet salesman, why not get my little Pakistani carpet assessed? So I hauled it up to the experts to ask what they thought it was worth. They looked at intently, counted the knots, and came up with a determination: $400 is the maximum worth of this carpet. And this was several years later, so the prices would have gone up substantially since I purchased it. To my horror, I was told I had probably paid at least double for the carpet than I should have.

Well, so be it. I take solace in the fact that at least I stood my ground with the $400 offer. A bit of patience on his part yielded him a 100% profit, I estimate. I really hope he paid a good portion of that to his helpers who really worked hard and, actually … were great actors.

TRAVELING IN VIETNAM

I was in Vietnam in 1990 to work on a WFP (World Food Programme) project. My task manager, Giuseppe Topa, an Italian who was with FAO (Food and Agricultural Organization in Rome) at the time, became a very good friend with whom I still stay in touch. He later moved to Washington, D.C. to work for the World Bank, and I collaborated with him many times in West Africa after the Vietnam experience. He is one of those very elegant and suave Italians with that distinct accent that people everywhere find so charming. Not only is he perfectly fluent in English, but also in French and Spanish. As a professional forester, he is one of the most competent individuals I have ever worked with, which is why he soon rose to become the head forester in the World Bank for Africa.

It was in mid-July when we were in Vietnam, and the likelihood of war in the Persian Gulf was increasing every hour. The entire world was on edge; people were reluctant to fly because of hijacking threats, and our team didn't know if we had the green light until the last moment. We finally got the word and headed to Bangkok, which was the only place we could get our visas to Vietnam. As the only US passport holder on the team, I had to get special permission to undertake this mission as a part of an international team, since the diplomatic relationship with Vietnam hadn't yet been formalized. We spent a couple of days in Bangkok getting the visas, and finally we were on the plane en route to Hanoi.

We arrived in Hanoi at the end of a very long exhausting journey. As we waited in the arrival hall for our suitcases to emerge, I noticed not one, but several rats scurrying between the legs of waiting passengers and along the walls, disappearing into holes and then reappearing to scurry around some more. I was told not to worry—rats apparently were abundant in Hanoi. It was impossible to control the infestation, they said, so they lived and let live.

We headed for the hotel. It was raining and cold, for which I was not prepared. Giuseppe had to loan me a sweater so I could stay warm. The hotel was supposedly one of the best in Hanoi, but for us westerners, it certainly wasn't. I would have given it only a one star had I been in the ratings business—there was only occasional electricity and virtually no hot water. At night sleep evaded me because the walls were infested with rats. Back and forth they scurried, with only a thin layer of sheetrock separating them from me. I checked every conceivable nook and cranny in my room and plugged every minute hole I could find before going to bed every night. But, sleep was still impossible—the rats were just too menacing.

We had four days of high-level political meetings in Hanoi before we were to head into the field to plan the project tentatively budgeted at $30 million. It was a WFP project to plant fuelwood trees in all eight regions of the country. I was the economist on the team tasked with the responsibility of determining the economic and financial feasibility of the proposed activities.

The meetings with the Vietnamese hierarchy were an experience in diplomacy. It was very clear that they really wanted the $30 million and so they rolled out the red carpet. There were lots of handshakes, lots of flowery language, and lots of accolades for the team members. We were all showered with small gifts and treated to elaborate banquets every day.

Together we planned the trip in detail, with the four of us on one side of a table and at least twenty of them on the other side. Each team member was asked what kinds of questions he would likely be asking, so they could prepare the field for our arrival in each region as we traveled south. We were to visit each region, spend at least a day and a half in each, meet and greet dignitaries, visit existing forestry plantations, and conduct interviews with local villagers. Everything was perfectly organized. An entourage of at least six Vietnamese foresters, administrators, engineers, and sociologists were to accompany us on the entire trip from Hanoi in the north to Ho Chi Minh City (the old Saigon) in the south.

The six Vietnamese were easy going, laughed aloud at jokes, patted us on the back, and spoke reasonably good English. They singled me out, however, because for some inexplicable reason they thought I was the spitting image of Mikhail Gorbachev. They even wanted to paint his characteristic birthmark on my forehead. At the banquets we attended as we traveled through the eight regions, they even reached the point of jokingly introducing me as Mr. Gorbachev to the hosting regional delegation of dignitaries.

Hanoi was the city in the first region, so after our initial diplomacy meetings we prepared ourselves for the fieldwork. High on our agenda was to meet and interview some fuelwood vendors in the city itself, so we could get a better feel for how the market functioned, the reliability of supplies, and price fluctuations. So off we went for our interviews. Oh, what a circus this turned out to be. We found a local fuelwood market and greeted the vendor, a diminutive man with a nervous tick that worsened when he realized what was happening. In Vietnam at that time the fuelwood market was closely controlled, all prices were fixed, and supplies were closely monitored.

Of course, all fuelwood vendors had found innovative ways to bypass the heavy hand of the government and earn some money on the side in thriving fuelwood black markets. This particular vendor was no exception, I assumed, so I wasn't surprised when he reacted by clamming up to an entourage of at least six Vietnamese officials, TV cameras, plus at least 200 onlookers who had gathered around us as I began to conduct the interview.

I was exasperated by this circus and tried to talk my Vietnamese counterparts into getting rid of the TV cameras, disbursing the crowd, and then for themselves to get out of the way. This, of course, was like herding cats. The TV crews moved away just a bit but then kept on rolling. This was news. The crowds moved some but then jockeyed for position until they were all as close to us as they had been before. It was impossible, so I gave up on getting any meaningful interviews. The poor vendor was scared out of his wits and probably anticipated going to jail or worse for engaging in black market activities (he probably assumed the authorities had sought him out because they believed he was guilty).

We learned very valuable lessons that first day, which we began to apply as we traveled south. Our Vietnamese counterparts had learned too, that no interviewee could be "random," they would have to be selected beforehand and briefed on the kinds of questions they would be asked and the answers they were to give. We, on the other hand, had learned that we should not conduct interviews with anyone our Vietnamese handlers selected. We rightly suspected that these "random interviewees" had been cherry picked beforehand and fed the right answers to all of the questions we would ask.

Everything was suspect. The dynamic between us and our handlers became pretty hilarious. They suspected that we suspected what they were doing, and we suspected that they suspected we were playing games with them. Our questions to their interviewees were perfunctory; then we would turn our attention to others around us to whom we would ask questions in private and without intimidation from our handlers. We did indeed get some good information from these people.

It was obvious that they were trying to rig things. While we were conducting the interviews our handlers listened intently to each question and soon realized that the same range of questions would be asked as we traveled between regions. In the beginning we received different answers to these questions; some would strengthen our decision to recommend the implementation of the project while other responses would not. Our handlers took copious notes, and we began to notice that some of them were absent from the inevitable banquet every night. It became obvious that they had traveled each night to the next province, selected and mobilized "random" interviewees, and coached them on the answers to give; answers strongly favoring the funding and implementation of the project.

To make a long story short, my handler that day took detailed notes as he always did, disappeared a couple of days, and then re-appeared two regions later to rejoin me as my handler. Well, we encountered the next "random" local interviewee and sat down to begin the questioning. Lo and behold, this semi-literate farmer interviewee responded perfectly to every question, including the question on when they harvested trees. He spoke eloquently about the Faustmann formulation—known to and used only by forest economists—as if it were something he had applied his entire lifetime. I glanced at my handler, but he studiously avoided me by keeping his focus on his notebook, writing furiously.

Our visit to Vietnam also coincided with the launching of the first Gulf War to liberate Kuwait from Iraq. When we weren't working we were in the car listening intently to our short wave radios—Voice of America, BBC, and other news outlets—to keep up with the news. The US launch of the war was imminent, and we wanted to know about it the moment it happened. I remember sitting in the car and discussing all of this with my team members. We all had different opinions on whether or not this would actually happen.

As we reached the summit and before we began the descent down the mountainside to Da Nang, BBC came on with breaking news—the US had launched the Gulf War. On the broadcast we heard the deafening roar of the fighter jets taking off from the aircraft carriers. At the crescendo of this loud moment on the radio, in which we were totally absorbed, we reached the summit—the border for entry into the next region. The car convoy slowed down, and an intense barrage of fireworks suddenly exploded all around us all. The entire team instinctively hit the floor of the vehicle—it had been a total surprise and instantly transported us into the Kuwait war zone. The fireworks kept popping, but after a while we regained our senses. Finally we peeked out the windows to see at least thirty smiling faces plus TV cameras bearing down on us. It was the delegation of dignitaries from the next region who had decided to greet us right at the summit border with loud celebrations. Behind us, our six handlers stepped out of their vehicle and joined their colleagues from the next region in line. We sheepishly exited our vehicle to meet and greet the dignitaries.

That night we attended the obligatory banquet where enormous amounts of food and drink were served, attended also by the ubiquitous TV camera crews. Worse, they showed the TV footage from the mountain summit and, there in clear view was our team ducking instinctively inside the car as the fireworks kicked off, followed by the sheepish expressions on our faces as we got out of the vehicle to greet the delegation.

The favorite beverage at the banquet was vodka and Johnny Walker Black whisky. Toasts were offered by everyone, and they were dutifully televised. Glasses were filled and refilled until all of us had bleary eyes and slurred speech. The game at each of the banquets we were obliged to attend had degenerated to a tacit competition over who would still be standing—our team or the Vietnamese. I quickly learned to respond to their bottoms-up 100% admonition accompanying each toast, by always saying "10%" meaning that 10% would be consumed by yours truly, not bottoms-up. After much teasing and scolding, I finally got away with it.

The Da Nang banquet had another distinction that stands out in my memory. The Vietnamese dignitaries were a bit older than the ones we had encountered in other regions, and their English was limited. Some of them spoke French, however. They paired me with an older and very distinguished lady who preferred to speak French, so I did my duty and engaged her in conversation. Well, we soon got into a discussion about the Vietnam War, and it came out that this lady had been a hostess for Jane Fonda when she did her treasonous tour in Vietnam. Up until then I had enjoyed conversation with this dignified lady, but that soon ended. I couldn't wait to get out of there and move on to the next province. I admit it: I intensely dislike Jane Fonda and everything she did during those days.

It became abundantly clear that the Vietnamese people were very industrious and smart. All of our handlers were from North Vietnam and were often referred to as bunker people. Most of them had grown up in underground bunkers constructed during the war years to protect themselves from the bombing attacks. I was the only American on the team, so it was very difficult for me to relate to them — the enemy — in the beginning. But it worked out well. My similarity to Mr. Gorbachev intrigued them, and that quickly broke the ice. As we traveled through small towns on the way south, the Gulf War became a favorite conversation topic. I know they were thinking about the days when the war had been in their own backyard. The Gulf War brought the past back to them in very clear focus.

In Vietnam as in Africa, nothing is wasted. In many children's playgrounds we saw merry-go-rounds fitted with old hollowed out bomb casings with seats inside them instead of the usual horse seats. Also notable were the fortified bomb craters which had been made into ponds for aquaculture operators. These ponds littered the landscape.

We wrote our report and it did favor the implementation of the project. From my perspective the proposed plantation activities were economically feasible, so as soon as the bureaucratic hurdles had been surmounted, they mobilized and began planting the trees to the exact specifications we had recommended. This included the selection of species, planting density, and harvesting at financial maturity, not biological maturity. If there's anything to learn from a communist regime, it is that whatever the government says you must do, you do it to the letter. Otherwise, capitalism is alive and well in Vietnam at the local levels, yet under the table!

CHAPTER 8: CARIBBEAN AND EUROPE

RIDGE-TO-REEF

Toward the end of my international consulting career, I had the privilege of working on several occasions in the Caribbean region, jetting from one island to another. I was on assignments that focused on preserving the integrity of the coral reefs around Jamaica and around many other islands in the region.

Now, what do I know about coral reefs? Not much is the short answer, but I am an economist, and we do have a lot of things to say about just about everything. My lack of knowledge of coral reefs was not a hindrance at all, so I wasn't unhappy about having been asked to work there. I got to travel to all of the most sought-after vacation spots in the world, and got paid to do it. How can you top that?

The ecological integrity of coral reefs is an indicator of how well the management of watersheds draining into the coastal areas is being done. Poor management adversely affects the reefs, good ecological management sustains them. Destructive land use management and overgrowth of tourism without proper management of the increased sewage loads will slowly but surely destroy the coral reefs. Tourism destroys tourism over time. It is a balancing act—too many tourists

result in crowding and ecological problems; too few stifle the economic well-being of the area. The existence of the reefs is one of the reasons
tourists come, and at that time they were in danger of becoming severely damaged.

I didn't have to be an expert on coral reefs, but I did need to understand the different kinds of land use management that would: a)
increase incomes for the participants, and b) minimize the ecological
damages inflicted upon the fragile coral reefs. I happily joined the team
of experts as the economist, blended in with the tourists, and stayed in
the great all-inclusive hotels while trying to get some work done. I am
a lousy tourist anyway, so I very much appreciated having some work
to do while in a tourist environment. I confess that to lie on the beach
for a whole day would bore me to tears. Five minutes of that is about
my limit, and then I would have to actually do something.

The work on these two USAID projects — the Jamaica Ridge-to-Reef
project and the Caribbean Regional Program — was interesting. We
conducted many interviews with farmers, foresters, and fishermen
in order to gather the data needed for the analyses. Out of this came
numerous recommendations on the alternatives these land users and
fishermen could pursue while earning a better living and preserving
the ecological integrity of the coral reefs.

One rather obscure alternative economic pursuit we recommended for upstream watershed farmers — the group that caused the most
siltation into the watershed drainage — was to harvest bat guano from
the literally dozens of accessible caves which all had huge populations
of bats. This extremely valuable fertilizer had accumulated over many
years and was prime for the taking. I was actually brave enough to
enter one of these caves through a small, well-hidden entrance behind
thick brush. It led into a large hall-like "reception area" with several
vertical hollows, all filled with sleeping bats. It truly was a creepy experience as we followed one of the small adjoining caves deep into the
mountain, treading gingerly on the valuable fertilizer along the way,
trying not to wake the sleeping hordes of bats. While inside the cave
my overactive imagination was giving me visions of blood-sucking
rabid bats descending upon me in fury for encroaching on their turf.

But I got out of there in one piece and headed to the hotel for at least two showers just to feel clean again. At that time I was grateful that I wasn't the one to be told that harvesting bat guano would be a very attractive economic opportunity for me. I couldn't have spent even one minute more in that claustrophobic cave full of what I perceived to be evil birds.

To make matters worse, in checking the market price for bat guano we discovered that the price was dominated by a thriving marijuana market in the US and Jamaica. The growers needed this fertilizer and paid premium prices for it. Well, this moved us into gray areas, so we first recommended this activity with a lot of qualifiers before we lost all courage and abandoned it altogether.

What looks good on paper, however, isn't necessarily so in reality. Two of our recommendations for the fishers were: a) sea moss farming, and b) aquaculture. The Jamaican fishermen had been overfishing for decades, which resulted in very poor catches from traditional fishing banks. It was time to let these areas recuperate in order to bring the fish population up, so fishing wouldn't disappear completely from the important industries in the islands.

Sea moss (Irish moss) farming occurs in calm seawater about 1-1.5 meters deep. The plant grows outward from a rope suspended in the sea and is used as an ingredient in many different and familiar food products. Aquaculture is simply fresh water fish farming. Both activities were deemed strongly economically feasible, and all of the fishermen we interviewed voiced their support for such fine recommendations. Indeed, they said they would organize themselves into cooperatives and launch sea moss and aquaculture activities in and around all of the bays in Jamaica while greatly cutting down on the fishing.

The fishermen, however, were all Rastafaris who loved reggae music and worshipped the deposed Emperor of Ethiopia, Haile Selassie. These were my clients, so to speak—the ones who needed alternative economic opportunities to augment their incomes while allowing the fishery resources to be restored. So imagine this: I, the consultant, am on the beach wearing my baseball hat, notebook in hand, accompanied by one of my team members, and interviewing twenty or so Rastafari fishermen with their dreadlocks and beards and listening intently to my every question. I took copious notes as they responded with answers that aligned very well with the recommendations we already had in mind. I concluded that this section of the report would be easy.

Gradually, however, it dawned on me that what we were talking about was all counterfeit. I was noticing a persistent and very distinct smell emanating from the group surrounding us. Good grief … it finally dawned on me (I am pretty slow in these matters), these guys were all stoned. Indeed they were, yet they were very lucid at the same time. I knew instantly that these guys would never get into sea moss farming or aquaculture, nor would they continue to pursue fishing, which had been their main vocation before. No, the most lucrative industry these days was ganja (marijuana) farming. This we had learned from interviews with others; we just hadn't connected the dots to discover that the fishermen were the ones heavily engaged in this industry. They were the growers and harvesters of marijuana, doing midnight runs with their fishing pirogues to haul bales of the stuff outside the twelve-mile international coastal boundaries to offload onto waiting boats. They didn't need the additional income; they already made plenty from the drug traffic.

Nevertheless, the sea moss and aquaculture recommendations remained in the report for the USAID readers and project planners, even though we knew that the income from drug trafficking would far outstrip the alternatives. But who knows, now some twenty-five years later it is entirely possible that conditions may have changed and that some fishermen may be engaged in both sea moss farming and aquaculture farming, making decent money. I'll ask around next time I am in Jamaica.

PICKLED PARROT

An X-rated story from Jamaica follows, so beware. Our team tried to eat lunch at different restaurants every day, so one Saturday in Negril, we chose the Pickled Parrot. It was located on the coast right by caves which were used as hiding places for Jamaican pirates. There was a sheltered bay with diving boards, swinging ropes, and water slides for tourists who might want a dip before lunch.

We arrived around 11:30 so the restaurant wasn't full yet. The scenery was breathtaking, the water crystal clear and inviting, and we all thought of taking a swim before eating. But the menu arrived so we abandoned any thoughts of swimming. Sitting in the shade under the restaurant awning, enjoying a view of the water and all the activities going on promised to be a very pleasant experience.

As we sat there and chatted while waiting for the food, we saw a huge catamaran approaching the bay where the Pickled Parrot was located. It was still far off, and we couldn't make out any details; there wasn't much wind, so they were motoring. Closer and closer they came, and it increasingly attracted our attention because the boat was so huge and something was going on the deck and in the cockpit.

As they came nearer we saw that the activity we had discerned on board was people moving about. Strange, we thought; do they all wear uniforms? We couldn't yet figure out why the color of their uniforms was so similar. Closer and closer they came, and then we all exclaimed in unison: "Oh no. They are all stark naked." We could finally make out the name of the boat: *Hedonism II*. Immediately it all made sense. The catamaran belonged to the infamous hotel that sported a nude beach up the coast a bit. Of course, they used the boat for excursions.

Sure enough, the catamaran was filled to the brim with, I'm not exaggerating here, probably a hundred or more stark naked people ranging in age from twenty to thirty. As soon as they reached an anchoring place in the bay, all one hundred of them (most of them were Germans) dove into the water and swam to shore. They climbed the stairs by the restaurant and began to use the water slides and swinging ropes to amuse themselves.

And so there we were, our fully clad team of five watching this incredible spectacle, squeezing mustard and ketchup and pickles out of our hamburgers and onto our pants without noticing. A few of the Germans tried to enter the restaurant but the owner said that it was off limits. This was an eating area, he said, and not entirely suitable for mass nudity.

The frolicking continued for at least half an hour, actually making us uncomfortable about being the only clothed people around. The restaurant owner told us that they came there every Saturday to use the water facilities. Well, we happened to be there just at that time. I certainly had no knowledge of what was about to happen, but upon reflection, I am beginning to suspect that our Caribbean counterpart did know, and that's why he recommended the Pickled Parrot that day.

I have often thought that I probably should have left the restaurant, but I didn't, nor did my team members. We had ordered the hamburgers and eaten half of them, but hadn't paid the bill yet, so we stayed. When some of the naked Germans asked us some questions I became aware of how awkward it is to strike up a conversation with a totally naked person.

As of this writing, I think the Pickled Parrot in Jamaica has gone out of business, but *Hedonism II* hasn't. I wonder where they take their catamaran tours of frolicking naked German tourists every Saturday these days. If you find out, don't tell me. Having that experience once is more than enough.

ALBANIAN PARANOIA

In my work in developing countries I often had to team up with consultants and donor organizations from different countries. So, I found myself in Europe frequently meeting with the Dutch, the Brits, the French, the Swiss, and others, all in the quest of solving development problems in Africa. The Third World development community in natural resources management is fairly small, and most of the folks knew each other and collaborated on projects. We held think tank-like workshops, shared experiences, ironed out conflicting approaches in different countries, and learned a great deal from each other.

But, I also had a chance to work in a few European developing countries: Bulgaria and Albania. Bulgaria was a poor and backward country behind the iron curtain when I made my one and only visit there at the beginning of my international career. Since then, however, it has quickly developed into a vibrant and dynamic economy, more so than the neighboring western European countries. Albania, on the other hand, was far worse, even after communism had collapsed a decade later than it did in Bulgaria. I can only speculate, but I think this is because the climb up to even a semblance of economic viability was so long and steep that it took a lot longer.

I had the occasion to work in Albania for one eye-opening week in 1994 to develop a proposal for a USAID forestry project in that country. Certainly, the same observations I made for the Russian Far East could also apply to Albania: the infrastructure was in bad need of repair or replacement, the people were desperately poor with little opportunity for meaningful employment, and the queues to buy anything were long and time consuming. But the differences were much deeper. Albania had been ruled for decades by one of the most paranoid Marxist-Leninist presidents ever: Enver Hoxha, a staunch communist who managed to alienate all allies in the Soviet Empire and China. North Korea was the only remaining friend he had before the regime collapsed. The country was hermetically sealed off from any interaction with the outside world — even Italy, its closest neighbor just forty-five short miles across the Adriatic Sea. After communism collapsed in Albania in 1992, it was a day of awakening for Albanians to discover how the surrounding world had moved on while they were left behind in a hopelessly underdeveloped state.

Upon arrival in Tirana, the capitol, my colleague and I opted to rent a furnished apartment downtown instead of checking into any of the few hotels accommodating the foreigners. We had been told that this was a much better arrangement and that the apartments were priced competitively with the hotels. The apartment owners were among the super-rich in Tirana. Very few had the means to own anything. When the foreigners came they would vacate their apartments and live with their relatives for the duration. The relatives would then share in the revenues generated from the rental arrangement — win-win for everyone.

The only problem was that the apartment was located on the top floor of a six-story apartment block with no elevator, maybe 150 square feet in size with one small bedroom, a sleeper sofa, and a tiny kitchenette. This was small to us, but to the owners, floor space this immense was pure luxury. Moving in with their relatives who made do with an apartment about 120 square feet in size was nothing but a small inconvenience. But for us, the small apartment was far better than what we could have expected from a tiny room at an overcrowded hotel.

We slept and cooked in this apartment while taking daily excursions to the field with our Albanian counterparts and getting small glimpses into what life under Hoxha had been like. First, the paranoia of being invaded was manifested in the Albanian landscape. Around the perimeter of any town and in the rural landscape itself the land was littered with concrete and steel bunker "bubble" defense installations. An estimated 700,000 of them were built and manned during Hoxha's regime. Since then, their most popular use has been as convenient places for trysts among young Albanians.

Second, the paranoia was manifested further in the farm fields. Tightly spaced inside the cornfields, for example, were spikes with sharp tips facing upward, designed to impale paratroopers as they landed. It truly was a bizarre sight.

Third, the people had lived in constant fear of not only the authorities, but also of family, friends, and co-workers. Everyone was spying on everyone. People could not hold normal conversations for fear of being reported for real or perceived infractions. Children in the schools had been shown TV test patterns and asked which patterns they recognized. And when they picked one, the family would get a visit from the authorities. The authorities now had proof from the school children themselves that they had been watching Italian television, which was forbidden. They needed to be punished with prison and hard labor, or worse.

Every adult we met during our week in Albania had had similar experiences. The authorities, fully aware that people had clandestinely watched Italian TV, mounted campaigns to convince them that what they saw was staged to derail them from what they clearly knew from propaganda: that the Albanian way of life was paradise on earth.

CHAPTER 9: ECONOMIC DEVELOPMENT LESSONS

What did I learn about development work in twenty-five years as an economist while I endeavored to improve the lot of the poorest-of-the-poor? What are some of the eye-opening facts about aid to developing countries that should be more available to taxpayers who ultimately foot the bill? The following lessons are limited to my own experiences which, I grant, may be a bit dated. But I stay in contact with my former development professional colleagues, so I know that the issues haven't changed a great deal. They still discuss the same problems and offer the same solutions.

Few of my colleagues are economists, even though in my considered and highly biased opinion, economists are by far the most important. Many of my colleagues gravitated to work in development because they were ex-Peace Corps volunteers. They had signed up for one- to two-year stints in the Peace Corps, so they knew the local (tribal) languages as well as French or Spanish or both. They also knew the cultures, and therefore had a significant competitive advantage in doing development work. Their solutions to development problems would typically involve government-to-government or NGO aid. A donor's *raison d'être* was to provide the funding for good development ideas, and to keep funding projects that worked well.

The crazy idea I had—that development aid should only prime the pump and get things up and running—didn't really enter their consciousness as a viable solution. And so, we had some lively discussions when we worked together in the field. My development experience didn't evolve from a Peace Corps background but from my interest in Third World development viewed through an economics lens. I strongly believe in the notion that all developing countries and individual recipients of project aid must keenly focus on weaning themselves from a dependence on foreign aid.

ECONOMICS AND POLITICS

The politics of development aid trumps economic feasibility analysis of proposed project activities. That lesson was learned early on. My job, of course, was to estimate the feasibility of specific proposed activities, and not to delve into the realm of politics. Somehow, however, I managed to skew things enough that the decision-makers became aware of alternative solutions. A case in point: fifty-two classified forests in Côte d'Ivoire, a fairly significant World Bank-funded project, were supposed to be rich reservoirs of species diversity of both flora and fauna, but as so often happens in many countries, the budgets were woefully inadequate and the forests didn't receive any management attention. Many were degraded because of encroachment by farmers who established clandestine cocoa plantations and other crops inside the forests to augment seriously degraded farmlands near their villages.

This is a fact of life in Africa. The government-owned protected classified forests were far more productive than the adjacent depleted farmland, because they were protected by law. Incremental encroachment was inevitable, even though it was illegal. The government simply didn't have the means to keep the neighboring villagers out. Every now and then they went on campaigns to kick them out, which caused big problems and often violence.

European donors had provided the initial funding for teams to visit these forests and prepare detailed management plans for each one.

They had done this with environmental-purist teams and did not engage the services of economists. The plans, of course, called for chasing the villagers out of the forests and restoring the currently occupied and degraded lands to the propagation of indigenous species to enhance the biodiversity of the forests. After many months of intense work, the World Bank agreed to fund the implementation of the management plans for the fifty-two forests. I was called in as the economist to effectively rubber stamp what had already been decided before full-scale implementation could begin.

This is the political reality of development aid. As a project moves down the planning pipeline it becomes increasingly difficult to dislodge. The political expectations for approval become almost impossible to overcome. When the economist arrives on the scene late in the game (as is the case more often than not), the pressure is on to demonstrate feasibility where there often is none. Some analysts cave to the political pressures and run scenarios that essentially rubber stamp feasibility.

I crunched the management plan numbers exactly as they were and discovered that if implemented as designed, all fifty-two natural forests would be economic disasters. Not only would zero revenues be forthcoming, but the costs would be prohibitive because the Ivorian forest service (SODEFOR) would have to beef up protection of the forests against encroachment by nearby villagers. The management plans had been designed by the biological diversity purists without any account taken of the economic realities associated with their plans. Biodiversity, we must all understand, is the Holy Grail — the science is settled (as the saying goes) and any contrary argument will be quickly dismissed.

And so, I was politely asked: "Are you sure your cost assumptions aren't too high?" "Aren't there 'in-kind' revenues that can be counted?" Their (slightly skewed) objective was to suggest cost reductions and/or revenue increases so we could assume that economic feasibility was in hand for all of the forests as dictated by the management plans, with implementation soon to take place and (politically) expected.

Trying to "obey," I re-crunched the numbers with different sets of assumptions, and none were feasible. Since I wasn't about to sacrifice any professional integrity on the altar of political expediency, however, I had to try something else. The management plans were not about to be revisited or redone; that much was clear from the donors who had funded them. I had to think of an alternative approach to reach economic feasibility, without doing any significant damage to the management plans.

Teak was the answer. Working on this project I had come across many recent reports about the very strong export market for teak poles and logs. There were several Asian buyers who were buying up every-thing that was produced. This wasn't just a blip in the present—the market had been strong for decades and there was no indication of any slowdown.

1. Fact: The foresters told me that many of the fifty-two classified forests in the country could produce fast-growing teak logs.

2. Fact: All of the forests had an average encroachment of approx-imately 5 percent of the land area in a degraded state.

3. My idea (brilliant, if I may say so): Instead of chasing the farm-ers out and reclaiming the five percent for biodiversity purpos-es, why not invite the farmers back in under contract to manage teak plantations instead?

So I re-crunched the numbers with just one change in the man-agement plans—commercial growth of teak on the degraded lands in each forest by farmers under contract, rather than propagating bio-diversity on this land. A huge change in the results was generated. Allowing some minimal commercial activity on the degraded land solved two problems.

The first: Growing teak on the already-small percentage of degraded land inside the forests was sufficient to secure economic feasibility in the aggregate (all fifty-two forests) managed in accordance with the (purist) management plans without having to incur any costs of restoring the degraded lands. The second: By contracting with the farmers to man-age the plantations, the farmers would be economically better off, and the government would not have to incur additional staff or equipment costs to protect the plantations from the neighboring villagers. The only negative was the sacrifice by the purists of the biodiversity on the tiny portion of degraded lands they had so carefully planned to restore.

Another example from forestry: A recommended tree plantation project by foresters or biodiversity experts would typically include species, planting density, and harvest timing — typically at biological maturity. An economist would then be invited to an already-set table to examine the economic feasibility. Many analysts would run the numbers on this one scenario alone and call it good. Sometimes the scenario would be marginally economically feasible.

As in the case of the fifty-two classified forests, however, there are always alternative scenarios.

1. First, foresters will recommend species A because it is biologically best suited to the site. An economist will suggest species B or C in addition which may be slightly less biologically suitable, but much more valuable in the marketplace.

2. Second, the foresters may recommend a 3-by-3 meter spacing between the trees (again for biological reasons), but an economist might suggest a 4-by-4 meter spacing to allow for crops to be growing between the trees for at least the first two years in order to generate short-term revenues.

3. Third, the foresters will recommend harvesting at biological maturity at thirty years; an economist might recommend harvesting at financial maturity, say at twenty years.

All of these different scenarios would provide a range of results that gave decision-makers several options, often leading to implementation choices different from the environmentally purist options.

The lesson: decision makers must be made aware of alternative solutions. In these cases, a small sacrifice of the integrity of the management plans would move the project from not feasible to feasible.

DEPENDANCE ON AID

In the collective opinion of most development experts, a good project is one that deserves continued funding for phase two and probably beyond. I would tend to disagree with this based on my conviction that the recipient countries were becoming dependent on infusions of foreign aid. A project requiring funding beyond phase one should most likely be viewed as a failure.

An economist's major task should be to work himself out of a job over the long term. No recipient country should need outside assistance in perpetuity; nor should any country ever allow itself to get into the position of becoming totally dependent upon foreign aid. Most African countries have done precisely this, particularly the West African countries. That's why it was so refreshing to hear Thomas Sankara's development aid philosophy for Burkina Faso: "We have to wean ourselves from dependence on foreign aid, rise to the task and do it ourselves."

Sankara's vision was unlike that of any other African president. Donors have suitcases full of money to give away, and the host countries are eager to receive them. Whatever the donors are willing to fund is always welcomed by recipient countries. Some accept funding from different donors for similar kinds of activities. It isn't unheard of to have one active USAID project in region A and a Japanese-funded similar project in neighbor-region B. Both projects may have similar objectives, but widely different approaches. One could be the preservation of the ecological integrity of the natural forests (region A), while the other for region B could be to eradicate the natural forests and replace it with fast-growing fuelwood plantations. How could these co-exist? They often did, and life went on—the coordination between donors was dismal at best.

Analytically, unlike the majority of economic development analysts, I would build the recurrent costs of a project into the analysis—including the project subsidies—to make sure that when all donor-funding had ended, the effort could continue into the future without any additional infusions of outside money. Otherwise I would be reluctant to demonstrate feasibility.

The lessons:

- Most projects are funded far too long (although we all had a strong incentive to continue our involvement in the project activities), why abandon an obviously successful effort?

- Donors are not coordinating their activities.
- Economists should always build recurrent costs into their feasibility analyses.

DON'T THROW THE BABY OUT WITH THE BATHWATER

Not all donor-funded activities are bad, counter-productive, or a misallocation of resources. Some activities are worthwhile and really make a difference. While a project may, as a whole, receive a failing grade (and many do), there are still nuggets of tremendous value buried within. Out of an expressed intent to benefit thousands (a metric to be evaluated), the project may end up with only a small handful of farmers/villagers who really get it and who then break the vicious cycle of poverty. Is it expedient for the donor to spend millions and get that kind of result? It depends. Yes, when the handful of farmers who get it could then become success stories that others could emulate; no, if we hold to the evaluation metrics of the project. A project evaluator would have to fail the project, given the rules of the game, because the quantifiable result—only 100 farmers succeeding in adopting the technologies and more than doubling their incomes per year—would fall far short of the stated goal of, say 2,000 farmers.

The reality, however, is that the 100 successful farmers could change the development dynamic in a region over the long run. Success or failure cannot be assessed satisfactorily over a time horizon lasting only for as long as the donor decision-makers are in office. It is very much akin to a politician's quest for positive results so long as they occur during his or her tenure in office. Success in an African context was strongly correlated with changes in the local culture—the kinds of changes that transition communities from dependence on external aid to a much greater dependence on their own efforts. Indeed, a few successful farmers could be a very strong catalyst for others who seek similar success in their lives. Some indviduals operating on a subsistence-level existence and faced with a promising new technology would respond with a desire to emulate what the successful farmers do.

One example from Senegal stands out. One subsistence level farmer in a relatively poor region near Dakar had the wherewithal to actually act on advice from Peace Corps Volunteers. Their advice was to do the following: a) irrigate your one hectare and grow vegetables to sell in Dakar (vegetables have a higher market value than do the grain crops); and b) protect your one hectare and greatly increase crop yields by planting *Leucaena leucocephala* all around the field to provide natural windbreak, fertilizer, nitrogen fixation for the soil, livestock fodder from the foliage, and fuelwood from branch pruning.

So, to get his supplies, he visited old project areas in his region where abandoned irrigation components were buried and unused. He dug up enough piping, repaired what had been damaged, and installed it on his one hectare. The system worked. The Peace Corps gave him some *Leucaena* seedlings, which he planted and maintained around his one hectare. He had a few head of cattle that he fed with the *Leucaena* foliage once the trees had reached maturity. By the second season, he was ready to get into vegetable production, focusing on cherry tomatoes and beans.

He met with spectacular success. Not only was his initial crop yield very high because he fertilized his field with composted *Leucaena* leaves and cattle manure, he also harvested two crops the first year, and then three crops per year for all subsequent years. Today, he operates a highly successful vegetable production farm of thirty irrigated hectares, all encircled by productive *Leucaena*-trees, plus an ever-increasing herd of cattle, producing enough manure to compost with the *Leucaena* foliage to add twenty to thirty tons of compost per hectare per year. His bean and tomato crop harvests three times per year per hectare are enormous; he has hired over 200 workers who pack crates of vegetables for export by air to Europe, and the farmer is now a millionaire—in dollars. He sells *Leucaena* seeds to neighboring farmers who now are doing the same thing on a smaller scale but with a view to becoming like him.

So, what may seem like failures early on could indeed prove to be highly successful endeavors in the long run. When this happens, everyone benefits—donor and recipient alike. But alas, the majority of projects or programs fail to generate these kinds of nuggets. I have seen many well-designed projects with good intentions failing miserably because of top-heavy bureaucratic intervention (noise really) from the donor side from beginning to end.

The lesson: There is a disconnect between project design and evaluation metrics. Many projects fail because the evaluation metrics do not match the monies spent. For a $5 million multi-year project complete with a long-term expatriate technical advisory team, vehicles, housing, etc., for example, one would expect results of more significance than what the evaluation metrics confirm. Either the project costs should be drastically reduced, or the evaluation metrics need to be more realistic.

DEMONSTRATION EFFECT

For rural Africans, seeing and meeting with white and foreign consultants from donor organizations meant money … lots of it. They all knew that everyone in the village would benefit greatly from the presence of a project. It was like Christmas when consultant teams arrived on their fact-finding missions. Local people eagerly said things they perceived the donors needed to hear so the region would be selected for a donor-funded project. The mere fact that we were foreigners, especially from the US, created inflated expectations.

In addition to creating expectations with the fact-finding missions, however, the beginning stages of any natural resource management project would also include the potential for the cherished "demonstration effect." Not only would the villagers lobby for a project to be located in their region, we added fuel to the fire by delineating a project region with potential for this deceptively simple effect. The logic is this: if a project activity is successful (doubling crop yields because of project-sponsored intervention, for example), nearby farmers should, under "normal" conditions, have their interest piqued and begin to adopt the technologies themselves. I (unwisely) subscribed to this in the early years because the "insider" development experts considered it an important external benefit of development aid, and I built it into my models in creative ways to analyze the economics of a project.

But after a few years of field experience, I soon learned that the demonstration effect was often strangely absent. We knew from our project implementation *inside* the project region that teaching farmers to do things differently would double their crop yields. This, as the argument goes, should have a powerful demonstration effect for farmers outside the project region. Surely, we thought and articulated in our reports, they would adopt the techniques taught en masse merely by observing what goes on inside the region.

But that does not happen. Most project-sponsored activities involve subsidies, such as making improved seeds and equipment readily available and free to the participating farmers. Farmers *outside* the region observe this and obviously want in on the action. So, if the village is outside the project region, the villagers actually have an incentive to make things worse for now. Since they don't receive any project assistance — the subsidies — which is what they want, why not make it obvious that they should be next in line as the project moves into phase two when the project region will expand? And this happens frequently — showing the donors the growing chasm between villages inside and villages outside the project region. This is what project evaluators will often document. Success *inside* the project region begets the expansion of the region in the second phase of the project so the success spreads. The lesson: The "demonstration effect" is closely related to the temptation to fund a project in perpetuity. The donors are being "played."

These are but a few development lessons I learned. Perhaps I will expand on these in another book with stories told from a field operative's perspective. I can do this now because I no longer have to play the political games that accompany all decisions for or against funding particular activities. Third World economic development today depends on the generosity of bilateral and multilateral donors. Most of my host country counterpart colleagues — the FSNs and professionals working in various minsistries — depend on the continued infusion of donor money for their livelihoods. Were it not for USAID, World Bank, UNDP funding or any other donor funding source, they would not be employed or receive the salaries they do. True, many of them are competent professionals and they earn every penny they get. But unless the system changes to include the assurance that all project activities funded by donors will continue without any further infusions of outside money, the demand for outside funding for economic development will be perpetual.

CHAPTER 10: CONCLUSIONS

Okay, here's my grand finale, aimed first and foremost at my kids and my wife. You've heard these stories over and over again, so you know them by heart. You encouraged me to write them down, so I hope I haven't embellished them too much. It has been fun to reconsider everything and to reflect on these moments of life and what they have meant to me and to us collectively over the years.

But I'm not done yet, so please stay with me as I get to the finish line of this small book. There's a bigger story to be told which I have reserved for last. Besides, I still have some come-clean moments, so here goes.

The story is this: in the preface I said I am a Christian and now, after having written some of my stories and crystallized my thoughts, I fail to understand how some people refuse to believe that the Triune God of the Bible is real. I have concluded that it actually takes a great deal more faith to be an atheist, or even an agnostic, than it does to be a believing Christian. During my travels all over Africa and Asia, I marvel at how God kept me safe during extremely dangerous moments, potential disasters, while flying on airplanes that should have been thrown on the junk heap decades earlier, while traveling on the rural roads in Africa and Asia, and from diseases and robberies. In human terms, the probability of passing through all of this unscathed without God protecting me would be extremely low.

My own walk as a believer hasn't been all smooth. My spiritual growth has been long and steady, but I can't say the learning curve has been particularly steep. In my case I think the seeds were scattered on the edge of the good soil where so many rocks were mixed in that my growth was slow. The good news is that my roots became extremely stubborn—God made sure He had a firm hold on me in fundamental ways. He also knew, however, that there was a lot of baggage He needed to root out and that this would take an inordinate amount of time. That process is still ongoing and will not be completed until after I have left this strange and temporary place for good.

Being a Christian is not a cakewalk. Yes, it completely changed my life over time, my outlook on life, how I dealt with situations as they emerged, how I lived, and how I will die. But we all live in the moment, which is where we fail miserably. I know the things I *should* do, but they are the opposite of what I *actually* do, as Paul says in the seventh chapter of his letter to the Romans. I know I have failed so many times as a Christian, and I often feel that God cannot possibly continue to try to infuse any sort of sense into me.

Of course I'm wrong, but the good news is that God never leaves me; instead I leave Him when I do the dumb things. Just by writing this I realize that my growth has not been optimal in any way; instead it has been (what's the word...?) stubborn. But over time even I have absorbed a fair amount of truth about God, about my own life, about how I fit in as a member of the body.

In my own reasoning, therefore, if someone asked me the question, "If you had to do it all over again, would you change anything?" my response would be a resounding YES. I would indeed want to change many things. In God's reasoning, however, He sees it differently (for which I am grateful). He didn't allow me to receive any of the things on my wish list of changes until late in life. I had to learn lessons, and learn them again and again, until some finally took root and became a part of who I am today. God is the Creator and we the creatures. What He does is perfect, what we do is ... um ... imperfect. Suffice it to say that God's guidance of my walk with Him so far has been perfect—I am exactly where He wants me at this very point of my life. That really is comforting ... to me ... but maybe not to those near me. So here's my coming clean moment, perhaps it is my revised "wish list" of what I would have wanted to do differently.

I started out as a Christian clandestinely. I didn't really want anyone to know that Roger, Judi's brother, had finally succeeded in planting good seed in good soil in Judi back in the early '70s, and then a few weeks later she communicated to me the change that had taken place in her life. The message He communicated to me through Judi then was very simple, and it prompted me to respond too as I was out jogging on a fall day in 1973. This is when I think God planted the tiny, tiny seed that fell on semi-good-but-somewhat-rocky-soil. The fact that I had heard the gospel and responded to it was sufficient.

Contrary to what I had heard—that new Christians want to change the world and shout for joy about their new-found faith—I had the opposite reaction. I didn't want to shout anything from any rooftop, nor was I particularly happy about the disturbance of my internal equilibrium with which I had grown very comfortable. The tiny seed of Christian faith that had entered my life became something of an annoyance to me as it nibbled at the edges of my finely honed and time-tested belief system dating back to my agnostic upbringing in Norway.

But there was a difference—I now believed that a "Supernatural Being" of some sort had created the universe, because that made sense to my intellectual bent. Therefore, I had no problem with the Genesis account of creation in general, except for the six days part. I tucked that enormous leap of faith deep down into my subconscious. So when discussions about this particular phenomenon surfaced, I would change the subject so I could avoid revealing any lack of faith in my newfound Christianity.

But it wasn't only the six-day part that bothered me; it was also all of the miracles that I tucked down deep and kept submerged. I realize now that it was like being in deep water trying to hold a hundred inflated balloons submerged to feign the impression of being a Christian while not revealing the true state of my unbelief. Come to think of it, it is quite stressful to maintain one foot in the Christian world and the other in the secular world simultaneously. While writing this little book my thinking became focused, and I concluded that for many years I had indeed believed all the fundamental truths in the Bible, but probably only cherry-picked that with which I was comfortable. The rest of it—the problem of the existence of evil, Jesus' miracles, literal six-day creation, and so on—I had conveniently tucked away.

God has been extremely gracious to me by showing me my unbelief over time, particularly as I have been writing these memoirs. There is still much baggage to expose, but I am also secure in the knowledge that He will eventually perfect what He has begun. He knows it all—the beginning, the middle, and the end, and He leaves no stone unturned.

Six-day creation, miracles, the problem of the existence of evil, Biblical descriptions and sanctions of wars all now unashamedly reside in my front and center consciousness and are no longer in a submerged state. What happened? Well, it's really simple—first, I am now on my seventh read-through of the entire Bible, from Genesis to Revelation. God does indeed remove the scales from our eyes so that scriptural truths become reality: He gives us understanding. It's not unintelligible or illogical. Every time I reread a passage, He reveals something new and fresh. It is very exciting. Second, the teaching in our church has been spectacular, adding layers of much deeper understanding of the Scriptures in the context of the full counsel of God—from both the Old and New Testaments. Third, our church family has been one huge exemplary testimony of how things in a community ought to be.

I was in my 30s when I became a Christian. I am now in my late 70s and have had ample time to reflect on what I could have done differently and wish I had. As a husband and father, I know I could have done a lot better. While God was busy rooting out baggage, my wife and kids were there living through all of my unwillingness to yield to Him as I had to repeat the lessons *ad infinitum.* They were there when I rebelled and had outbursts of anger and impatience. All of this, obviously, is relative, because we all know we could have done better. Nevertheless, it doesn't diminish my sometimes overwhelming regret for time lost and the wish that I had a chance to do it over again differently.

I grew up with an unkindness trait. Kindness in my family was actually perceived as weakness because it didn't fit the mold of competitiveness. Winning was everything — competition was the fuel that advanced us, and advance we must, even at the expense of leaving others in the dust. It manifested itself in all sorts of ways, not only in the sports arenas, but also in traffic as we tried to outsmart other drivers to gain that one-car advantage here and there, in queues of all sorts trying to get to the checkout before others … in everything really. It permeated my very being while growing up, and we all thought it was healthy — the more of it the better. It meant you had ambition and ambition was good, yet my ambition was misguided, to be sure.

I wish I had been there a lot more for the kids. My job, I would always rationalize, was the reason I was on the road so much — after all you have to feed the family. And my business — consulting work — meant that some client out there would have to pay for my time. The nature of this business is such that you must submit to the god of "billability." When working for a beltway bandit in Washington D.C., billability is the alpha and omega; if you are less than 70 percent billable, you are in the danger zone and risk being laid off. The best of all worlds was to be fully engaged on a project so you could be billable 100 percent of the time.

I was usually very successful in the billability department, yet sometimes I had dry periods when the clients weren't lining up to hire me, and I would really agonize and take it out on my family (funny how my wife and the kids sort of disappeared from my presence during those times). I obviously hadn't developed any real trust in God's ability to provide.

I wish I could have long ago developed my wife's keen sense of the current moment, her joy in noticing and caring for the little things — smelling the roses, knowing plants and flowers and animals — all of God's creation around her. I have truly admired this; in fact, I think I have envied her for this most extraordinary gift from God, so different from my own way of living. I can be in the most breathtaking

place and up to my neck in God's beautiful creation yet still be thinking about some new analytical twist in my work, or be worried about
some deadline or another.

Sure, I have epiphany moments when everything makes total sense
and gives me an enormous peace in my soul, but they are often interrupted by work-related inanities. This inability to switch work on and
off, I think, is some sort of Norwegian-wired mentality that is extremely difficult to shed.

Finally, I wish I had developed a much better ability to listen more
and to talk a lot less. Born and raised in Norway, I think I am geneti-
cally disposed to experience "uff da" moments, realizing after the fact
that I hadn't listened properly to the questions and had therefore provided the wrong answers. If I could do it over again, I would be much
more focused and attentive to what's happening at home than I was to
the happenings in my work.

The good news: God isn't finished with me yet. Every day that
goes by now I am increasingly thankful to Him for His blessings. In
my work and in some of the stories I have told here I know that God
protected me from harm many times. When I experienced these incidents I didn't reflect much on what God did for me; I was only glad I
survived and lived to tell about them. Now, in retrospect, however, I
know in my heart that God was there in very real ways. That realization is what I want to nurture now, not only for the past, but also for
the future — in all things.

A new unexpected understanding of my place in creation has occurred, and is occurring, because of these reflections on my past, and
as a result of viewing my life as a whole from past to present, and
comparing all of that to God's ideal. I am truly grateful for that and
for God's never-ending patience with me. Today I am a different man
than I was yesterday, and tomorrow is yet another day. I hope and
pray that God will draw me ever closer to Him each day I remain on
this earth, and that He never stops showing me the baggage I keep
trying to drag around with me.

ACKNOWLEDGMENTS

None of the stories told in this book would have seen the light of day without the involvement of my closest friends and colleagues. I had the privilege of teaming up with some of the finest professionals in their respective disciplines. My respect and admiration for the vast majority of them are very high—they are smart, dedicated, fun, and hard-working folks who have a love and passion for their work unlike I have seen anywhere else.

So here's to you guys—my closest co-workers, antagonists, political adversaries, and above all, friends:

To **Fred Weber**, the most prominent and pragmatic development specialist that ever lived. He was my mentor. Rest in peace, Fred—you did a lot of great work and your legacy is very much alive today. Without you, none of the above stories would have happened, and I probably would have ended up teaching at some university somewhere and worrying about my retirement plan.

To **Bob Winterbottom**, colleague for several decades—although you've taught me many things over the years, I would have wanted you to learn a bit more about economics in our work together. Thanks for all the good times, and for your tremendous hospitality for letting us stay for weeks in your home in Niamey (in exquisite air conditioned bliss) during TDYs. I miss our times together in the field, and particularly our endless discussions about economics vs. biology and sociology.

To **Juan Sève**, my fellow like-minded economist and colleague, I can't think of anyone I had more fun with in the bush than I did with you. Your linguistic capabilities and knowledge of field realities are surpassed only by your abilities to tell good jokes. Thanks for letting me have at least one co-worker who had notions about development similar to mine. It was often lonely out there.

To **Asif Shaikh**, my fellow sometimes unlike-minded economist (on some of the bigger issues at least), and boss for many years, we sort of grew up together in this business and, I think, learned loads from each other. I don't think I've ever met anyone so completely at ease with both the lowliest peasant in the bush and ministers at the highest level of government. Replacing you in Abidjan on the EIA project was a tough act to follow.

To **Giuseppe Topa**, forester par excellence and World Bank boss, you have the passion for doing the right thing and doing it well, wherever you are and whatever you do. You were a great client because you held me accountable and just so you know — my gas tank was always empty after completing an assignment for you. I could never figure out your obsession with that one piece of dark chocolate and bread after dinner, however. What's with that?

To **John Heermans**, forester, jack-of all-trades, supreme development specialist and colleague, I know we're politically as far apart as the east is from the west, but I still love you and respect you. I have never met anyone (except perhaps Fred) who could get along better with host country teams and counterparts than you did. You and Cece are true field people and the development world will sorely miss you when you finally decide to retreat to the mountains of Vermont.

To **Roy Hagen**, Chapeau Rouge — what can I say? How many countries have you worked in by now? 100? 150? How many political unrest scrapes have you escaped from by now? Working with you was always an experience that kept me on my toes with my various economic analyses. If I said X, most people would say, OK, I'll accept that. You would say: why? And then I would have to explain, and that wasn't always easy.

To **Ed Karch**, well now, you're a special case. Working with you in Abidjan and beyond was how I learned the most about charcoal and fuelwood. Your unorthodox approach to things was totally devoid of the kind of arrogance exhibited so often by many other development experts, and was very refreshing. Thanks for the good times.

To **Gerry Hawkes**, inventor and out-of-the-box thinker and doer par excellence. How many patents do you have now? I remember the contraption you built in Bobo Dioulasso out of discarded bicycle parts for making fences out of eucalyptus coppice cuttings. I thought you were nuts—but the thing worked. It is probably there still making fences since it was virtually indestructible. Most vividly, though, I remember in Niamey, Niger, when you wanted to try out that pepper spray you had brought to fend off would-be robbers (and 800 robbers had recently been released in Niamey as a gesture of goodwill). You aimed at the tree trunk and it ricocheted right back in your face. That was the only time I saw you dance.

To **Tom Catterson**, your field experiences may even surpass Fred's. Working with you in Kenya, Guinea, and probably many other places (at least we worked on the same projects at different times), you taught me a lot and I hope it was a two-way street. If I recommended A, you would invariably recommend B, and so we ended up in heated arguments as to why A was better than B, or why B was better than A. Often we agreed to disagree and our reports would so reflect—but the recommendations were a lot better documented than if we hadn't had those discussions. Just for the record, though, I still think A is far superior to B.

To **Mike McGahuey** and **Tim Resch**, I can't think of one of you without also thinking of the other, and with great fondness. You were perpetual clients on the USAID side, but not of the kind we were nice to just because you controlled the purse strings. You were, first and foremost, colleagues with an intimate knowledge of field realities which permeated everything you did.

To **George Taylor**, I wouldn't want to go through a coup d'état with anyone but you. Our intense time in the US Embassy chancery in Ouagadougou will be seared in my memory forever.

To **Susan Gannon**, working with you on my team in Niger along with Gerry was a delight. It was a team that really clicked. Rest in peace, Susan. It was great to get to know you before you left us all far too early.

To **Barry Rands**, Niger and Senegal wouldn't be able to get along without you. You had a knack for sorting through USAID's impossible data files on different projects and doing the analysis on what had worked, or not worked. Thank you for letting me be the economist on your teams.

To **Hassan Mazzoudi**, or should I say Fidel — which is the nickname we gave you in Morocco. You were the spitting image of a young Fidel Castro, complete with the cigar and the mannerisms. Thanks for staying in touch while in Africa and later after you returned to Morocco.

Finally, the biggest thank you goes to you, Judi, who lived through all this and tolerated all of my flaws for so long.

PHOTOS

Following are some pictures that give life to some of the stories and people I've introduced in this book. Mind you, the pictures are not top quality because they are scanned from old and grainy photos I had lying around. So here goes:

Home, sweet home — the downtown apartment building (with no elevator) where I lived in Oslo, Norway. Our apartment is on the top floor — with the balcony.

With my sister and her husband by the old sandbox (now landscaped) where we used to have our brutal ice hockey games and play cowboys and Indians.

My brother on the left, sister in the middle.

Where Judi and I lived in Norway while working for Norconsult.

Börsen, my best friend in Norway with whom I sailed for two months in a small boat at the age of fifteen.

Our friend Midi—the Touareg—who regularly came by to sell us handcrafted art pieces.

Ed Karch, my co-worker in Abidjan. He is the world's foremost expert on traditional wood to charcoal conversion techniques.

A picture from somewhere in West Africa of some of my long time colleagues, friends, and all-round great guys. John Heermans to the left,
Roy Hagen on the right, and Bob Winterbottom (seated).

Fred Weber, my mentor, friend, and probably the most knowledgeable
West Africa expert on natural resources management and forestry ever.

A typical day in the life of most West African women in the rural areas—this is just one of the chores—carrying headloads of harvested crops from the farm fields, fuelwood, always with one or several kids in tow.

Women collecting fuelwood in West Africa.

"Sawmill" in West Africa—this is how they make 2x4s. No people in this picture—they were all hiding in the woods nearby thinking we were officials trying to arrest them. The forests are heavily poached. The more entrepreneurial poachers add value by processing the logs into lumber this way.

Our neighbors in Bobo Dioulasso, Burkina Faso.

Kari, our oldest daughter, with our pet rabbit in Bobo Dioulasso. This rabbit became a notoriously productive bunny rabbit producer after we had left.

The kids' French tutor in Bobo Dioulasso, Burkina Faso.

Our closest neighbor in Bobo was a local medicine man—he stopped
to greet us.

Bertrand Zida, one of my forester colleagues in Burkina Faso.

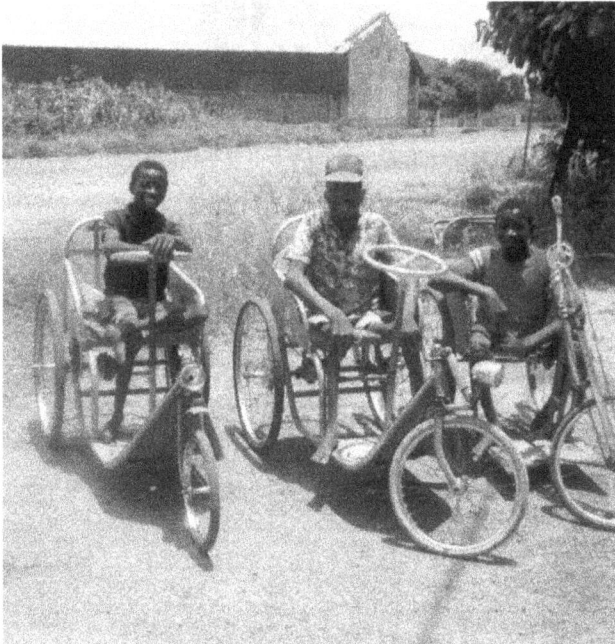

Three of our beggar friends from downtown Bobo arrived at our doorstep the day we left for good. They wanted to say goodbye ...and get a little parting gift (which they did).

We often visited Yao, our friend and local basket maker in his "office" in the bush while we were on our biking excursions in Abidjan. He made about a dollar per day for his efforts.

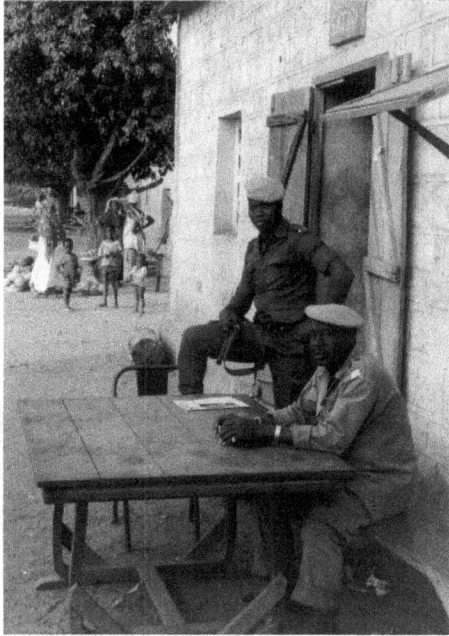

Border guards somewhere in West Africa.

Hassan Mazzoudi (right), friend and colleague from Morocco. We appropriately called him Fidel because of his spitting image to a young Fidel Castro.

Traveling up-river to visit the chimp rehabilitation project in Congo-Brazzaville. It got worse—more overhanging branches and narrower—after this stretch.

Denis Alaire, relaxing on the porch the night before we headed up river to visit the rehabilitated chimps.

Mme Jamar, the chimp rehabilitation lady (on the right) in Congo-Brazzaville, en route to the project site. On the left is the sociologist team member.

At the chimp rehabilitation site destination up river in Congo-Brazzaville. It is a very swampy and mosquito-infested area with project staff housing on stilts.

These guys were heading out to hunt an old man-eating lion in Tanzania. The lion had recently killed four people. George Jambyia, one of my Tanzanian team mates is on the left.

Lions feeding on a recent kill (Tanzania).

Our team in Tanzania. I worked with Roy Hagen (with the hat) in many different countries over the years.

My African journeys weren't all plagued by discomfort—this is the view from my hotel room in Dar Es Salaam (Tanzania) where I always stayed when on TDY there.

The elephant that crossed the road just ahead of us (in Tanzania); many others were crossing right behind us. We were stuck in the middle of the herd.

Meeting with the headhunter tribe in the Philippines. My translator (priest) is the one kneeling on the left. The one on the right in the white t-shirt is the one that had tried to take his head twice in the '70s.

Yours truly in front of our rented Jeepney in Lake Sebu, the Philippines.

Taken from my hotel room—the pool area at Hotel Mille Collines in Rwanda where nearly a thousand refugees were spared from death.

Rwandan children

Our team in Vietnam. Giuseppe Topa, our fearless leader and task master is second from the left.

One of the (daily) banquets we had to attend with the Vietnamese officials as we traveled south through all of the provinces.

Traveling somewhere in Indonesia.